Death of the Dinosaur

Death of the Dinosaur

HOW WALL STREET HAS CHANGED
AND WHERE IT IS HEADED

● ● ●

Jory Berkwits

ISBN-13: 9780692054321
ISBN-10: 0692054324
Library of Congress Control Number: 2018931033
Atlantic Publishing, University Park, FL

For Kandy

Table of Contents

Preface

● ● ●

DURING MY YEARS ON WALL Street, I was an advisor, an executive, a life coach, and a psychologist. I rubbed elbows with nobodies and notables, saints and scoundrels. My experiences were varied, often memorable, sometimes bizarre, and I accumulated war stories by the dozens—just by showing up for work. Often, I would regale friends and neighbors with them, each one, at least in my mind, more amusing and astonishing than the last. As time went on, I toyed with the idea of writing a book composed entirely of such anecdotes, but I ultimately decided against it, having become convinced that a book of humorous vignettes—and nothing else—would have no lasting value. In truth, I would be creating a bathroom book, a Wall Street *Believe it or Not*.

It was at this point I decided to make the *Death of the Dinosaur* a bit more nuanced. Wall Street has experienced a fantastic amount of change during my lifetime. These changes have occurred on many levels: regulatory, technological, and cultural. They have collectively transformed the securities industry, making it almost unrecognizable in the space of a few generations. Not surprisingly, they have also had a huge impact on investors and their attitudes toward the financial markets and the people who lead them. In the end, the book became a collage of memoirs, anecdotes, facts, and opinions, all focused on changes that have impacted the industry and how those changes have influenced individual investors. The *Death of the Dinosaur*, then, is a literary menagerie of sorts; seemingly disconnected subjects—from sex discrimination and flash crashes to online trading and regulatory compliance—are all part of the Wall Street experience. Humor remains present in many of the narratives I have chosen to include, but it does not occupy center stage.

I have tried to be as truthful and accurate as possible. All the events referred to in the *Death of the Dinosaur* are, to the best of my knowledge, authentic. This is in no way a fictional representation of reality, where the broad assumptions are generally accepted, and the details are fabricated. Here, the details are real, though I have changed several names and omitted a few others; this was done only to spare those individuals and their families embarrassment and hurt.

Many of the events I describe took place at Merrill Lynch, and most of my personal sources worked there at one time or another. Yet this is in no way a book exclusively about Merrill and its culture. Merrill was just the securities industry in microcosm, even though that wasn't the case during my childhood. In the years immediately following World War II, the company was something of an outlier, a unique creation of Charlie Merrill. It was a company that reached out to plain people with modest bank accounts in small towns. However, by the time I joined the firm in the early 1970s, if it wasn't already behaving just like its white-shoe brethren, it was well on its way to doing so. At the end of its run, Merrill was successfully chasing the wealthiest, most influential investors in the world, just like all its competitors. The company recruited traders, analysts, investment bankers, and financial advisors aggressively from its rivals. They even established—as did its competitors—a separate division and network of offices (Private Wealth) to focus exclusively on the ultra-high-net-worth market. When the millennium arrived, Merrill didn't look much different than Goldman Sachs or Morgan Stanley. That's because it wasn't. Its demise during the 2008 credit crisis showed how much it had in common with other Wall Street victims of that era like AIG, Fannie Mae, Bear Stearns, Lehman Brothers, and others. What happened at Merrill happened everywhere.

Investors today have almost instant access to information and can trade in the stock markets at extraordinarily low commission costs. They also have benefited from being able to choose from an extensive menu of investment products and services. Financial advisors are far better trained and more knowledgeable than were the so-called "customers' men" of old; these people are now considered industry dinosaurs, little more than order takers and stock jockeys. Regulators at the federal and state level are extremely active in protecting the interests of investors. The industry itself has a self-regulatory body, FINRA, whose mission of enforcement is much the same. In addition, investment firms spend an enormous amount of money within their own compliance departments; compliance is the one area of employment on Wall Street where hiring seems to increase every year without regard for business conditions in the industry. Naturally, one might think to ask: "If investors have better access to information, lower costs, and the protection of multi-tiered regulatory oversight, why aren't they any more successful than they were fifty years ago—and why do they keep getting scammed?" Why indeed?

Forming an opinion is easy. Getting at the truth is something else. In the *Death of the Dinosaur*, I examine change on Wall Street from a variety of perspectives. This is a challenging exercise. Many of us tend to resist change, and those that don't rarely agree on a course of action. Managing one's way in an economy with many moving parts can be equally demanding. None of us can foresee the future; historians don't even agree on the past. Consider the credit crisis and the Dodd–Frank reform legislation that followed it. If one asks what caused the credit crisis in the first place, one is likely to get a laundry list of answers: Republicans, Democrats, bankers, mortgage brokers, the Federal Reserve, Bush, Obama, realtors, naïve investors, speculators, crooks, ratings agencies, hedge funds, or even Barney Frank himself. To fully understand how the pieces of this puzzle fit together requires both legwork and an open mind.

The trust deficit that exists throughout many elements of our society is nowhere larger than on Wall Street. A recent poll revealed that firemen, paramedics, and farmers hold the three most admired occupations in our country. Near the bottom are insurance salesmen and Wall Street executives. In this case being "near" the bottom is not much to brag about. Drug dealer and crime boss occupy the two rock-bottom positions.

The industry's ability to restore public trust must be its number one priority. There is a widespread belief that the system is "rigged." I have often heard this sentiment expressed by sophisticated, experienced, highly educated investors. Even if such convictions are largely untrue, their very existence points to the challenges the industry faces in attempting to resurrect its reputation.

I have tried to present not just an insider's view of the state of the financial markets, but one from thirty thousand feet as well. Does the little guy, whoever he may be, really have a chance? Is the investor playing field level? Does the competitive culture that virtually defines Wall Street create a conflict of interest so large that it can never be bridged? Do financial advisors offer the public genuine value, or are they little more than well-spoken croupiers offering up trite clichés and broad generalizations? These questions, and many others, plainly reveal an industry in crisis, one that must be willing to take corrective action now if it is to flourish in the future.

The History of Money

• • •

IT HAS BEEN SAID THAT money is the root of all evil, that it can't buy happiness or love. We read in Ecclesiastes 5:10, "Whoever loves money never has enough; whoever loves wealth is never satisfied with their income…" Pope Francis has spoken out against what he called the idolatry of money. Senator Bernard Sanders railed against the Wall Street "billionaire class" throughout his unsuccessful 2016 presidential campaign. It might be noted that the Pope and Bernie Sanders have little in common with each other— or with Joseph Stalin, for that matter. He was no fan of capitalism, either. The Dalai Lama has said, "Man sacrifices his health to make money, and then he sacrifices his money to recuperate his health." Religious and political leaders have made this point for centuries. So did my mother.

For all the well-meaning observations that have been handed down through the years concerning greed and materialism, the lure of wealth has exerted a powerful influence on civilization. Today we may think of money simply as a bank account, or the cash in our wallet, but money is any medium of exchange people use to acquire goods and services. Sacks of grain or heads of cattle were used as "money" by early agricultural settlements as long ago as 15,000 B.C. After that came precious metals, then minted coins, and finally paper currency (that was initially backed by gold or silver). Today, "money" can exist in the form of bank deposits, overnight repos, credit cards, or money market funds. One thing is certain: throughout human history, people were drawn to the idea of acquiring wealth.

Even Karl Marx had nothing against money per se—his wrath was directed solely at the folks who had it, the bourgeoisie. For him, the problem was simply that peasants and workers were exploited, and that wealth was not distributed equitably. Interestingly, Marx, a German intellectual, had his own financial challenges, depending partly upon royalties from *Das Kapital* and mostly on the generosity of his wealthy collaborator, Frederick Engels, to help him make ends meet.

For much of recorded history, most of the world's economic activity was based upon agriculture, with wealth concentrated in the hands of a few landowners—the landed gentry or noblemen of those times. A merchant class did begin to appear in some cities during the Renaissance, but it would be many generations before a sizeable middle class emerged in Europe and America.

The first stock market, the Amsterdam Stock Exchange, was established in 1602 by the Dutch East India Company to provide a venue where investors could trade securities. There was only one company listed on the Amsterdam Exchange—the Dutch East India Company. The story behind its fantastic rise and dizzying fall is worth retelling and serves as a symbol of the wildly unpredictable nature of financial markets. It is also a lesson for today.

Originally, the Dutch government had granted the company a twenty-one-year monopoly on that country's spice trade, and it quickly grew in stature and power. It maintained a vast fleet of ships, more than the rest of Europe combined. The company was authorized to establish its own military forces, and it soon achieved dominance in what is now Indonesia and surrounding areas. The Dutch East India Company in some ways was the world's first multinational company, and during its life achieved phenomenal success and wealth. Yet in the end, it was weighed down by corruption, its insistence on paying a rich cash dividend to shareholders, competition in Asian trade, and a series of wars with England. The firm was ultimately dissolved in 1800, and its remaining holdings were nationalized. A company that once owned nearly two hundred ships, maintained a private army of ten thousand soldiers, and employed fifty thousand people was suddenly worthless, and its investors suffered a loss of 63 million guilders. The unthinkable had happened.

The collapse of the Dutch East India Company was the first of what was to be an almost endless series of spectacular business failures and stock market wipeouts that have occurred since that time. There is no real formula for failure. Sometimes, technological innovation by one company (say, a railroad) can instantly erode the business of another (Pony Express). Occasionally, the road to implosion is slower and subtler; in such cases, initial success may lead to arrogance, and arrogance, in turn, can lead either to poor decision making or inertia (no decision making), or both. There are countless examples of this in contemporary times, like Howard Johnson's or F.W. Woolworth or Encyclopedia Britannica. Failures like these, if not inevitable, are commonplace in a free-market economy. It seems self-evident that all companies cannot be successful all the time, and invariably competitive changes and/or a misguided response to them can lead to an unfortunate ending.

Just as individual companies have a life cycle, so do economies and financial markets. Every business expansion has been followed by a contraction, and every bull market by a bear market. Public awareness of the concept of a business cycle grew slowly over time as economies became more complex and as stock exchanges became more firmly established. Then, in September 1873, lightning struck. A financial panic on Wall Street was precipitated by the sudden failure of Jay Cooke and Company, just as it was about to market a $300 million issue of bonds for Northern Pacific Railroad. A crisis in confidence caused the New York Stock Exchange to close for ten days; this was the first such closure in its history. A chain reaction of bank failures followed. Within two months, over fifty of the country's railroads failed, and another fifty ceased operations a year later. The economy cratered and remained mired in depression for six years. Unemployment climbed over 10 percent and stayed at that level for the rest of the decade; those that were able to hold onto their jobs saw wages drop over 20 percent. The *New York Times* wrote of Cooke's failure:

The brokers stood perfectly thunderstruck for a moment, and then there was a general run to notify the different houses of Wall Street of the failure. The brokers surged out of the Exchange, stumbling pell-mell over one another in general confusion and reached their offices in race horse time. The members of the firms who were surprised by this announcement had no time to deliberate. The bear clique was already selling the market down in the Exchange, and prices were declining frightfully.

Within a matter of weeks, over seventy NYSE members and approximately five thousand financial firms failed. The Cooke failure that precipitated the subsequent economic collapse marked a critical turning point in our history. The Panic of 1873 was a Wall Street creation, caused by a credit crunch and a stock market collapse. The hard times that followed were thought to be the obvious aftereffect of the bad behavior—if not sophistry—that many believed typified Wall Street's values. The parallels with the credit crisis of 2008 and the reaction to the government bailouts that followed it are striking. For the first time, brokers and investment banks became scapegoats of the first degree.

Severe market declines or crashes have occurred infrequently but with regularity in modern times. In the United States alone, we can look back at 1893, when a Wall Street panic induced a five-year recession with unemployment remaining at double-digit levels. The Crash of 1929, the mother of all crashes, gave birth to the Great Depression of the 1930s. More recently, we have witnessed major bear markets in 1973-74 (Watergate, interest rates, oil embargo, recession) and the market crash of 1987, one that produced a 20 percent decline in one trading day; after these, we endured the dot-com bubble (and bust) 2000-2002, and the credit crisis of 2008-2009. History suggests that boom-bust cycles with speculative bubbles and panic-driven crashes are rather normal occurrences, not freakish aberrations.

Virtually all financial reform legislation in the past one hundred years has occurred as a direct response to panics and market meltdowns. The

Federal Reserve Bank was created in 1916 after a series of severe market declines and recessions in the 1890s and early 1900s. A plethora of legislation similarly followed the Great Crash of 1929. The Securities Acts of 1933 and 1934 represented the first meaningful steps for federal regulation of the securities industry, which until then had operated as freely as cattle ranchers in the American Wild West. More recently, Dodd–Frank similarly represented a broad response to the credit crisis of 2008-2009. Most financial legislation like this has but one goal — to protect the public.

Often financial panics or market crashes have been precipitated by scandal or fraud. Fraud is as old as civilization itself and is addressed frequently in biblical passages. It was in no way originated by Charles Ponzi, whose early twentieth-century fraud was so spectacular the phrase "Ponzi scheme" is now part of the American lexicon. Yet it seems clear that during the American Industrial Revolution, as wealth was created and a large middle class began to emerge, fraud increased. Why not? There were more potential victims in the United States than anywhere else.

One of Ponzi's contemporaries, George Parker, spent much of his life selling real estate he didn't own (usually landmarks in New York City). He sold the Brooklyn Bridge several times, once for $50,000. Parker was perhaps outdone by Victor Lustig, another con man who managed to sell the Eiffel Tower on two separate occasions. Ulysses S. Grant, former Commanding General of Union forces during the Civil War and a former president of the United States, died virtually penniless; his fortune had been vaporized by the scandalous failure of the investment firm Grant and Ward. Buck Grant, the president's son and one of the firm's principals, found out too late that his partner, Ferdinand Ward, was a fraudster of the highest order, pilfering millions from the company's treasury and leaving his partner, employees, and customers hanging out to dry.

In recent years, however, fraudulent activity has cropped up with frightening consistency. Many (though not all) of the frauds that have been perpetrated have occurred on Wall Street, and more than anything else this has sullied the image of the industry. Individual scams have routinely reached $100 million and on several occasions more than $1 billion.

Bernie Madoff orchestrated the biggest fraud of all time—over $40 billion with more than four thousand clients. His name is a household word not because what he did was so unusual, but rather because his victims, mostly well connected and very rich, lost an astonishing amount of money.

Madoff, a brazen sociopath, ran nothing more than a classic Ponzi scheme. He took in billions from clients, but he conveniently neglected to make legitimate investments on their behalf. When potential clients looked at his operation, they were presented with fabricated financial statements. (Of course, the statements Madoff's clientele regularly received were bogus as well.) Sometimes Madoff even gave a live personal presentation to show his clients how their money was managed. They were able to observe (or so they thought) how his trading desk was linked up with the NYSE, other electronic markets, and the DTC (Depository Trust Company). This must have been quite impressive to his star-struck investors, almost like a laser light show. Unfortunately, the presentation was a total fake, an electronic fantasy designed only to seduce his victims.

The securities industry is almost tailor-made for fraud since it deals in intangibles and because so much of the business is conducted informally via unrecorded conversations. Fraud can present itself in many ways and in varying disguises. Misrepresentation, churning an account for commissions, and recommending unsuitable investments are all forms of fraudulent behavior. Not-so-distant cousins are mortgage fraud and insurance fraud.

In a very real sense, your garden variety "rogue broker" is perpetrating a fraud by making exaggerated claims and promises. Recently, one such individual named Anthony Diaz achieved unwanted national publicity. In June 2016, the Associated Press reported that he had just been criminally indicted for fraud, after having worked for eleven different securities firms in a fifteen-year period. Five of these firms had fired him, yet he always managed to land on his feet. During this time, as many as fifty different customers filed formal complaints with FINRA for virtually every wrongdoing imaginable: fraud, misrepresentation, churning, unauthorized trading, unsuitable recommendations, and more. He was accused of frivolously exchanging dozens of annuity contracts for many of his clients only to generate commissions, as there was no apparent benefit for his customers in making the switch.

Today, no top-tier firm like Morgan Stanley, UBS, or Merrill would touch someone with Diaz' history, but there are apparently smaller, sleazy broker-dealers that would—and did. This reality, of course, gives the entire securities industry a black eye, but what is even more distressing is that Diaz was able to avoid the "death penalty" by securities regulators for so long. Ultimately, he was permanently barred from the industry by FINRA—but this came much too late as far as his victims were concerned.

It is difficult to describe how deflating and demoralizing it has been for my industry colleagues and me to learn about financial fraudsters. Compared to Bernie Madoff, Anthony Diaz was a small-time petty thief. His misdeeds, however, were no less notorious. The failure of industry regulators to take firm, prompt disciplinary action against him was inexcusable. It was not uncommon for long-term clients of mine, after reading about the fraud *du jour*, to comment about it by prefacing their remarks with "You guys...." Not Madoff, or Milken, or Boesky, or Diaz for that matter—just "you guys." The inference was clear.

Cyber crimes, identity theft, and internet phishing are all relatively modern forms of fraud that make George Parker's peddling of the Brooklyn Bridge seem primitive by comparison. In these examples of modern fraud, predators and victims never meet. Old-fashioned fraud typically involved a criminal mastermind and a victim who trusted him. Whatever form fraud takes, there seems to be no stopping its growth. CNBC originated a documentary television series, *American Greed*, some years ago—and it has never run out of material.

Still, it would be both inaccurate and irresponsible to believe that financial fraud has been the primary cause of market volatility and investor panics. Fraudsters may find it easier to operate during an investment bubble, but they don't create bubbles. Legitimate investors do. The bubble occurs when society becomes convinced that continued success is certain and inevitable.

Investment bubbles, from the Dutch Tulip mania to the dot-com froth of the 1990s, have almost always met with devastating results. Real estate investors before the 2008 credit crisis never thought of themselves as crap-shooters, even though a rational person could have intuitively understood that the homebuilding/mortgage bubble of the early 2000s could not last forever. The rise in real estate prices was being sustained by lax mortgage lending standards and widespread speculation—not a shortage in the nation's housing stock. The bust was called a credit crisis for a reason.

Perhaps the biggest bubble of all occurred in the United States during the 1800s. Bankers and investors had a love affair with railroads during the so-called railroad mania, which lasted much of the nineteenth century. It rivaled if not exceeded the internet frenzy of recent times. In both cases, a new technology with obvious game-changing potential attracted a tremendous amount of investment capital—too much, as it turned out. We can say so with certainty today because we have the benefit of hindsight. Yet in its early years, the growth potential of the railroad industry seemed to be as inevitable as the underlying growth in the American population and economy.

The first railroad company, the Baltimore and Ohio, featured train cars pulled by horses. The route covered a little over sixty miles between Baltimore and Sandy Hook, Maryland. Within fifty years, in 1869, Union Pacific had completed construction of the nation's first transcontinental route, at which time fifty thousand miles of track had been laid throughout the United States. By 1900, there were four additional transcontinental railroads operating on nearly two hundred thousand miles of track. (By comparison, the entire interstate highway system in the United States covers approximately forty-six thousand miles.) The failure of Jay Cooke and Co. and the subsequent Panic of 1873 were not omens indicating that the end of the railroad boom was imminent, any more than the dot-com stock market bubble and its subsequent collapse foreshadowed the end of the internet. The reality is that no investment mania lasts forever, and when they run their course, the ending is not a happy one.

The plain fact was that investors in both cases felt that this time it would be different, that the opportunities in railroads (and later, in the internet) were virtually limitless, and that success was assured. The belief in the certainty of such success warped the judgment of investors and led them to throw enormous sums of capital into anything that looked or smelled like a railroad. Railroad stock investors, instead of becoming more cautious as prices rose, became more optimistic and enthusiastic. A feeding frenzy, and then a speculative bubble, soon took shape, one that sowed the seeds of a climactic bust. Fraud had nothing to do with it. The culprit was greed.

When I was in high school, a history teacher attempted to explain the difference between a "United States dollar" and a "United States Treasury note." He revealed that the older dollar was backed by gold and that for every dollar printed there had been a dollar's worth of gold safely tucked away in Fort Knox. On the other hand, he said, Treasury notes were backed by "nothing." He had paused dramatically before saying the word "nothing." I questioned him immediately. They both looked pretty much the same to me, and in my mind (and in the real world) both had equal value. He then ripped the Treasury note in half. "Nothing," he repeated, to make his point even more clearly. I was horrified, as was everyone in the class, but this particular history lesson was learned well and never forgotten. Years later, it is interesting for me to recall how a schoolboy with no job, no financial responsibilities and no bills to pay could have had such an emotional connection with a piece of paper money—and it wasn't even mine.

It seems that the insatiable desire to acquire more and more wealth, currently measured by amounts of money, is an inseparable part of what makes us human. Most mammals are happy enough to be secure, comfortable, and well-fed, but for many people, that's not nearly enough. We desire material wealth and the intangible benefits of power and prestige that accompany it. On Wall Street, where the business of business is money, extreme behavior around money is the norm. To paraphrase Vince Lombardi, "Money isn't everything. It's the only thing." Its constant presence in our thoughts and conversation can have a toxic influence on our behavior and spiritual values.

The case of Jack Grubman is a perfect example. For some time in the 1990s, he was Salomon Smith Barney's leading telecom analyst and the highest-paid analyst on Wall Street, earning about $20 million annually. Brokers and investors alike felt that he walked on water. A recommendation from Grubman typically resulted in an immediate surge in that stock's price. His influence was immense, and he acted as a magnet for investment banking business. Citigroup, then Smith Barney's owner, earned approximately $1.75 billion on debt and equity deals between 1996 and 2000.

Ultimately, the good times came to an end. The decline in telecom stocks was severe—identical to that experienced by their internet cousins. Grubman and Smith Barney, conflicted by the prodigious fees they were earning on the investment banking side, appeared to be in a state of paralysis. Grubman consistently reiterated buy recommendations on a number of telecom companies—especially those with ties to Smith Barney—long after it became obvious that the tide had turned against them. Privately, he harbored different thoughts. In an email that was later uncovered, Grubman referred to one of his buy recommendations as "a pig."

Grubman was scarcely the only individual who lost his moral compass. Henry Blodget, a star internet analyst at Merrill Lynch, similarly referred to one of his own recommended stocks as a "piece of crap." Once, when asked by a client what made a particular internet stock attractive apart from banking fees, he replied, "nothing."

In any event, five of Grubman's top ten recommendations in March of 2001 were virtually worthless within twelve months' time. Among them were WorldCom and Global Crossing, both of which soon went bankrupt. Eliot Spitzer, then Attorney General of the State of New York, took aim at Smith Barney and other companies as well, and he was successful in exposing the inherent conflict of interest that was common among Wall Street firms that engaged in investment banking as well as research. Wrongdoing was also uncovered at Merrill Lynch, Lehman Brothers, Morgan Stanley,

Goldman Sachs and others—ten firms in all. Subsequently, Grubman (and Blodget) were permanently barred from the industry, and each paid heavily. Blodget had to write a check for $4 million, and Grubman had to cough up $15 million.

The Grubman narrative, however, didn't end there. During Spitzer's investigation, more embarrassing information came out. It was revealed that in 1999, Sandy Weill, the CEO of Citigroup, asked Grubman to take a "fresh look" at his research opinion on AT&T. Weill sat on AT&T's Board of Directors, and while there is no evidence to suggest that he had a dark, hidden motive in making this request, he had no business bringing the subject up in the first place. How can an analyst be truthful if he has been asked by his boss to issue a favorable opinion?

A timeline of events that occurred shortly thereafter speaks for itself. Grubman soon upgraded his opinion on AT&T to a "Buy," and Smith Barney secured a lucrative investment banking deal with the company. At about the same time, Grubman asked Weill to see if he could use his influence to help get his twin daughters admitted to a prestigious nursery school, the 92nd Street Y, in New York City. (Readers should note that the tuition for this school in 2016-2017 was $33,600.) Among certain social circles in Manhattan, being admitted to the 92nd Street Y is looked upon as a prerequisite for an Ivy League degree and perhaps for life after that as well.

Citigroup then pledged to give $1 million to the school, paid in installments over the next five years, and Grubman's daughters were subsequently granted admission. While there is no concrete evidence directly linking the Citigroup donation to the Y's acceptance of Grubman's daughters, just as there was no clear connection between Grubman's research upgrade on AT&T with their choice of Citigroup as an investment banker, this sequence of events just doesn't pass the smell test, or even come close. *The Wall Street Journal* called the episode "kid pro quo."

Jack Grubman was by all accounts an extraordinarily bright, committed, hard-working research analyst who possessed unusual talent. His career ended in tatters, his reputation destroyed. One would be hard-pressed to identify a clearer picture of the corrupting influence of money and its potential consequences. In this narrative, there were no winners. Everyone—from Grubman to Citigroup stockholders to public investors in all of the failed telecom companies—lost in the end.

The investigation launched by Spitzer ultimately (in 2003) resulted in a global settlement that tied in the NYSE, the NASD, and ten investment banks. Collectively, these firms were assessed over $1.4 billion in fines–$900 million in restitution to investors, and the balance for investor education and third-party (independent) research. The firms all agreed to formally separate research and investment banking to provide greater transparency in their operations.

While $1 billion is hardly a trifling sum of money, when spread among the ten firms that were punished, it represents a very manageable amount. Citigroup, the parent company of Salomon Smith Barney, was assessed the highest penalty, $400 million. In 2003, it earned a record $17 billion. In other words, Citigroup's punishment amounted to a little over one week's profit. Merrill Lynch was fined $200 million; it earned $3.7 billion in the same year. Goldman Sachs was forced to pay $110 million, compared to that firm's $3 billion in profit. Taken together, the fines represented little more than a rounding error on an income statement. Wall Street's reputation, however, took a very big hit. Citigroup's decision to drop the *Salomon Smith Barney* moniker in favor of *Citigroup Global Market Holdings* didn't fool anybody and infuriated that firm's brokers and traders.

Grubman's fall from grace must have sent a strong message at that time, but ethical lapses among research analysts have nevertheless continued to make news. In 2012, star internet analyst Mark Mahaney was fired by Citigroup (Grubman's former employer) for sharing some non-public information on YouTube with a French business magazine. This appeared ironic to some because years earlier Mahaney purportedly had been fired by hedge fund Galleon for *failing* to acquire nonpublic (inside) information. Not so surprisingly, Galleon founder Raj Rajaratnam (Mahaney's former boss) was convicted of insider trading in 2011, and his firm was closed. He is still in federal prison. Mahaney managed to resurface and was subsequently hired by RBC Capital, where he is currently their lead tech analyst.

In 2015, Goldman Sachs and JP Morgan found themselves in a similarly embarrassing situation. Together, they ended up firing thirty young research analysts who had been cheating on tests. The analysts in question were mostly freshly minted MBAs just beginning their Wall Street careers, and the tests themselves were a routine part of each firm's internally administered training programs. There is no way any of these junior analysts should have had any difficulty in passing the exams in question, and of course, there is no way they should have been tempted to take a shortcut—but they did.

Sometimes investment firms are themselves victimized. Yes, it's true! We live in a litigious society, and there are many cases where customers who have not been taken advantage of in any way bring legal action against their financial advisors and/or their employers for alleged wrongdoing. These complaints typically contain the usual verbiage—deceitful, unauthorized, false, misleading, unsuitable, reckless, etc.—when the client knew all along what he was doing and why he was doing it. At some point, he became a sore loser and called his lawyer. Thousands of such complaints are litigated every year. They are like white-collar slip and fall cases. I was peripherally connected with one where legal fees for all parties concerned approached $2 million, and the advisor and the firms he worked for were completely exonerated.

Ayn Rand said, "So you think money is the root of all evil. Have you ever asked what is the root of all money?" She poses a challenging and interesting question, one that is in many ways part of a larger paradox. If greed and selfishness are evil, what then is the desire for profit? How can Wall Street recalibrate its moral compass if it places such tremendous emphasis on winning at virtually any cost? How can Wall Street rediscover its soul? Did it ever have one in the first place?

These questions and others are addressed in an important new book by Kim Ann Curtin, *Transforming Wall Street*. Curtin has taken a very unusual approach, offering interviews with fifty prominent individuals she calls the Wall Street 50 (although a number are academics, futurists, or religious leaders). She then intersperses their responses with her own thoughts and experiences. The result is more than a good read—it's an effective if unconventional call to action, encouraging a change from what she calls crony capitalism to conscious capitalism, i.e., capitalism with a conscience.

I will be referring to Curtin's work several times later in *Death of the Dinosaur*, but the central focus of her book is that capitalism, as it has been practiced in America and on Wall Street, has lost its way. Crony capitalism does not serve society. Unless we can practice capitalism with a conscience, the entire system is at risk. She spoke with author and futurist Patricia Aburdene, who called out acclaimed economist Milton Friedman for writing that the *purpose* of capitalism is to produce profit; Aburdene says that while profit is an essential result of a successful business, it in no way represents the primary purpose of the business itself. To some, this distinction may seem to be a trivial argument in semantics. Not to me.

Healthcare giant Johnson and Johnson issued a credo in 1943, the type of proclamation we call a mission statement today. It was created by Robert Wood Johnson, former CEO and a member of the firm's founding family. Here is some of what was said:

"We believe our first responsibility is to the doctors, nurses, and patients, to mothers and fathers and all others who use our products and services. In meeting their needs, everything we do must be of high quality. We must constantly strive to reduce our costs to *maintain reasonable prices* (my italics). Customers' orders must be serviced promptly and accurately. Our suppliers and distributors must have an opportunity to make a fair profit."

The credo goes on to say that the company must be responsible to its employees, who should have a sense of security about their jobs. Beyond that, the firm must be mindful of ways to help employees fulfill their family responsibilities. Next, "We are responsible to the communities in which we live and work and to the world community as well. We must be good citizens—support good works and charities and bear our fair share of taxes..."

Finally, at the end of the credo, there is talk of profit. "When we operate according to these principles, the shareholders should realize a fair return." One may debate what constitutes a fair return, but it should be noted that since Johnson and Johnson's IPO in 1944, the company has split its stock on multiple occasions, and a hundred-share investment made then would have grown to over two hundred thousand shares today. Robert Johnson believed that if his company placed the interests of customers, employees, suppliers, and society first, his company would prosper over time—and so it did. For whatever reason, Wall Street has found it difficult to embrace these ideals, something that has cost it dearly.

On a subtler level, individuals who have made their careers on Wall Street have paid a steep price as well. I don't know of many of my former colleagues who could not identify at least to some degree with the story of Sam Polk. Polk, a Columbia University graduate, walked away from the investment business when he was thirty. He was a successful senior trader at an elite New York-based hedge fund who became bitter and angry that an annual bonus of more than $3 million "just wasn't big enough." That moment represented an epiphany in his life. He realized his value system had been overwhelmed by the culture of Wall Street. He moved to California and wrote a revealing memoir, *For the Love of Money*. Polk's publisher noted that his "becoming a Wall Street trader had been the fulfillment of his dreams, but in reality, it was just the culmination of a life of addictive and self-destructive behaviors, from overeating to bulimia to alcohol and drug abuse. His obsessive pursuit of money papered over years of insecurity and emotional abuse." Polk rediscovered the idealism of his earlier years. Soon he founded *Groceryships*, a nonprofit committed to providing low-income communities with access to healthy, unprocessed foods. Shortly after that, Polk and a business partner created *Everytable*, a "grab and go" eatery that serves up healthy snacks and meals in areas where such restaurants don't typically exist, namely poor urban neighborhoods. His first store opened in South L.A, formerly known as South Central.

Polk's story is inspirational, but it also haunts me to some degree. I remember saying on many occasions after I turned forty that I wanted to get out of the business by the time I was fifty and run a nonprofit. I was sincere when I said it, but I didn't put my thoughts into action. In fact, I never even tried. The money was just too good.

The Death of the Dinosaur

• • •

I saw my first glimpse of the Wall Street dinosaur in 1968. Still in college, I was working a summer job at the Marine Midland Bank's stock transfer department in New York City. In the same year Neil Armstrong became the first person to walk on the moon, Wall Street seemed to be lost in space, in a time warp, so to speak, where trade clearing and bookkeeping were still done manually. Paper stock and bond certificates were the norm. Share volume on the New York Stock Exchange averaged less than ten million shares per day, but the Street's leading firms couldn't keep pace. The NYSE's answer was to close on Wednesdays.

Marine Midland's stock transfer department employed hundreds of people, all of whom were involved with stock issuance and shareholder recordkeeping for a variety of different companies. Paper certificates were typically sent out after each stock purchase, and a manual record for every shareholder was handwritten and then stored in a giant bin of file drawers that worked exactly like a giant Rolodex. I remember that clerks called "signing officers" had but one job—to sit at their desks all day and sign stock certificates before the certificates could be sent out to the owner of record. Of all the clerks, they earned the highest salary, because once they signed a certificate, it became as negotiable as cash. Important mathematical calculations were done on an electro-mechanical calculator. These machines were extremely slow and noisy to boot. They now appear in museums.

For those of you who find this scenario mind-boggling, consider this: during my junior year in college, I held a part-time work-study job at Columbia University's Graduate School of Business. I was assigned to the Alumni Relations office, and my job was to keep track of the address changes of Business School graduates. I did so by making pencil entries on 3x5 cards and storing the cards in a tin box. Thinking about this sometimes makes me feel old and irrelevant.

Some of the idiosyncrasies of this era were, if nothing else, quaint. The US Treasury issued bonds in bearer form, meaning that the securities weren't registered in the holder's name. If such a bond was lost or stolen, the owner was simply out of luck. Equally surprising, brokerage firms were not required to issue 1099s to their clients. Dividends, interest, and capital gains were reported on the honor system.

1968, of course, was a year like no other. It was marked by the assassinations of Martin Luther King and Robert Kennedy, violent riots in several American cities, and almost continual turmoil related to the war in Vietnam. My university and many others across the country were scenes of active protest and confrontations with police. The country was divided as never before, and this continued for several years. In addition to Vietnam and civil rights, a cultural revolution was taking place, and it encompassed issues from gender equality and sexual freedom to psychedelic drugs and alternative lifestyles. While opinions on the value of these cultural changes differ, there is no doubt they caused a lot of social and generational friction. To make matters worse, the economy began to sputter, and as the decade turned, the phrase "urban decay" began to appear with alarming frequency. The promises of Lyndon Johnson's Great Society were proving to be elusive.

On a personal level, my life went in a direction I could barely have imagined just a few short years before. I got married, and soon afterward I completed college and a year of graduate school. My first child was born in 1971, and I quickly became the sole support of my family. In less than three years, I moved from New York to Seattle to New York to Boston. One adventure led to another. My first job was in the publishing industry.

It turned out to be a poor idea, given my temperament. I was young, ambitious, tremendously independent, and impulsive to boot. Rather abruptly, I decided to make a career change. Serendipity intervened, and I found myself in the investment business. The story behind that life-changing event is worth telling.

I was earning about $8,000 per year at my publishing job. That worked out to about $32 per workday—before taxes. While pondering my next step, I had one immediate need: sell an odd lot of Kodak stock (at the time my entire net worth) to come up with a down payment for a home purchase. So, on a sunny winter day, I walked across the street to Merrill Lynch's Boston office; I stopped at Merrill only because it was the first brokerage firm I came upon. It was cold, and I needed to get out of the wind.

The receptionist was very friendly, and within a minute a young broker named John Mattivello greeted me with a warm handshake and said that he'd be happy to help me dispose of my holdings. I pulled a stock certificate out of my trousers, all thirty-six shares worth, and handed it to him. He couldn't have been nicer. While opening an account for me, he explained that it would cost about $50 in commission to sell my stock. This was my first epiphany. Merrill Lynch would make more money on this trade than I would earn in the next day and a half.

I asked John if he liked his job, and he said he did. Then I asked him if Merrill had any openings in its training program, and he said yes, they absolutely did. He suddenly became very engaging if not outright enthusiastic. He told me how to apply for the job and suggested I use his name. I probably sent in an application as soon as I got home. My cover letter went something like this:

"I am applying for a position in your account executive training program. I have spoken extensively about this opportunity with John Mattivello, and based on his knowledge of my qualifications and skills, he has strongly urged me to apply for this position."

At the time I possessed a master's degree in history, had never taken a course in economics or business, and had no relevant work experience. I knew nothing about the securities industry or what I was getting myself into. Much later I learned that Mattivello stood to receive a $1,000 finder's fee (adjusted for inflation, nearly $6,000 today) if I were fortunate enough to get hired, pass my registration exams, and go into production. Were it not for this bounty, I am certain I would never have gotten past the starting line.

Ultimately, I had to take a written exam and sit through four different interviews before Merrill gave me an offer. I later learned that the firm hired two people out of a pool of two hundred applicants, and I was one of them. I became extremely proud—perhaps too much so—until I finally found out about John's finder's fee. That was something I was not very anxious to talk about. So, I didn't. It was more enjoyable to fantasize. One day, an account executive trainee, the next, CEO.

Obviously, I was thrilled to have been given this opportunity. As was the custom at the time, the job offer was made via a special delivery letter sent on stationery that had the look of a wedding invitation. When the postman handed it to me on a Saturday morning, my wife stood next to me. She was staring at the envelope and whispered excitedly, "You got the job! You got the job." Arrogantly I said, "Of course. They wouldn't turn me down with a special delivery letter." But I wasn't sure until I opened the envelope. It took me months to come down to earth. Forty-five years later, the memory of that moment is still vivid.

Merrill had always been recognized for an excellent training school, and its managers, who did not themselves handle customer accounts, were completely invested in the success of their branch offices and its associates. Nevertheless, on "Day 1" I felt as if I was entirely on my own—and in many ways, I was. My mission was to make as many as one hundred cold calls a day and open as many accounts as I could. I was told that all my hard work would somehow pay off, but it would most likely take two or three years. My boss told me that he went through it, that everyone went through this rite of passage. I was all in, committed to success.

The work environment for rookie brokers was almost feral. I felt as if I was in a ferocious, daily competition with every broker in Boston, working days, nights, and weekends. The culture was wildly macho and cutthroat.

Once I was told by a coworker who had brazenly attempted to poach one of my accounts that there was no reason to be upset. After all, "this is a contact sport." He reminded me of The Godfather's Michael Corleone saying, "It's not personal; it's strictly business."

My first day of work was March 6, 1972. I was wearing wing-tipped shoes and a dark suit. Our sales manager took me to lunch at the Fort Hill Club, a men's luncheon club. Yes, there really were such places in those years. I ordered a glass of scotch and a sirloin steak medium rare—thank you very much. I was exhilarated beyond words. My host ordered a double Jack Daniels and a double shrimp cocktail. He said he was on a diet.

Shortly thereafter, I heard the following words: "Gentlemen, we are not an eleemosynary institution." So intoned David Palmer, the Resident VP at Merrill Lynch's flagship Boston office. He was speaking at a sales meeting of retail brokers, virtually all of whom, like me, were young, inexperienced Type-A males, bursting with excitement and a bit of bravado. Sadly, most of us were also destined to wash out of the investment business altogether, temperamentally unsuited to cope with the hard times of the 1970s as well as the responsibilities that come with managing another people's money.

I was one of those fortunate enough to hang on and make it. For me, 1972 turned out to be the first year of an unforgettable forty-year run in the securities industry—all with Merrill. That alone made me something of a freak of nature in a business known for job-hopping and opportunism. Perhaps a genetic defect allowed me to stay in one place so long. On that day, however, my immediate concern was trying to figure out what "eleemosynary" meant. My colleagues were all equally clueless. After a few minutes of awkward silence and blank stares, Palmer told us that it is a seldom-used, old-fashioned synonym for "charitable." For the balance of that day, and during the weeks and months and years ahead, we would remember the broader meaning of what we had just heard.

Palmer's pronouncement was a pithy way of saying everything one needed to know about how the investment business works. It explained why Charlie Merrill and Ed Lynch started their company in the first place.

It revealed why I and my co-workers chose to become financial advisors rather than teachers or diplomats or artists. It goes without saying that everyone who has a job wants to get paid fairly for his labor, but on Wall Street, making money (lots of it, preferably now) is the central tenet of its culture. If you can help a client in the process, that's simply a bonus.

The first war story I heard could have been written by Damon Runyan. It concerned a man who had walked into our office to open an account to dispose of some shares of IBM. After the stock was sold, several employees in the "cage," where securities were processed locally, noticed irregularities on the certificate. It turned out to be counterfeit. When the "customer" came back to the office a few days later to pick up the proceeds of the sale, he was met by FBI agents and promptly arrested, brought to trial, and sentenced to a prison term.

In a situation like this, the firm would ordinarily "bust" or cancel the trade in question, but in this instance, the broker beat Merrill to the punch. Noticing that IBM had dropped in price since the original sale took place, the cunning broker went ahead and repurchased the stock in the customer's account, thereby earning two commissions for his trouble. The decline in IBM's price was enough to cover the two commissions and then some. Amid all the excitement, this financial skullduggery was overlooked by management but became legend to future generations of brokers. I don't recall if he was actually paid on this business, and I never wanted to find out.

In 1972, not much had changed on Wall Street since my 1968 summer job at the Marine Midland Bank. One notable difference involved the Centralized Certificate Service, the harbinger of today's electronic book-entry transfer system used by the Depository Trust Company. The NYSE established the Centralized Certificate Service in 1969, its first baby step toward modernization. It allowed for a centralized depository of paper certificates for the exchange's member firms, thereby streamlining—to some small degree—the process used in settling trades. Exchange President Robert Haack announced, "We are going to automate the stock certificate out of business by substituting punch cards." He was an optimist. The

NYSE made participation voluntary, and well over 50 percent of broker-age firms refused to go along. They preferred conducting business the old-fashioned way, dispatching runners carrying paper stock certificates and miscellaneous trade documents.

I found myself immediately attracted to the competitive culture of the boardroom. If my new employer had asked me if I were a team player, I would have said "yes"—no doubt omitting the qualification that on my team I would need to be coach, general manager, or president. Fortunately, the question never came up. This was not a team sport. It was made crystal clear that my success in the industry was entirely dependent upon my abil-ity to build a book of business. (If I didn't, I'd quickly be shown the door.) After a period of training and a year or two of financial subsidy, my paltry salary would be replaced by what was called incentive compensation. I had no idea how to accurately forecast what this would be, nor did anyone else. Whatever the case, I would now be facing a very uncertain future.

Where to begin? Our sales office was located on the ground floor of a relatively new building in Boston's financial district, with back-office operations on the second floor. Orders were written on paper tickets and then sent through pneumatic tubes to the wire operator upstairs, who would then transmit the order to the floor of the exchange. In fast mar-kets, there could be a delay of several minutes in order entry while the wire operator struggled to keep up with the order flow. Occasionally the plastic carriers (small tubes) would get jammed somewhere in the system, and more than once this resulted in extensive delays and large trading errors. No, you cannot tell an investor his order was ignored for a few hours because it got stuck somewhere in a pneumatic tube. If that happened, he would have to be made whole at the firm's expense.

Information was transmitted over teletype. There were two wires, A and B, and both machines made a tremendous amount of noise. (This clickety-clack sound was like boardroom music, only partially drowned out by even louder metallic snaps from a commodity quote board.) The A wire transmitted general domestic news from press agencies like AP, UPI, and Reuters. The B wire was an internal wire, containing research opinions, market analysis, bond inventories, corporate policy bulletins, personnel announcements, and so on. All the information was available on an (almost) real-time basis, but only if you happened to plant yourself in front of the teletype machine and stand there all day reading what it spit out. In practice, someone had to take scissors, cut out the information deemed relevant, photocopy it, and have it passed out by hand to every registered employee in the office. It was almost an everyday occurrence to discover that a research opinion went from buy to sell (or sell to buy) several hours after the fact. Bond buyers were constantly dismayed to learn that an issue they wanted to buy had gone up in price or been traded away and was no longer available.

Municipal bonds created special challenges. Most of them were traded regionally because many of the issues were small and had largely local appeal. New England bonds were traded in Boston, Mid-Atlantic bonds in Philadelphia, and so on. The Boston trading unit was located on the second floor of the branch office where I worked, and the inventory was posted entirely by hand. To see what was available, one had to walk upstairs, grab a leather-bound inventory book, and look at dozens of 3X5 cards in plastic sleeves that contained the details of every issue that was available. Some intrepid souls would wander in early in the morning and pull out a card or two so that they could contact their clients without running the risk that the bonds would be purchased by someone else.

Even getting a fresh, accurate quote was sometimes a challenge. In the very early days of the stock market, of course, prices were written on a chalkboard. By the 1900s, information like this was disseminated nationwide via teletype machines, but only the largest trades of the most liquid issues were reported via teletype. For example, at 11:30, one might scroll back on a roll of teletype paper (just like pulling on a roll of toilet paper) to learn that at 9:45, ten thousand shares of GM traded at forty-five, but to get a more meaningful quote, one would need to send a wire (via teletype) to a trader and wait for a response. If a large order were pending, one would place a telephone call to the trading floor. This was as good as it got. Prices of thinly traded NYSE stocks and all OTC stocks were simply not readily accessible, nor were those of many government, corporate, or municipal bonds. In many cases, this led to inefficient markets, wide spreads (sometimes obscenely so), and abusive trading practices.

The Bunker Ramo Corporation was one of the pioneers in electronic price reporting for the financial services industry. The first machines appeared in the 1960s and featured small screens that were hard to see clearly. By the early 1970s, one could obtain very basic real-time price information on listed stocks and a few hundred OTC (NASDAQ) stocks. If you were looking for last trade, bid, ask, and volume, you were in luck; if you needed any additional information on a company—its financials, investment prospects, price history, earnings estimates and the like—you would need to take a trip to the library.

I worked in an office with perhaps fifty or sixty registered employees and approximately fifteen Bunker Ramo machines. Each machine was placed on a swivel and could be spun in a 360-degree circle. If your desk was ten or fifteen feet away from the nearest machine, you were furnished with an extra-long telephone cord.

Customers and non-customers alike would call the office to get quotes. There was no other way to get them. One of the duties of the "broker of the day" was to cheerfully give quotes to any and all individuals who called in. Sometimes they would call in with their entire portfolio, simply saying, "Quotes, please" and then reading off a list of securities in alphabetical order. If it took more than two minutes to get from Avon to Bethlehem Steel to Clorox, you could plan on missing lunch. Lengthy quote calls like this contributed to traffic jams near the Bunker Ramo machines, with several brokers and their assistants queued up waiting for their turn.

There were no private offices except the few reserved for managers. Our branch office was essentially one gigantic boardroom—just a sea of desks, credenzas, and Bunker Ramo machines. Office equipment featured rotary telephones and manual typewriters. A Trans-Lux ticker was centrally located and visible virtually everywhere. A seating gallery made it possible for the public to settle in and watch the ticker during market hours. In active markets, it was not uncommon for people to shout out the name of a stock that was really moving, the same way that racetrack devotees encourage horses. The stock symbols on the ticker tape, just like the horses, didn't pay much attention. Occasionally someone would simply blurt out "moon shot!" or "go!" or "all right!" The boardroom was always active and noisy, and tremendously entertaining.

It also had the ambiance of Grand Central Station. The scent of cigar smoke was mitigated only during lunch hour, as the odor of steak bombs and pizzas filled the office. No conversation was private, either face to face with a client or on the phone with a spouse. Often phone calls were announced by shouting. ("Hey, John, it's your mother!") There may have been a pretense of civility, but it didn't go very far. I remember that one broker's desk butted up against a water cooler that in turn was situated next to an exterior wall of the men's room. That wall was paper thin, and it was easy to pick up the sound of a flushed toilet. For a while, my friend Dick Greene happened to sit there. He was soon to become a legend as Merrill Lynch's largest producer in the United States.

The culture was infused with alcohol. Eighty-proof liquor was routinely served up at lunch. Happy hour was in truth two hours, perhaps three. The company Christmas party was paid for by employees because of a shared belief—true enough—that if the firm sponsored the event, it wouldn't be wild enough. The office was always deathly quiet the morning after, with dozens of employees hungover, barely making it in by lunch. One of my co-workers failed to come in for three days, and once it was determined that he was not in harm's way, the whole incident was recalled with widespread merriment, especially when it was learned that his wife had called in on the second day of his binge to see what had become of him. Hilarious!

Companies that issued new shares of stock would embark on corporate road shows, stopping in major money centers like New York, Boston, or Chicago to make presentations to brokers, portfolio managers, and analysts. The 4:15 pm "due diligence meeting" was typically standing room only because these meetings always had open bars. Occasionally people in the industry would arrive late, but no one ever left early. During one Q&A

session, I recall that a clearly impaired individual asked former astronaut and then Eastern Airlines CEO Frank Borman, "How many pushups can you do?"

Drinking was an integral part of doing business. I don't recall anyone ever being counseled for drug or alcohol issues in the early 1970s. Back then what passed for substance abuse treatment was generally limited to drying out in a hospital or a psych ward. Nowadays, people struggling with addiction may no longer feel quite as stigmatized as they did in the past, and they can get help from their employers as well as from public and private treatment facilities; forty years ago, alcoholism was seen not as a disease but a choice. The industry's chief concerns were limited to what is today called "optics," meaning the impact that someone's behavior might have on the reputation of his or her employer. It was expected that you hold your liquor, manage your behavior, make it appear that you were not under the influence even if you were—and keep a breath mint handy at all times.

Trading errors were commonplace. Such errors occur when a customer loses money as a direct result of something that an employee did incorrectly or forgot to do altogether. These errors can occur for a variety of reasons—buy for sell (and sell for buy), wrong quantity, wrong symbol, or wrong account number. Sometimes an order might have been set aside and never entered, or an order that had been sitting on the books for days or even weeks was forgotten and never canceled as it should have been. (This usually resulted in buying or selling the same stock twice; in rare instances, orders were mistakenly executed after a customer had died or after he had transferred his account to another firm.) Policy dictated that as soon as an error was discovered, it was brought to the attention of management and corrected immediately. Any time a customer suffered harm, he was made whole—no questions asked—unless, of course, the broker responsible for the error attempted to intervene and mastermind the situation. Masterminding was very uncommon, but desperate people sometimes do desperate things.

One such incident stands out in my mind. The broker in question, whom I shall refer to as Max the Magician, was widely regarded as error prone. This extended to his personal life as well, as he had been divorced three times before the age of thirty, twice by the same woman. At work, he was leading the pack in trading errors, and rumor had it that he had committed close to thirty within a twelve-month period. He had without question earned his reputation for sloppy work and inattention to detail, and his employment status was anything but secure.

One of Max's clients was about to buy a house, and he needed to sell one thousand shares of then high-flying Polaroid to finance the transaction. Max mistakenly bought one thousand shares, bringing his client's total to two thousand shares, and as a result, he put his customer into a margin call. When the client called the office, Max told him that they could wiggle out of the trade quietly by selling two thousand shares, and because the stock had risen slightly in price, his client would end up with more money in his pocket. The customer consented, but Max proceeded to make the same mistake *again*. Faced with a new margin call, twice as large as the first, his customer blew the whistle. Not surprisingly, Max left the investment industry and was forced to seek employment elsewhere.

Women began to pursue Wall Street careers in meaningful numbers in the 1950s and 1960s, most commonly in securities research or perhaps in other areas like marketing, HR, or training. Sales and trading positions remained male-dominated. It was assumed (by males, of course) that only they had a reasonable chance of success in a sales career. This was rarely said openly but was nonetheless believed to be true, in much the same way that some white football aficionados quietly presumed that African-American quarterbacks did not possess the intelligence or leadership skills necessary to succeed in the NFL. In 1972, every retail and institutional broker working in my branch office was male, as was every manager and trader. Even as attitudes (and the law) changed, relatively few women sought out sales careers in the 1970s, and by then females were being actively recruited on Wall Street. Perhaps gender stereotyping had to some degree become ingrained in their minds as well. Or, more likely, many women may have felt uncomfortable, understandably so, in the locker room, frat house culture that prevailed during those years. Truthfully, there were many days I did as well.

Registration with the NYSE took a minimum of six months. At Merrill, the first four months were spent in the branch office preparing for a variety of examinations, some of which were quite exacting, and others embarrassingly easy. At that time, the Massachusetts licensing exam consisted of twenty multiple-choice questions, and every candidate got precisely the same questions in the same order. That one was hard to fail.

On my first day at work, I was shown to my desk and told to open the box that was on it and read every book packed inside. Reading these books represented my pre-class training assignment in its entirety. There was no apparent timetable and no preferred order of completion. When I wasn't reading, I was obligated to do whatever was asked of me—answer phones and take messages, make reservations, clean out closets, fetch coffee or address envelopes. My manager also required that I become involved in the Greater Boston Chamber of Commerce by soliciting new members for the organization. My principal task was to cold call professionals, executives, and business owners and pitch the benefits of membership in the Chamber. It was a wonderful introduction to my future career. I also quickly learned the meaning of rejection.

The final two months of my initial training were spent in New York City, attending formal classes. Exam preparation was certainly a key component of the program, but I also had a chance to learn about the Federal Reserve banking system, tax law and regulations, and complex financial statements as well as fundamental and technical analysis. It was a terrific program and in the eyes of many the best on the Street—in a way, perhaps, too good, because it seemed that half the world got its start at Merrill Lynch and then moved on to a competitor.

The primary reason behind this exodus was compensation. Founder Charlie Merrill was both a visionary and a maverick, and many of the principles that Merrill Lynch was guided by, at least in its earlier years, were quite revolutionary. Merrill wanted to bring Wall Street to Main Street and made a concerted effort to educate and actively court middle-class investors. Although the firm was private at the time, he insisted on publishing an annual report that disclosed how the firm earned its profit and how much it earned. He forbade the sale of mutual funds to retail investors, believing that their sales charges and fees were unjustifiably high— and at the then- customary 8½ percent level, he was correct. He prohibited the firm's branch managers from producing business or in any way competing with its retail brokers. Finally, he insisted that brokers at his firm be paid salary plus bonus, not straight commission. Until the late 1970s, Merrill Lynch brokers were paid something called supplemental compensation twice a year. The actual amount, of course, was closely related to an individual's level of revenue, but other factors, many of them quite subjective, were brought into the equation as well. The company was ultimately forced to break with this tradition because competitors offering higher payouts and monthly commissions could—and did—recruit a healthy number of the firm's brokers. Merrill brokers went on straight commission in the late 1970s.

Other things started to change during the 70s as well. The company began selling mutual funds in 1971. Not long after that, it got into the asset-management business and began to offer its own in-house mutual funds. Managers in all but the largest branches were required to maintain a practice with individual clients in addition to their other duties. As time went on, the firm's commitment to the small investor began to wane. Initially, the goal was to be all things to all people. That morphed into "all things to some people." Small accounts were shunned, as were small individual orders; in some of these instances, broker compensation was reduced dramatically and in time eliminated entirely.

However, many years before Merrill Lynch changed its modus operandi, it operated in lockstep with the principles laid out by its charismatic founder, Charlie Merrill, and this meant keeping its focus on serving the average American small investor. The *Sharebuilder* account was created to allow customers to save as little as fifty dollars a month in individual common stocks; this was later broadened to include precious metals when the sale of gold bullion became legal. Educational seminars targeting first-time investors were commonplace, and they were often held in public libraries of small towns. The so-called Sales Promotion department produced an enormous number of educational brochures and white papers for public consumption. Scripted seminars were supported with slide projectors and compliance-approved advertising. The company's logo and "Bullish on America" theme created a powerful brand identity. The firm even owned a small fleet of buses that operated as mobile offices, visiting towns and small cities that were at least a two-hour drive away from the nearest branch office. The ML bus may have looked like a giant snack truck, but in the end, it proved to be a success.

I appreciated all the support I was given, but what I remember most about my early years in the business was fear and financial insecurity. Fear was a constant motivator. For all of the training and mentoring I received, this much was plain: when I began my career, I had no customers. On Day 1, I took a seat at my desk. I had a rotary phone, a copy of the Boston Yellow Pages, several Chamber of Commerce membership directories, and a yellow legal pad. My manager stopped by to give me a pat on the back and said, "Go get 'em, tiger." I called someone whose name had been given to me by one of my training school classmates. The prospect was my co-worker's cousin. My colleague had told me that I most definitely should make this call—he insisted upon it if truth be told—and said that he could not place it himself because he felt awkward soliciting a family member. I went ahead and made the first outgoing call of my career, and then I heard three words: "Not today, Sonny." My life in the securities industry had begun.

A few weeks later, my boss exhorted me "to get out of the office." No, he wasn't giving me my walking papers, but instead was suggesting that I get in my car, drive somewhere far away from Boston and start walking up and down Main Street, calling on business owners, handing out cards, shaking hands, and smiling. I looked at my map and picked Athol, MA, a town known primarily for its unusual name. (The "a" in Athol, by the way, is not pronounced like the "a" in the word paste.) Athol was a small, dreary, isolated place, and I assumed its residents hadn't been approached by a retail broker in the past fifty years. I was wrong. Within a few minutes, it became obvious that someone just like me, from my own firm no less, had gone through the town a few days before.

It got worse. Not only was I young, inexperienced, and unsure of myself, the economy was awful, and the stock market reflected this reality. The Dow dropped almost 50 percent in two years' time; the American Stock Exchange and NASDAQ experienced even greater declines. The market struggled from late 1972 until the fall of 1973 when, in October, all hell broke loose. The Yom Kippur War saw the United States provide Israel with arms, and OPEC retaliated by instituting an oil embargo against America. This led to an immediate spike in oil prices, a genuine energy crisis, a deep recession and a bear market of epic proportions. Inflation and interest rates both rose to painfully high levels. The Vietnam War dragged on, and so did all things Watergate. Nixon resigned the Presidency on August 9, 1974, six days after my daughter was born. Now there was one more mouth to feed. It was in this environment that I began my practice, trying mightily to be optimistic, exuding energy and confidence; but sometimes it was hard to get going every morning, to feel the way I needed to feel, to walk the walk. Often, I felt bewildered and discouraged, but I soldiered on.

Unlike most sales or business development jobs, retail brokers do not have protected territories or a clearly defined universe of prospective customers. In a sense, anyone with a pulse and some money was fair game. Poaching accounts that had already established relationships with Merrill Lynch was highly discouraged, but apart from an occasional scolding, there were no adverse consequences for doing so—at least not in those years. This type of behavior, sometimes called "eat what you kill," persisted for a long time. It was more than embarrassing. Advisors in different offices and sometimes even the same office would go to war with each other over the same account. Teamwork proved to be elusive.

Don Regan was the firm's CEO throughout the 1970s. He was a compelling figure, brilliant, decisive, and intimidating. He was the son of a Boston cop who received a full tuition scholarship to Harvard University and worked as a theatre usher and campus tour guide to cover expenses for room, board and books. He graduated in 1940 before going on to Harvard Law the following year, but after Pearl Harbor, he dropped out and joined the Marines, serving in five Pacific campaigns, including Guadalcanal and Okinawa. He earned the rank of lieutenant colonel in his mid-twenties. After the war, he began his career at Merrill Lynch. At thirty-five, he became the youngest partner in the history of the company and later became its youngest president and its youngest CEO. It is no wonder that he left a powerful impression on everyone he met.

He had a tradition of speaking for a half hour or so to each of the account executive training classes during the New York portion of the instruction. At the session I attended, he told us how hard he expected us to work—days, nights, and weekends. He stressed that our spouses (he may have said wives) should understand that our jobs would be extraordinarily demanding and affect the amount of time we would be able to spend with our families. He went on to say that our future with the firm would be based upon the results we produced—just as it would be for him—adding that the security of his position as CEO was entirely in the hands of Merrill's Board of Directors. He stressed that if the Board members didn't approve of the job he was doing, they would fire him. Then he paused for dramatic effect, leaned over the lectern, and with a steely-eyed look, said, "They wouldn't dare." He had a smile on his face, but he meant what he said.

Once he was in town in the mid-70s to speak at the Harvard Business School. One of the eager young brokers in my office—I suppose that described all of us at the time—went to Cambridge to hear him speak. Afterward, she introduced herself and told him how much she enjoyed his talk. He looked at her and said, "How come you're not back in the office prospecting for new accounts?"

As blunt as Regan was, he is best remembered as an agent of change. He often took unpopular stands, the most controversial of which was his support of the deregulation of the securities industry. Among other things, this meant the end of the fixed commission structure that had been a staple feature of the business for several hundred years. Generally, regulation is designed to protect consumers, but in a sense, government regulation of pricing protected brokerage firms just like it did airlines, railroads, electric utilities and telephone companies. Regan spoke up for deregulation and the end of fixed commissions. He believed successful brokerage firms would become diversified financial supermarkets. We'll be examining deregulation in the securities industry and Regan's role in it later, but I am bringing his name up now because it was through his vision I learned how my job would be transformed in the future—or if I did not adapt to change, who I might become. Let me put it simply. I did not wish to become a dinosaur.

Call it what you will. Job descriptions such as customer's man, stock broker, account executive, investment broker or registered representative were all commonly used phrases to describe my work in 1972. The goals were simple: solicit and open new accounts. Perhaps one might add to that: do more business. Cold calls, direct mail, seminars, investment clubs, networking, and/or teaching adult education classes were all common techniques to establish a business, but cold calling was by far the most indispensable activity. It was never fun, but in 1973 and 1974 it was a near torturous experience.

The cold call practically defines the old-school stock broker, who was pretty much a hawker or a stock jockey. Today, the cold call has begun to be de-emphasized, mostly because of federal legislation ("Do Not Call" lists) and the influence of social media, but for many years it was an ever-present part of the business. I am sure that many cold call recipients thought Wall Street brokers were not much more than well-dressed and well-educated croupiers. Perhaps they even imagined us wearing green eyeshades (casino visors). Once I was introduced by my boss to a prospective customer as "one of our salesmen." I still remember the feeling of embarrassment and awkwardness. What in the world was I? Was I a real-life version of Professor Harold Hill, the central character in *The Music Man?* (Hill arrived in River City promising to teach the townspeople to play the musical instruments he sold them; in fact, he was a con man, who had no intention of giving music lessons—he couldn't even read music.) I had a sinking feeling that many investors believed that the stock brokers of that era had a little bit of Professor Harold Hill in their DNA.

Rule 405 was the "know your customer" mandate of the New York Stock Exchange. It required member firms to exercise reasonable due diligence in obtaining essential facts and records about customers who wanted to open a brokerage account. Such information, of course, was thought to be an indispensable first step in determining if an investment was suitable for a customer. In truth, that's what it was—a first step. Information asked for included name, address, date of birth, occupation, social security number, income, net worth, and a bank reference. Often customers would refuse to provide data on income and net worth, and banks would rarely confirm any information at all. Additionally, prospective clients were asked to provide us with an investment objective, but they were given only two choices: growth or income. Many chose both. The information was filled out by hand on a three-page carbon paper form and became part of the company's permanent books and records. Rule 405 did not cover investment strategies, decisions to sell securities, or decisions to hold them. There were no expanded investor profiles encompassing strategic goals, temperament, liquidity needs, and the like. (That came much later, after the credit crisis, with FINRA Rule 2090.) In 1972, a typical new account application could be completed within a minute's time.

Monumental effort was put into sales training along with honing and perfecting our communications skills; these would be essential components of our ability to succeed. Larger offices had full-time non-producing sales managers who spent most of their time recruiting, teaching, motivating, mentoring, and otherwise coaching inexperienced brokers. The importance of this professional guidance cannot be underestimated; without it, none of us stood a chance.

Most rookies in the investment business are eminently teachable for a very good reason. They arrive without any industry experience and have absolutely no idea what they are doing. First year law associates at least went to law school; doctors similarly attended medical school, and professional athletes prepared for their careers as amateur athletes. By contrast, I majored in American history, had no real sales or relevant business experience, and never took an economics course. One associate of mine had been an NCAA athletic coach. Another was an officer in the US Navy.

Virtually every element of the job was measurable, so it is easy to understand why almost everything one did was carefully analyzed. That has carried through to the present. Today's advisors have goals for new accounts, net new money, client retention, client satisfaction, assets under management, and many other variables. In the 1970s, newly minted retail brokers had one goal: opening new accounts. At Merrill Lynch, the typical standard of measurement involved carving out a group of brokers with similar lengths of service (say, less than two years' experience) and then ranking them in quintiles. Being in the fifth quintile was a ticket to Siberia, while landing in the first quintile was a pathway to the Promised Land. My primary concern during my first few years was acquiring new clients and earning membership in the first quintile. I asked my boss, "How many accounts will I need to open to be in the first quintile?" He said, "It's hard to predict. Just make sure you're in the top 20 percent." Again, I asked what, exactly, that would take. He replied, "Well, we won't know precisely until the end of the year. That's when we get the numbers."

Armed with this knowledge, I went cheerfully off to work, and luckily for me, I did end up in the first quintile. Obviously, 80 percent of my colleagues were not so fortunate. Underperformers were disparagingly referred to as "five-fives," meaning that they were in the fifth quintile in both new accounts and production. They were considered to be near-hopeless cases and found themselves constantly in the hot seat. Five-fives were frequently called into our manager's office, and with an open door and glass walls, it was easy to figure out what was going on. Sit-downs like this were designed to be counseling sessions, and they were, but each one also featured a stern warning about job security. We referred to this as "getting the lamp treatment," something that conjured up images of the interrogations in *The Manchurian Candidate*.

Sales contests have been frowned upon for some time and disappeared almost entirely after the 2008 credit crisis. Stories of Wall Street brokers romping in Hawaii or the Mediterranean on exotic incentive trips did not sit well with Congress or the American public during the Great Recession. The use of sales contests and incentive trips reached a crescendo in the 1980s and 1990s, but even in the early 1970s, contests were fairly common and thought to be an indispensable tool for motivating retail brokers and driving their behavior. Generally, they involved new business development (new accounts or new assets), and in subsequent years—as the business was transformed—they encompassed new products or innovative services like central asset accounts or financial plans. Even though I was never coerced to push a particular security, I wasn't entirely comfortable with the contest mentality. In my mind it tarnished the profession.

In any event, these contests, like all contests, had winners. Initially, a typical prize might have been a free dinner for two or a modest travel voucher, but as the years went on, the perks became more lavish. By the 1980s, luxurious trips to venues like Aspen, Hawaii, San Francisco, or Palm Springs became commonplace. In addition, the firm's biggest producers were rewarded each year with their own trip, one based solely on annual revenue. Before the dot-com bubble and the credit crisis, many brokers could attend two trips a year. Elite producers traveled to places like Beijing, Sydney, Florence, and Paris. We became very spoiled. Travel to Europe was booked business class, but domestic travel was always economy. Flying coach from Boston to LA provoked outcries from some. Sometimes life can be very cruel.

Syndicate business (new issues and secondary stock offerings) was popular with investors and brokers alike. In the early 1970s, the IPO market was virtually nonexistent; the stock market seemed to be in a state of perpetual freefall, psychology was negative, and more investors were getting out of the market than getting in. Still, established companies needed capital from time to time, and if they needed to raise equity, they would go to an investment banking firm like Merrill, Goldman Sachs, or Morgan Stanley. Electric and gas utilities were in the marketplace constantly. They needed capital to build new power plants and upgrade old ones, and since interest rates were sky high at the time, they chose the more economical alternative of selling stock.

One of those companies was Bay State Gas. Bay State was a small Massachusetts gas utility that currently operates under the name of Columbia Gas. It was purchased by NIPSCO (formerly Northern Indiana Public Service, now known as NiSource) in 1997. The company was largely unknown outside of Massachusetts, and as a result, stock allocations were limited to offices within Bay State's local service area. Honestly, it was hard to get excited about anything in 1974, and investing in Bay State Gas was not on the top of my list.

An informational office meeting was scheduled just before the Bay State stock offering. After a few perfunctory remarks about the company's operations and prospects, a door at the rear of the conference room opened and in sauntered a lovely young woman in stiletto heels and a blue bathing suit. I believe this occurred at approximately 8:30 a.m., a rather unusual time for an exotic dancer to go to work. Draped around her body was a ribbon that identified her as "Miss Bay State." Someone then said, "Gentlemen, may I present Miss Bay State!" At this point, the introduction seemed quite unnecessary. Music began to play, and she started to dance. Her movements were somewhat restrained—something on the order of a buttoned-down cha-cha, but at the end of her performance, she plopped herself in the office manager's lap. A rollicking good time was had by all.

For the next week or so, Miss Bay State proceeded to call every broker in the office to see how each of us was doing. These incoming calls were discreetly announced by the switchboard operator, "Miss Bay State would like to speak with you." However, if the call ended up getting bounced around the boardroom—as happened from time to time—someone would shout, "Mike, I've got Miss Bay State on my line for you!" And so it went. The offering was an unqualified success, and in fact, Bay State Gas turned out to be an excellent investment. Still, some forty-plus years later, I feel uncomfortable writing about the experience. Indeed, when I first witnessed it at the age of twenty-seven, I felt much the same way. This was hardly something I would want to run home and tell my family about.

Putting Miss Bay State aside, stock offerings like Bay State Gas were widely used by inexperienced brokers as a door opener and prospecting tool. Bay State Gas customers would be called on Bay State, in much the same way that hardware store owners would be approached on Black and Decker or pharmacists targeted on Bristol Myers. Additionally, such offerings were appealing to investors and brokers alike, partly because new issues like this were sold without the standard commission attached—the underwriting fee was paid by the company issuing the stock. Sometimes these were so popular that the same prospects were called three or four times a day by different brokers, often working at different firms, on the same deals. God help you if you owned a business in Fitchburg when Fitchburg Gas and Electric needed to raise capital.

Tuesday nights were work nights. Many of us would head across the street to a local watering hole on Pearl Street, the 99 Bar and Grille, and grab a hamburger and a beer, or perhaps a hamburger and several beers. Calling would begin in earnest around 6:30. Busy signals, no answers, or hang-ups were the norm. The friendliest, most welcoming people were almost always those with a preexisting Merrill Lynch relationship. One or two percent of the time we would stumble upon that rarity—someone genuinely interested in the financial markets, friendly, an engaged conversationalist and maybe, just maybe, willing to establish an account down the road. For the most part, though, work nights were like work days. They were long, hard, demanding, and filled with rejection and disappointment. Those of us who survived and went on to establish ourselves with some measure of success could never have done so without a sense of humor and the camaraderie that grew out of—how else can I say it?— the miserable experiences we all shared. Years later I saw the film version of *Glengarry Glen Ross*, a dark, disturbing David Mamet play about high-pressure real estate salesmen. A Siskel and Ebert review described Mamet using a "language in which the routine obscenities and despair of everyday speech are transcribed into a sad music." Strangely, I found the film oddly amusing, as did all my former co-workers who have seen it. It brought back a lot of memories.

I have mentioned several times that it was very hard for my colleagues and me to get established in our careers. In many ways, building a business from scratch—which is what I had to do—was the hardest thing I've done in my life. Attrition was (and is) high, especially in the first two or three years one spends in the business. Some brokers would join a competitor, thinking that if their new employer were a little bit smaller, perhaps somewhat paternalistic, they would be able to flourish in this new, friendlier environment. In most cases, this belief was naïve. Mediocre performers at Merrill became mediocre somewhere else. Other advisors left the business altogether, unable to deal with the pressure, the rejection, or the responsibilities that presented themselves. Whatever the case, whenever someone resigned, the next step (and by far the most pressing order of business) would be to reassign his accounts.

Reassigning accounts is like dropping a chum bag into a tank of piranhas. The feeding frenzy became especially acute if the departing broker resigned not to leave the industry but join a competitor and receive a fat signing bonus. Resignations almost always took place on Friday afternoon. There was no such thing as giving notice. Clients were contacted immediately, often during the weekend that followed the departure. You can imagine the thoughts and conversations that followed. Receiving broker: "They gave me some crummy accounts. I deserved better." Departing broker: "My old boss is hammering me and trying to hold up my registration; people who used to be my friends are picking apart the investment decisions I made." Clients asked, "Why did so and so leave?" The answer was usually a cryptic and dramatic, "I am not at liberty to comment." This led the departing broker to say, "I left because the research was poor; XYZ has a better research department." All of this was bogus, because it was always about the money.

Women who were unhappy with accounts that were handed over to them sometimes complained about sex discrimination, and members of minority groups would also have occasion to question the process of account distribution. Frankly, white males would bellyache just as much, perhaps more. Everyone seemed unhappy about the accounts he received. While no doubt some gripes were legitimate, many of the claims and counterclaims, accusations and retorts, were bogus. Whether justifiable or not, much of the dissatisfaction with customer account reassignment was revealing for one reason: it showed me, from my very first years in the business, that selfishness was the norm. The ways in which larger firms now reassign accounts has changed. The process is more transparent, orderly, and merit based. Nonetheless, the focus on "me first" is still front and center. This is one characteristic of the business that has remained a constant throughout my career.

Dinosaurs disappeared from the earth sixty-five million years ago. Their extinction was sudden, something unprecedented in the evolution of life on earth. Most scientists believe that a cataclysmic event, probably an enormous asteroid colliding with the earth, was responsible for the severe climate change that ensued. The death of the dinosaur allowed evolution to proceed in an entirely different direction.

This metaphor is something I have chosen to apply to the world of financial services. I didn't know it at the time, but when I was hired in 1972, the days of the dinosaur were about to end. The extinction process began only a few years later, on May 1, 1975. May Day marked the end of fixed commissions and the dawn of a new era along with the beginning of the democratization of Wall Street. In subsequent years, internet-based services like online trading and the repeal of the Glass–Steagall Act turned the industry upside down, and by 2000 the stock jockey of old had largely disappeared.

The customer's man we remember had two products to sell: stocks and bonds. He earned his income solely based on commissions that were both fixed (standardized) and high. The more you traded, the more your broker made. Sometimes this conflict of interest led to trouble, as one can easily imagine. At best, however, it appeared that the interests of Wall Street and investors were strategically misaligned, even if the arrangement worked for both parties, as it often did. Broker jokes abounded:

"It was so cold I saw my broker standing outside with his hands in his own pockets." Or, "My broker and I are working on a retirement plan. Unfortunately, it's his."

Deregulation and the advent of online trading led to a collapse in transaction costs, forcing Wall Street firms to switch gears. Brokers became advisors, commissions were largely replaced by asset-based fees, and the limited stock and bond menu was turned into a potpourri of items—commercial and individual lending, financial planning, corporate services, trust management, private equity, hedge funds, retirement plan design and administration and more.

Investors soon had lower prices, more choices, and better access to information. Stock jockeys began to age and fade away, and by the 1990s, the fate of the "old world" stock broker was sealed. Twenty years later, the Wall Street cowboy was gone, replaced by fee-based consultants, advisors, and planners. Yet for all the positive changes that have taken place, and there are many, Wall Street is more vilified than ever. The individual investor is alienated. Bankers and brokers are objects of scorn and ridicule. Often this feeling of contempt is without justification, because Wall Street is far from a society of monsters; nevertheless, it is both widespread and real. The dinosaur may have disappeared, but the world is not entirely secure and comfortable. Change is rarely easy or certain.

May Day

● ● ●

IN A SENSE, THERE WERE two May Days on Wall Street. The first occurred on May 17, 1792, when twenty-four brokers signed the so-called Buttonwood Agreement that formally established the New York Stock Exchange. On this day, the signatories established a floor on commission rates, and perhaps more importantly they also bound themselves to trade with each other on an exclusive basis. The NYSE was soon able to establish a dominant position in securities trading within the United States, and if anything, its influence grew as time went on. The exchange's member firms gave American companies much-needed access to capital and provided investors in publicly held securities a centralized and highly efficient marketplace for trading. The NYSE was no doubt an instrumental part of our country's growth and emergence as an industrial superpower—and there is also no question that the exchange and its insiders accumulated a fabulous amount of wealth in the process. That's not necessarily scandalous, but rather a simple statement of fact. The NYSE evolved into a monopoly whose members were protected from competition.

Each firm was able to create its own commission schedule, but since minimum rates were set by the exchange, the differences were trivial and largely meaningless. Commission rates were not published and were closely guarded secrets of every member firm. To make matters more opaque, the formulas used to calculate rates were complicated enough to challenge most math majors. Imagine something like this: "1.45 percent of the amount invested, plus $0.15 per share up to 2,000 shares, then $.10 per share for the next 3,000 shares, then $.05 per share on the excess, plus $50 for orders with a total market value of no more than $5,000, less $100 for orders with a total dollar value in excess of $50,000." Notwithstanding the above, the maximum commission on a single round lot (a hundred shares) of stock might be set at $65 and the minimum at $30, but trades of two hundred, or five hundred, or ten thousand shares would have their own minimums and maximums. Easy.

For all the complexity, one thing was immediately obvious: the rates were steep. Institutions got a break only because large orders were subject to a slightly more favorable schedule, not because most mutual funds or money managers had any ability to cut a deal. Larger institutions could skirt this through a form of rebating called commission splitting, now illegal. The SEC did move to loosen restrictions on orders over $500,000 in value a few years before May Day II, but prior to that there was absolutely no wiggle room. The old schedules employed a sliding scale where transactions were priced on a cents-per-share basis, not a flat rate. An order for twenty-five thousand shares would have a much lower (cents per share) rate than an odd-lot order of twenty-five shares, and in a sense, this represented some form of volume discounting. The bottom line, though, is that the commission charges on all orders—small, medium, or large—appear almost obscenely high when compared to those available today. I remember that an order for three hundred shares of AT&T, then trading about $50 per share, carried a commission of approximately $200. At the time my mortgage payment was $200 a month, and I was earning $200 a week.

Since the early 1970s, inflation has occurred in the prices of almost all consumer goods and services—what cost $100 then would on average cost nearly $600 today; but in the securities industry, we have seen *disinflation* of an unimaginable magnitude, a collapse of as much as 99 percent in retail transaction costs. Today, trades can be placed with an online discount broker for as little as $5 to $10, regardless of size. Full-service brokers have had to reinvent themselves and their business models to survive. Even if they had been able to retain their dominant market share over the years (and they haven't), the decline in transaction costs and trading revenue would have overwhelmed them several decades ago.

May Day II occurred in 1975. It arrived with much fanfare and some uncertainty as well, much like the opening of the Berlin Wall after the collapse of the Soviet Union. This particular May Day also marked the end of an era. From this point forward, Wall Street became, at least from the perspective of commissions that NYSE member firms could charge their customers, fully deregulated. The New World began with a simple administrative order from the SEC that came at 10:00 a.m. on Thursday, May 1, 1975.

On the tenth anniversary of May Day, Leslie Wayne wrote in the *New York Times* that when "fixed brokerage commissions were abolished...venerable (old school) houses crumbled and inestimable fortunes rose. Money flowed into Wall Street on a scale not known before, creating huge financial powerhouses. If someone had fallen asleep on May Day, only to wake on its tenth anniversary this week, he would find a restructured Wall Street, where the rules of the jungle prevail as never before, and only the fittest survive."

Smaller, privately held regional brokerage firms began to lose traction and relevance in this new world. Some failed to fully comprehend the changes that were taking place and how they would affect the concept of doing business as usual. How could something that had worked so well for two hundred years suddenly stop working? Perhaps these were the same people that thought Encyclopedia Britannica would successfully ward off competition from the internet because their customers would always prefer to use big, heavy, leather-bound books. After all, they were elegant and dressed up a living room.

I suppose Darwin's theory of evolution—the survival of the fittest—is always at work in a capitalist or free-market economy, but after Wall Street's May Day, all bets were off. Leslie Wayne's rule of the jungle metaphor was right on the money. Within a few years, many firms entered into a death spiral and perished. Whether it was through shotgun marriages or liquidation, the process of consolidation on Wall Street got a jump-start on May Day. Within a generation, dozens of companies, many with long, proud histories, simply disappeared.

One such firm, Moseley Hallgarten Estabrook and Weeden, is a good example. New York-based Hallgarten and Co. and Boston's F.S. Moseley merged in 1974. Both firms traced their roots back to the nineteenth century. Shortly after they combined, Weeden and Co. was acquired, and the new firm, now known as Moseley Securities, was listed on the New York Exchange. The firm had a nice split of institutional and retail business, a meaningful footprint with thirty branch offices, and a good name (Hallgarten) in investment banking. None of this mattered. Within fifteen years, Moseley was dead. Its retail business and branch office network were sold to Gruntal and Co. at a fire sale price after a prior deal—set at only $15 million—fell through. After the 1987 crash, it gave up on plans to continue in the institutional market segment and ceased operating altogether. By the way, Gruntal and Co. ended up being acquired by Ryan Beck, and Ryan Beck was, in turn, purchased by Stifel Financial. This game of financial musical chairs took place constantly, creating uncertainty and anxiety for employees, vendors, customers, and shareholders. I knew someone who was recruited by a regional firm on a Friday; when he went to work on Monday, he had a new employer. In a sense, he was lucky. Another acquaintance found the doors locked on what he thought would be his first day of work.

Transaction costs for institutions began to decline almost immediately after May Day, and they continued to drop without interruption for the next forty-five years. Institutional brokerage used to be a very lucrative business, and institutional account managers were looked upon with jealousy and awe by retail brokers. Institutional brokers arrived early, read the *Wall Street Journal*, and listened to a daily morning research call that went out to branch offices on a speakerphone known as the squawk box. These brokers would then proceed to call upon their clients—mutual funds, investment advisors, insurance companies, bank trust departments, etc.—to relay the highlights of the morning call they had just heard.

I don't wish to make light of it, but this was largely an exercise in regurgitation, e.g., "We changed our price objective on Boeing from 84 to 92; we went to a sell on MMM; we lowered our earnings estimate on IBM by five cents a share; we initiated coverage on Baxter." Information was always relayed using the third person plural. Then came lunch, usually with a client, and in the afternoon a few more calls. When the market closed at 4:00, the office emptied.

The old business model was simple. Full-service firms "earned" their commissions by providing research. For years, research was disseminated just as I have described, through a veritable army of institutional brokers serving a clearly defined and finite group of clients. Analyst reports were typically communicated via the telephone, one call at a time. Fax machines did not come into widespread use until the mid-1980s, and the internet was another ten years away. If you learned of a buy recommendation or earnings estimate change at 9:00 instead of 11:00, you felt fortunate to be on the A-list.

It is important to bear in mind that financial institutions like mutual funds do business with many brokers. They also employ analysts themselves. As such, they were not utterly dependent upon any particular brokerage firm for insight or analysis. The relationships they maintained with a brokerage firm were far different than the connections experienced by individuals. Individual investors may have been just as price sensitive as portfolio managers who oversee billions of dollars, but they had far less negotiating clout. Large financial institutions held all the cards, and they used them.

There were few discount brokerage firms in waiting before May Day. Charles Schwab was the exception. Chuck Schwab's company did well from the outset and perhaps could have grown even more quickly had it not been for a number of factors beyond its control. In 1975, Schwab had no physical branch offices, only an 800 number. The company had not aligned itself strategically with investment advisors, a major source of their revenue today. The firm had no 24/7 customer-service capability and an extremely limited menu of products and services. To make matters worse, the 1970s represented a very difficult investing environment. It is estimated that six million people pulled out of the market during the decade. Finally, this being the pre-internet era, many customers were skittish about depositing their securities with a name that was largely unknown, especially since they couldn't "see" their accounts online. In 1975, at least, saying you did business with Schwab was like saying you got a loan at Fred's Bank.

Despite these obstacles, the firm met with almost immediate success, and its later ascendancy was nothing short of remarkable. Joe Nocera describes founder Charles Schwab as "the luckiest entrepreneur" in one of his bestselling books, *A Piece of the Action*. I can't argue with Nocera that Schwab was in the right place at the right time, but the firm's timing was not entirely an accident.

Before he established his discount brokerage firm, Schwab himself had tried to bootstrap several different investment businesses as a young man. Unlike most entrepreneurs, he was weak on operational management, and he hated to sell. On the other hand, he was a visionary thinker, highly opportunistic, and by all accounts an exceptionally affable person, someone to whom people were instinctively attracted. Schwab got an early start, in 1973, when NYSE member firms were allowed to offer discounts on a very limited basis to small investors trading odd lots (less than one hundred shares). On Wall Street, these investors were looked upon as lepers, but Schwab felt that they represented an opportunity to get a jump-start in the nascent discount brokerage business. He began to take small ads in the *Wall Street Journal* advertising discounted commissions on odd lot trades, often posting his rates next to those of a full-service broker.

Most established firms must have thought he was mad. If the big boys couldn't make money on odd-lot trades with relatively high commission rates, how could Schwab expect to produce a profit if he was offering discounts of fifty percent or more? The answer soon became plain. Schwab did not employ offices full of highly compensated retail brokers, and the representatives in his one call center in Sacramento gave no advice. The provided one service and one service only: cheap trade executions. As it turned out, there were enough odd-lot traders who signed up with Schwab to convince the company that it was onto something that had real promise. When May Day arrived, Chuck Schwab was ready—a step ahead of his would-be competitors.

The establishment was not convinced. Full-service firms did not take the threat of defection of retail clients seriously. It was widely believed that given a choice, any sane investor would willingly pay up for professional advice and personalized service. Affluent investors did not shop at Walmart, travel by bus from Boston to New York, or go to a clinic for medical care. Why would they call an 800 number for matters concerning their personal investments? It was felt that the relationship between client and trusted advisor was impenetrable. Not one wire house cut its standard commission rates after May Day. In fact, the opposite was true—commission rates went up.

Retail brokers, called investment executives or account executives in the 1970s, were given some latitude to address competitive situations. In the beginning, this was done only as a last resort, principally to keep a client from running out the back door. That said, a typical response to a client seeking a discount was, "I'm sorry. I wish I could accommodate you, but we are not a discount brokerage firm." If the client persisted, modest discounts of 10 or 20 percent might be offered as a salve. Discounts of more than 35 percent were virtually unheard of, and often required regional or even national approval.

It took a while for Schwab to gain traction, and the company experienced many speed bumps long after it became the established force in the discount brokerage industry. In the summer of 1975, the firm was processing less than one hundred trades a day. Schwab opened its first brick and mortar branch office in Sacramento five months *after* May Day. Business jumped as soon as customers could visit a branch office and see live representatives face to face. As time went on, more branches were opened, but it was another three years before an office outside California was established. This was in every respect a start-up company, and it was chronically short of capital; Chuck Schwab on more than one occasion turned to his uncle, Bill Schwab, for a cash infusion. Initially, the firm's expansion was somewhat slow and measured, but ultimately, Schwab was able to create a national footprint.

As Charles Schwab and Co. grew, it needed even more capital to finance its growth, and in 1980, plans for an initial public offering of common stock were drawn up. An embarrassing computer failure forced the company to shelve the offering, and in 1983, Schwab was sold to Bank of America for $53 million. Five years later, Bank of America sold the company back to Schwab for over $280 million, with Schwab borrowing heavily to finance the purchase. At the time, Chuck Schwab said, despite being on the wrong end of this trade, "I am tickled pink." He was ever the optimist. In September of 1987, he finally got to take his company public at $16.50 a share. In October, the market crashed. One of Schwab's customers couldn't pay a $40 million margin call. By the end of the year, the stock was trading at $6. Chuck Schwab soldiered on.

The leading retail firms of the time—Merrill Lynch, Paine Webber, E.F. Hutton, Shearson, Bache and Dean Witter—were hardly shaking in their boots. In 1979, Schwab had thirty-three thousand customers—no mean feat—but still a drop in the bucket compared to the big wire houses. What's more, many of these customers were very small, or they traded infrequently, or both. Several years later, the entire discount brokerage industry had gained only a 5 percent market share of all retail commissions earned by Wall Street.

The term "value proposition" has been overused so much it has become terribly clichéd, like "disruptive." When it comes to May Day and the emergence of the discount brokerage business model, however, these words fit perfectly. Discounters were disruptive, of course, to a traditional, high-cost, full-service firm that had no intention whatsoever of competing on the basis of price. The discounters forced Wall Street's white-shoe firms to look inward, and, as such, identify exactly what their—please forgive me—value proposition was. This encouraged the established firms to diversify, something that many were in the process of doing anyway. They

began to offer enhanced products and services as well as more sophisticated account features in order to attract and retain affluent clients.

Merrill Lynch, then the dominant wire house and an industry leader,
was once looked upon as a blue-collar firm by the rest of Wall Street. It
used to think of itself as the firm that brought basic stock and bond investing to Main Street. In fact, it did. Small investors were welcomed with open
arms, but as the competitive environment changed, so did Merrill. Soon
it was attempting to connect with a smaller universe of affluent investors
while offering a larger and more diverse menu of financial services—not
just stocks and bonds but also mutual funds, options, cash management,
insurance, lending, real estate, fully managed private accounts, and limited partnerships. Retail brokers were now referred to as advisors or consultants and became heavily involved in gathering assets and cross-selling
more complex products. Branch offices everywhere became more opulent,
with mahogany desks and private offices. Firms sponsored golf tourna-
ments, operas, and ballets. No one sat next to a water cooler. By 1990, the
dinosaur was on its way to extinction.

Schwab and other leading discounters began to court the haves as well.
It made no less sense for them than it did for the old guard. Cutthroat competition among discounters brought commissions steadily lower. Schwab
was often the leader in this regard and created quite a buzz when it began
to offer trades for a flat rate of $29.95, and shortly after that $19.95. Of
course, $19.95 proved to be a very temporary floor. Transaction rates are
now typically between $5 and $10 throughout the discount industry, and
some firms offer free trades to extraordinarily large accounts. Discounters
realized it would become harder and harder to grow if they remained
entirely dependent upon transactional business where prices were falling
faster than trading volume was increasing.

Chuck Schwab was a visionary, and his company did a lot more than
cut rates in the 80s and 90s. The company introduced a mutual fund marketplace in 1984 that gave its customers centralized access to one hundred
forty no-load funds. In the same year, Schwab created proprietary software that enabled investors to manage and monitor their stock portfolios.

Remember that in 1984, Apple first introduced its Macintosh computer, and widespread use of the internet was another ten years away. This was just one example of Schwab investing early in technology to give the firm a leg up on its competition.

Schwab soon rolled out a touch-tone quote system, and a few years later a touch-tone order entry capability. The stock market had a decent run in the 1980s, and many investors who fled the market in the 1970s returned. Trading activity increased; Chuck Schwab's handsome, smiling face continued to grace print and television advertising, and the company continued to expand its branch office network. By 1994, Schwab achieved two milestones: $1 billion in revenue and $100 billion in customer assets—and this was only the beginning.

Widespread public use of the internet began in the mid-1990s. I still remember when Amazon announced sales numbers on a Monday after Black Friday—I believe it was 1996—and the market went on a historic tear. To me, this was a seminal event. It gave the concept of e-commerce instant credibility and was a major catalyst behind the huge run-up in tech stocks during the late 1990s. Amazon, which had been founded by Jeff Bezos just two years earlier, is now the nation's largest retailer in terms of market capitalization, having surpassed Walmart in 2015.

Schwab's growth was similarly exponential. The company's massive investments in technology were soon to pay off beyond Chuck Schwab's wildest dreams. Online trading was a spectacular success. You could trade anywhere, anytime, just like the big boys. It was easy, fast, convenient, private and inexpensive. What's more, from 1995 to 2000, the stock market enjoyed an unprecedented bull run, in some ways more frenzied and speculative than the 1920s. It was impossible not to make money. All investors felt they were geniuses, and many Americans quit their jobs to concentrate full time on day trading. I remember IPOs priced at $12 that opened at $150. Online trading was cool, no question, but making money in the process was even cooler. Investors poured into the market, and many became Schwab customers. In the five years between 1995 and 2000, Schwab's assets had ballooned from $100 billion to $1 trillion.

The rest of Wall Street blinked…. hard. Schwab's stock price was soaring, more than doubling in 1998 alone. At the same time, Merrill's stock was sinking, losing over half its value in six months' time. While this decline principally related to separate market forces—the Asian currency crisis, Russia defaulting on its debt, and the collapse of the hedge fund Long-Term Capital Management—it was clear that the dot-com boom and the spectacular increase in Schwab's market share were having an enormous impact on Merrill's core businesses and employee morale. That summer, Merrill's Private Client President John "Launny" Steffens caught a tremendous amount of flak when he said, "the internet should be regarded as a serious threat to Americans' financial lives." He was talking about day trading, especially in high-risk technology and internet stocks, but his intended message (one that turned out to be quite prescient) was lost in the noise. By the end of the year, Schwab's market capitalization exceeded that of Merrill Lynch. Within two years, Steffens was replaced by Stan O'Neal as President of Merrill's Private Client Division. Yes, this was the same Stan O'Neal that later became the company's CEO, the person widely believed to be responsible for the firm's collapse during the 2008 credit crisis.

When O'Neal took Steffens' place as President of Merrill's retail business, he also gained substantial influence and power; a year after he was bumped, Steffens walked away from Merrill Lynch. Steffens could sometimes appear to be a bit aloof to Merrill's army of brokers, but he was smart, fair, and universally respected. At first, he may have responded a bit slowly and cautiously to the competitive threat of Schwab and the other discount houses, but in the end, he helped to reshape Merrill Lynch to successfully meet this challenge. Under his watch, Merrill introduced a flat-fee brokerage account where a customer might pay 1 percent annually and can make unlimited trades without additional charges. Initially unpopular with the firm's advisors, this alternative ultimately proved to be highly successful in retaining (and attracting) customers who otherwise would have become someone else's customers. Also rolled out was Merrill Edge, a $29.95/trade Schwab look-alike that at the very least helped to stem attrition among the firm's most price-sensitive retail accounts.

The NASDAQ index peaked at 5048 in March 2000, a level it was not to see again for another fifteen years. The bear market that ensued was painful for all investors, but customers of online discount brokerage firms were hit especially hard. They traded heavily in internet stocks, and when those stocks cratered, shareholders experienced staggering losses. For Schwab and firms like it, this resulted in a loss of customers, a loss of market share, and a loss of capital.

The dot-com meltdown forced Schwab to implement massive layoffs beginning in 2001, and the company shuttered all of its operations in Japan and Australia. ETrade, Ameritrade, TD Waterhouse and other discount firms were engaging in a seemingly endless price war. In addition, there was the looming presence of Fidelity Investments, always a major player in the discount brokerage business and an absolute powerhouse in mutual funds and corporate retirement plans. Schwab was seeing declines in the number of customers, the number of trades, and the average revenue per trade.

The company decided to pivot and moved upscale. Schwab Private Client, in a sense a firm within a firm, was created to serve clients with more than $500,000 in assets. Clients with less than $50,000 in assets were subject to a commission increase, much to their dismay. This shouldn't have been too surprising. The same thing happened to small investors at Merrill Lynch, Morgan Stanley, and every other wire house on Wall Street. In some ways, the distinctions between "full-service" firms and bare-bones discounters began to disappear.

Branch office employees received additional training, and for the first time, customers who were looking for advice could come into a Schwab office and get it. Some of these offices became franchises, literally—independently owned and operated like McDonald's, 7-Eleven, or Hertz. Most important, though, was the commitment Schwab gave to Schwab Advisor Services, a unit created in the mid-1990s to provide back-office support (trading, clearing, custody, and recordkeeping) for independent investment advisors. Under this arrangement, Schwab and each advisor shared in fees paid by individual clients. In practice, it was not much different from what clients of Merrill or Morgan Stanley experienced. One individual provided advice, and one very large firm provided everything else. Today, Schwab Advisor Services, by itself, maintains 2.5 million accounts with $1.2 trillion in assets. Not bad.

In the summer of 1972, I was finishing up Merrill's account executive training program in New York City. One session was designed to familiarize the class with mutual funds and how to sell them on a cold call. It was presented by two Pioneer Fund wholesalers. One wore a string tie, the other a loud sports jacket and a white belt. Their presentation consisted of a scripted, make-believe telephone call between a salesperson and a prospect. I will never forget it.

"Mr. Jones, please?"
"That's me."
"Mr. Jones, thank you."
(silence)
"Mr. Jones, this is Goober Wilson from XYZ Securities."

At this point, the class was asked what it had just heard. Someone said sarcastically, "You just said the guy's name three times." At this point, the men from Pioneer got pretty excited, complimenting us on our listening skills, and quickly revealed that the best way, really the only way to begin a cold call is to say the prospect's name three times. Why? People like to hear their names. It makes them feel good about themselves and well disposed toward the person saying their names. The message was clear. Do you want to build trust and rapport? If you say a prospect's name three times at the beginning of a cold call, you have a better chance of making the sale.

It got worse. We heard a lengthy explanation of the Pioneer Fund's track record (by the way, it was a very good one). The fund began in 1928 and produced stellar returns despite depressions, recessions, World Wars, and Cold Wars. It was pointed out repeatedly that a $10,000 investment with dividends reinvested grew to a staggering amount. I recall something reaching into the mid six figures. Of course, it took forty-five years, and yes, there was a small sales charge (8½ percent), but that was thought to be a mere trifle compared to the bonanza waiting at the end. Our prospect asked, "How can you charge so little for such a wonderful investment?" At this point, we were informed, "Gentlemen, you have just heard a buying signal. Stop talking. Now all you need to do is fill out these forms to open an account. Are there any questions?" If I was left speechless, I wonder what Chuck Schwab would have said if he had been sitting in on this performance.

Deregulation, of course, not Chuck Schwab, was singularly responsible for the emergence of the discount brokerage industry, but Schwab had a colossal influence on the way in which the industry evolved. Schwab was a risk taker, as are all entrepreneurs. He was also a visionary. He instinctively knew that if his company were to have staying power, it would have to offer investors something beyond cheap transactions. While cutting commissions from $50 to $25 to $10 and lower helped to boost market share, it also represented a pathway to oblivion. Schwab quickly realized that his firm would have to diversify and scale up to stay relevant. And that's exactly what he did.

Schwab had plenty of critics. In the early years, he expanded very fast—some would say too fast. While he invested heavily in technology, he leveraged his company's balance sheet to do so, and the company almost failed as a result. He was chronically short of cash but remained committed to his vision for the business, something that few on Wall Street shared. He built his firm in a most unorthodox way—direct marketing. In the beginning, he had no salespeople and attracted clients exclusively by advertising in newspapers and on radio and television. The firm's advertising, by the way, always featured Schwab's handsome, smiling face. Other Wall Street CEO's may well have scoffed at the sight of his visage, thinking that his marketing strategy was laughably lowbrow. Whatever the case, it worked, just like Merrill Lynch's roving bus thirty years before.

On balance, the benefits made possible by discount brokerage and later online investing were inestimable—enhanced transparency, greater choice, immediate access to information, and (obviously) lower costs. May Day was clearly a defining event for our time, but it was not the only event. May 1975 hardly marked the dawn of investing utopia. Some things changed for the worse, and others didn't change at all.

Boys Will Be Boys

• • •

WHEN MARTIN SCORSESE'S *THE WOLF of Wall Street* was released in 2013, it became an instant commercial success, grossing almost $400 million in its initial release. Based upon the shameful history of the now-defunct brokerage firm, Stratton Oakmont, and its sleazy founder, Jordan Belfort, the movie shocked and titillated its audience. The film contained countless scenes of orgies, drug use, drunkenness, and misogynistic behavior. The word "fuck" or some iteration thereof was uttered at least five hundred times, setting a record for a mainstream Hollywood film that will likely never be broken.

I have been asked many times if the film was an exaggerated work of fiction, or if it represented an accurate depiction of life on Wall Street. What can I say? Sex sells. John Lefevre's *Straight to Hell* and Turney Duff's *The Buy Side* are practically a matched set of contemporary literature— two hush-hush "inside stories" about deplorable behavior on Wall Street. Lefevre, interestingly enough, had originally gained notoriety for his @ GSElevator twitter feed, writing about conversations that he claimed to have heard riding up and down the elevators at Goldman Sachs. (Later, he admitted he never actually worked at Goldman.)

In any case, both books read like never-ending narratives of drinking and debauchery, similar to the plot line of *The Wolf of Wall Street*. Picture *Animal House* with Tim Matheson and John Belushi as thirty-something sales traders in wingtip shoes and Brooks Brothers suits; Duff and Lefevre, unlike Belfort, had the degrees (and pedigrees) of Wall Street's best and brightest. Their shenanigans and high jinks went on seemingly without end, as did the partying with tequila, cocaine, and prostitutes. The front covers of each book don't leave much to the imagination either. *Straight to Hell* promises "true tales of deviance, debauchery, and billion-dollar deals." *The Buy Side* offers up an image of a striped blue tie, upside down, formed in the shape of a hangman's noose along with the tag line, "a Wall Street trader's tale of spectacular excess."

Much less well known than *The Wolf of Wall Street* is Ben Younger's *Boiler Room*. The film is entirely fictional but having been released in 2000, four years after the failure of Stratton Oakmont, the parallels could not be clearer. Giovanni Ribisi plays a college dropout, Seth Davis, desperate to gain the approval of his father by pursuing a legitimate career as a stockbroker. He naïvely joins a Long Island chop shop that preys upon gullible investors through an army of young, wildly aggressive, cold-calling white males. When they are not cold calling, they drink, party, gamble, and spend money recklessly. They are consumed by the idea of making as much money as possible as quickly as possible. As time goes on, Seth learns that his employer, J.T. Marlin, is really a criminal enterprise, taking fake companies public and manipulating their stock prices afterward. In the end, he has a spiritual awakening of sorts and brings in the FBI. The government ends up closing the firm, and with it also closes a tragic chapter in Seth's life.

To be truthful, this extreme level of behavior was not and is not the norm among established Wall Street firms, although it was probably the case with Stratton Oakmont. Certainly, major investment firms and banks are not criminal, fraudulent enterprises that manipulate markets and launder money; and most Wall Street professionals are fully committed to their work. Yet it is undeniable that Wall Street was and in many ways still is a good old boys' club, where profit and productivity trump all, and egregious behavior in the workplace has been quietly ignored. I might add that such behavior outside the workplace until very recent times has been similarly overlooked and often winked at. Even today, in an era of relative enlightenment, incidents of sexual harassment and sex discrimination occur with numbing regularity. Wall Street may have no monopoly on bad behavior, but its reputation in this realm has been well earned.

Years ago, I was friendly with someone who had loads of talent, a lovely family, and a bright future. He was also upbeat, outgoing, and full of positive energy. That he squandered it all is undeniable. He fell victim to a trifecta of addictive behavior—sex, alcohol, and compulsive spending. He once had a lavish lifestyle that included two vacation homes (summer and winter) and two boats (power and sail). When he lost all the toys, and his house was foreclosed on, he had to move into a small apartment. He drifted from firm to firm, always failing to meet expectations, cutting corners, womanizing, and disappointing all of his employers by performing poorly. He mismanaged his own financial affairs and bounced checks in his own account. He found himself in constant trouble due to formal customer complaints. His career took him from large reputable firms to small reputable firms to small not-so-reputable firms to bucket shops. Through it all, there were sexual peccadilloes, sometimes with other employees or even subordinates that inevitably affected office morale and his employer's reputation in its community. Finally, nearly seventy years old and after yet another customer complaint, he was banned from the industry by FINRA, which chose not to impose a fine after recognizing he had no assets with which to pay it. Through it all, despite being dismissed by a series of employers or forced to resign on many occasions, he always was able to land on his feet and convince yet another firm to give him one more chance, explaining that "this time it would be different." It never was. He lived his life as if he were a nineteen-year-old college student on a never-ending spring break. Apparently, until FINRA applied the death penalty, all was forgiven.

Sex discrimination laws have been on the books for a very long time. The Civil Rights Act of 1964 was without question a transformational piece of legislation, the signature achievement of Lyndon Johnson's *Great Society*. Title VI forbade discrimination in the workplace on the basis of race, color or national origin; Title VII similarly prohibited sex discrimination and created the Equal Employment Opportunity Commission.

More legislation both on the state and federal level followed the Civil Rights Act of 1964. Affirmative-action hiring quotas, still controversial, were mandated as early as the late 1960s. In 1972, the subject of civil rights was again addressed in Title IX legislation, parts of which applied directly to women's college sports programs. Senator Birch Bayh, who shepherded Title IX to passage, said, "We are all familiar with the stereotype of women as pretty things who go to college to find a husband, go on to graduate school because they want a more interesting husband, and finally marry, have children, and never work again. The desire of many schools not to waste a 'man's place' on a woman stems from such stereotyped notions. But the facts absolutely contradict these myths about the 'weaker sex' and it is time to change our operating assumptions." Title IX was signed into law by none other than Richard Nixon.

The Declaration of Independence proclaimed, "We hold these truths to be self-evident, that all men are created equal, that they are endowed by their Creator with certain unalienable Rights, that among them are Life, Liberty and the pursuit of Happiness..." Equity, fairness, tolerance, and freedom have always been core American values. As our nation grew, these principles were applied more broadly throughout society, not just among English-speaking white males. Slavery was abolished. Voting was extended to women and minority groups. A variety of social programs were created in the 1900s. Social Security and Medicare are just two examples of the federal government becoming an active advocate and protector of the wellbeing of *everyone* who calls the United States his home. In this respect, it is not surprising that landmark civil rights legislation—focused upon the rights of women—became the law of the land.

Still, the path to genuine equality has been a slow one. Phrases like "glass ceiling" and "gender gap" will likely remain part of our lexicon for many years to come. It may not be easy to pass controversial legislation, but it is much easier than trying to change attitudes and behavior. Tom Wolfe's *Bonfire of the Vanities* was a hugely successful and entertaining novel about Wall Street in the 1980s and the powerful, wealthy men at its center. He called them Masters of the Universe. The moniker still lives on today. After the Lehman bankruptcy in 2008 and the onset of the credit crisis, Wolfe was asked what would become of the so-called "Masters." He wrote in the *New York Times* that there were "ambitious young men (note his choice of words) who, starting with the 1980s, began racking up millions every year — millions! — in performance bonuses at investment banks like Salomon Brothers, Lehman Brothers, Bear Stearns, Merrill Lynch, Morgan Stanley and Goldman Sachs. The first three no longer exist. The fourth is about to be absorbed by Bank of America. The last two are being converted into plain-vanilla Our Town banks with A.T.M.'s in the lobby and, instead of Masters of the Universe, marginally adult female cashiers with wages in the mid-three figures per week, stocked with bags of exploding dye to hand the robbers along with the cash. American investment banking, the entire industry, sank without a trace in the last few days." Perhaps I am taking him too literally, but when Wolfe talks about his "Masters" being replaced by marginally adult female cashiers, he seems to be in a bizarre state of mourning because his *padrones* of Wall Street were knocked off their perches. Maybe his tongue is embedded in his cheek, and I can't appreciate the intent behind his words. Maybe not.

I have observed more than a few instances of questionable behavior during my career, and in most cases when a truly egregious offense was brought to light, an appropriate punishment was meted out. All large firms today have a heavy investment in regulatory compliance and a zero-tolerance policy toward major infractions. In fact, that was the case at Merrill long before I joined the firm. Sexual harassment, however, was treated differently, and rarely if ever were consequences suffered if the issue at hand could be explained away by saying "boys will be boys." If the "boy" in question was a star analyst or a highly productive sales trader or retail financial advisor, he might be scolded. Or not.

I once saw a married broker strip down to his speedos during an evening dinner/dance attended by several hundred people including his wife, his manager, his manager's manager, and the manager of his manager's manager. There were no consequences, and he continued his career without interruption. On another occasion, a branch manager repeatedly hired limousines for himself and several brokers for what can perhaps best be described as a boys' night out at Providence, Rhode Island's 10,000-square-foot strip club, the Foxy Lady. He was never reprimanded.

Some years ago, I attended an office Christmas party at which a local manager arranged for a male stripper to entertain all those in attendance; the guest list included his sixteen-year-old daughter. The executive's boss, a close friend of mine, called me the next morning to corroborate what he had heard and what I had seen. I confirmed the sordid details. He was genuinely horrified but hesitated in pulling the trigger, choosing instead to give the manager another chance. Later, he assisted him in finding comparable employment in another area of the country, where he could get a fresh start. If given the opportunity, I could very well have done the same thing. At this point, our erstwhile party planner became involved in a sexual harassment lawsuit brought by a former subordinate and was forced to resign after embarrassing revelations of his behavior became public.

I was also privy to an instance of sexual harassment where the perpetrator was a client! This occurred one year before the Christmas party incident described above. As was the tradition throughout the 1970s and 80s when long distance calls were expensive, we opened our offices one Saturday morning every year to allow our clients to make holiday calls anywhere in the world. One family group—grandpa, parents, and children—entered together, but grandpa, a sweet-looking man near eighty, propositioned every woman in sight, in very graphic terms. He described body parts and sex acts in disturbing detail. No one encouraged him to keep it up, but no one forced him to leave either. Perhaps he felt right at home.

Public awareness of sex discrimination and harassment on Wall Street increased significantly after the 1980s. The so-called first wave of feminism appeared about one hundred years ago and concerned itself primarily with suffrage and property rights. The second wave was launched with the publication of Betty Friedan's groundbreaking 1963 book, *The Feminine Mystique*. To Friedan, the mystique was that women could be fulfilled by being housewives and mothers. At the time, this "mystique" was (almost) universally accepted as fact. The second wave was witness to a number of genuine advances in gender equality, but there was also an element of stridency that turned off broad segments of the population. Second wave radical feminists were looked upon as man-haters and spoken of pejoratively as "women's libbers" or "bra burners." Feminism's so-called third wave began in the 1980s and is still active today. Among other things, it expanded the focus of feminism to include sexual harassment in the workplace.

Often sexual harassment and sex discrimination occur hand in hand. One case I am intimately familiar with is that of a former co-worker, Teresa Contardo, who sued Merrill Lynch in 1984. She was represented by Nancy Gertner, then a practicing attorney specializing in women's rights and civil liberties; later, Gertner became a federal judge. She now teaches at Harvard Law. The case did not go to trial until 1989, and after years of preparation, discovery, and depositions, the outcome was somewhat inconclusive.

Contardo v. Merrill Lynch did not involve an enormous financial award, nor did it evolve into a class action involving dozens or hundreds of brokers and many different investment firms. In the end, Merrill Lynch was assessed actual damages of one dollar and punitive damages of $250,000, the latter amount at best little more than Contardo's legal expenses. I think it is fair to say that both parties lost. Contardo could not have been pleased with her financial award, and Merrill Lynch's reputation took a big hit as the details of the lawsuit became public. The trial itself created adverse publicity for Merrill and had a demoralizing affect within the firm.

To me, the case is noteworthy for several reasons. First, it was one of the earlier sex discrimination lawsuits filed by a female broker. The broker in question was successful and secure in her employment. Most important, Contardo v. Merrill Lynch showed how hard it is for a plaintiff to "win" a sex discrimination lawsuit, or at the very least to win big. There are no fingerprints, murder weapons, or other elements of physical evidence. Much of the testimony can be categorized as "he said, she said"; there are rarely smoking guns, and very little in the written record is strictly black or white. Corporate policies and actions can be rationalized or justified for a variety of different reasons—many of them perfectly valid, others not. In the end, every fair-minded person must realize this: not every woman who claims to have experienced bias in the workplace has in fact been victimized in this way. Allegations like these are hard to prove.

Gertner's 2010 book *In Defense of Women: Memoirs of an Unrepentant Advocate* makes for engaging reading. Her cryptically titled chapter "Sexual Harassment Pays; Sex Discrimination Doesn't" focuses on the Contardo case. I was deeply interested to learn of her interpretation of events that occurred more than thirty years ago and to compare it with my own memories and assumptions. She writes, "There was the usual fare—pornographic pictures left on her desk, conversations laced with sexual innuendoes, a flood of sexist jokes." Yes, that was the environment at the time. That's the way it was in 1972 when I was first hired, years before Teresa was employed. There may not have been female brokers then, but there were plenty of female employees.

Contardo was rejected by Merrill Lynch when she first applied for a job as an account executive trainee. Gertner assumes Merrill rejected Contardo "because of her reaction to their written employment test, which included such classic questions as 'What qualities appeal to you in a woman?'" Let's understand that Contardo first applied to Merrill in the mid-1970s, when a question like this—one that may seem laughable if not outrageous today—was considered common fare at the time. Putting that aside, is such a question relevant in determining an applicant's suitability for the job? No. Is it helpful? No. Can it in any way make a female applicant feel empowered to answer it? No. Yet it's a big leap of faith to assume Contardo was summarily turned down by Merrill because she may have given the "wrong" answer, or just squawked about the question on this psychological test. It is twisted logic to connect the dots in this fashion.

Here's where we can get lost in the weeds. It is entirely possible that Merrill Lynch had stronger candidates at the time, especially from the kind of applicant it was laser-focused on hiring—an individual with a consistent history of successful business experience, especially in sales. Or perhaps they just made a mistake. Who can say? In my career, I have hired plenty of men and women, and I have rejected them as well. Sometimes the people I hired didn't pan out, and others I passed on found their way into the business and built successful businesses with a competitor. One never knows.

Gertner goes on to talk about the last straw, so to speak, the one that led Contardo to file a formal complaint. In the late 1970s, Merrill, like many other wire houses, began to promote tax shelters. These were typically private real estate syndications for apartment or office buildings; each deal could accommodate a small group of affluent investors—perhaps forty or fifty in every transaction—who would pony up upwards of $100,000 apiece to participate. Because of the generous tax benefits they offered at the time, these offerings were always in short supply, much like a hot new issue. Brokers and customers would queue up in advance, clamoring for a piece of the pie, and they were almost always disappointed.

Contardo believed that she was denied the opportunity to participate in these deals because she was female. She felt she was similarly mistreated when the accounts of a departing broker were reassigned throughout the office, or when any of the local professional sports teams were playing at home and she couldn't get a few of the firm's tickets to entertain her clients. I am certain that at her core she believed that sex discrimination disadvantaged her.

At that time, I experienced much the same treatment as did Contardo over the distribution hot issues, account reassignments, and sports tickets, and like her, I stewed with resentment on every such occasion. Frankly, so did everyone else in the office. Do the math. If there are four tickets available to a World Series game, and a few hundred employees with tens of thousands of clients want them, someone is going to be disappointed. It might have led me to dismiss her claims out of hand as having no basis in fact—just an example of pettiness and sour grapes. Yes, I did get some goodies occasionally, but I always understood this to be a function of performance, not gender. That's my honest opinion, but I do understand that an opinion is not a fact. That's why the case went to trial.

Was Teresa Contardo's claim frivolous? I think not. It was just hard to prove. The blurry nature of the testimony, which was often contradictory, made the issue of assessing damages especially problematic. I can think of no other reason why the actual award was one dollar, while punitive damages were set at $250,000. There were instances, many instances, of gross and sometimes outrageous behavior that took place during her time in Merrill's Boston branch, but no clear proof of any financial price that she paid as a result.

Gertner herself knew this was no slam-dunk case. She writes, "On the eve of the trial I was worried. What were the damages?" She goes on, "How could we show what she would have earned had she received the same advantages as the men did?" Gertner rightly understood that it would be foolish to base a claim on the value of Celtics tickets or access to a handful of tax shelter investments. She says, "the reassignment claim was key," thinking it would be relatively easy to place an economic value on a "retired broker's accounts." Gertner blames Merrill Lynch for keeping poor records (true enough), something that made her task of establishing a fact-based claim next to impossible. The records may have been poor, but as a practical matter, Gertner misses a pretty big point—during the time in question, hardly anyone retired. During the 1970s and early 1980s, I recall only one individual in the office where Contardo worked, Paul Dusossoit, who actually bowed out in this way. Most brokers were in their twenties and thirties. Successful brokers who left the firm did so to join a competitor and took the lion's share of their accounts with them. Unsuccessful brokers, whether they were terminated or left the business of their own volition, had small books of business filled with small accounts. No one would want them.

In any event, there was no science applied in the reassignment of accounts. Managers generally attempted to oversee a balanced and fair distribution, if for no other reason than to avoid an office mutiny. They were almost never successful in this public relations effort, and virtually every broker felt mistreated when the reassignment process was completed. That said, the best accounts by and large went to the most productive brokers. This made sense in theory. It also meant that the most successful senior advisors (white males) would end up with the most lucrative accounts.

Sex, age and race discrimination lawsuits have changed all of that. Today, most large investment firms reassign accounts based on a formula that combines many strategic metrics. One would think that reassignment by such a formula would remove any possibility of favoritism or discrimination. Human nature being what it is, those that find themselves at the bottom of this new, transparent pecking order often feel as if they are victims of a rigged system. In their minds he metrics themselves must somehow be unfair.

Today, $250,000 doesn't seem like a lot of money, and it was far from a staggering sum twenty-five years ago. The importance of this case cannot be measured in money. When the verdict was handed down in 1990, the *Boston Globe* reported,

> In one of the largest punitive damage awards ever handed down in a sex-discrimination case, the first woman stockbroker at Merrill Lynch & Co. in Boston won a $250,000 award against the brokerage house yesterday.
>
> Teresa Contardo, a 53-year-old Charlestown native who worked at Merrill Lynch from 1972 to 1984, said she is "elated" by the US district judge's decision and hopes it will encourage other women to fight sex discrimination in the workplace.
>
> "Merrill Lynch was barbaric in their treatment of women. They treated me immorally and illegally, and it tormented me for years," said Contardo, who said she was driven to drink and had to seek psychiatric help.

If Contardo did not achieve a knockout win in the judgment, she certainly could claim victory in the court of public opinion. Merrill Lynch's reputation was badly tarnished by many of the disclosures and attendant publicity. In the years that followed, more and more women became active litigants in sex discrimination lawsuits. None was bigger than the so-called "Boom Boom Room" lawsuit first filed in 1995 against Smith Barney. The tawdry details that emerged from this made the Contardo case humdrum by comparison.

It doesn't take much imagination to figure out how the "Boom Boom Room" got its name. The room itself was located in the basement—yes, the basement—of Smith Barney's office in Garden City, NY. Calling it a party room would be charitable. All of the gory details can be found in Susan Antilla's *Tales from the Boom Boom Room: Women vs. Wall Street.* Antilla is a well-respected financial journalist and deserves kudos for heightening public awareness on this very difficult subject. The atmosphere described was akin to that of an 1800s saloon when pioneers, gold prospectors, and itinerant cowboys would gather for a bit of adult entertainment. Maybe worse.

Initially, the lawsuit was limited in scope, much like the Contardo case. It was first filed by Garden City broker Pamela Martens, and she was soon joined by two of her co-workers. In 1996, twenty other women joined the original three in a gender discrimination class action, and a settlement was reached the following year that carried a price tag of $15 million. Martens and a few others did not participate in the settlement, choosing instead to soldier on. Over time, they were joined by some twenty-five hundred other women, and in 2008, Smith Barney was finally able to close the door on what had become a profoundly embarrassing nightmare, and an expensive one at that. The final cost was upwards of $150 million.

The early-mid 1990s and early 2000s saw an exponential increase in sex discrimination and sexual harassment lawsuits; every major Wall Street firm was hit with hefty financial judgments and adverse publicity. UBS, Morgan Stanley, Goldman Sachs, Wells Fargo and Merrill Lynch were all sued successfully. Even though most of the cases were settled, and in all of the settlements the usual qualifier—"without admitting or denying guilt" appears—these firms together wrote checks for over $500 million. In addition, the firms were forced to make a number of material changes in their internal policies and operations.

At one point the Equal Employment Opportunity Commission (EEOC) even joined a former star broker, Allison Schieffelin, one who had been making $1 million annually, in her lawsuit against Morgan Stanley. Schieffelin had claimed the firm had passed her over for a promotion. She then had a few run-ins with her manager and filed a formal complaint alleging sex discrimination. After some months of stressful negotiations, Morgan fired her. Apart from the fact that it is highly unusual for a firm to terminate someone after the filing of a sex discrimination complaint, Morgan seemed to have a defensible position. First and foremost, the job that Schieffelin wanted, the one she said was denied her due to gender bias, was given to another woman. Schieffelin, the top producer in her unit, was made out to be a petulant if not disruptive prima donna by Morgan Stanley. Her manager wrote she was verbally abusive and insubordinate.

Sometimes appearances can be deceiving. Shortly after negotiations between Morgan and Schieffelin broke down, other Morgan Stanley female employees joined her complaint against the company. We will never know all of the evidence that was collected during discovery, nor do we have access to testimony given in depositions, because the case was settled on the eve of the trial for $54 million. Even on Wall Street, that's a lot of money. Schieffelin received $12 million, $40 million was distributed among the other women who had joined in the lawsuit, and $2 million was set aside for diversity training.

Perhaps recent revelations of gross sexual misconduct by politicians and celebrities will prompt a meaningful change in workplace behavior. However, until now few women, even those no longer active in the business, are comfortable in talking publicly about this subject—understandably so. Roz Goldberg is not one of them. Smart, resourceful, and resilient, Goldberg started her career at Merrill Lynch in 1975 as an account executive in New York City, moved over to a junior position in the tax shelter area, rose to run that department's marketing staff, and later to oversee the department itself. Before retiring in 2001, she was responsible for all private equity deals distributed through the firm's Wealth Management division. She worked tirelessly on behalf of the firm's clients, shooting down as many as four hundred deals because they didn't meet the standards both she and Merrill had established. She had a great run and is justifiably proud of her accomplishments. Besides that, she has many fond memories of Merrill and the relationships she established during her tenure there.

I was surprised then by some of the stories she told me when we met in 2015 because Roz Goldberg is not an angry, bitter former employee, the kind that would spew venom if given a chance. She was just being honest. When she started her first job with Merrill, she was, like the rest of us, new to the business, anxious and uncertain. She approached one of the office's established brokers at the suggestion of her manager and asked this individual if he would be available for coaching and guidance. He said, "Sure, let's have lunch," and then proceeded to come on to her very aggressively. She made it clear she wasn't interested. The man, who happened to be married, continued his pursuit, and in Goldberg's words it became "obsessive." Notes and phone calls followed without letup. Then she received a phone call from the broker's wife, who angrily told her to "leave my husband alone" because "you are destroying my family." Confused and somewhat paralyzed, she briefly left Merrill Lynch, fearing that if she complained, no one would listen, and her status at the company would become even more uncertain.

She described many other incidents of harassment over the years. She remembers investment bankers talking about their erections or her nipples. Comments of this nature didn't crop up every week or even every month, and the vast majority of the men in the firm treated her with respect, but of course, it is the few that did not whom she remembers. Even though a relatively small group of men harassed her in this way, they did it constantly and apparently with impunity. That didn't surprise me at all. I have seen people fired, and I have fired them myself, for any number of reasons: poor performance, chronic absenteeism, disruptive behavior, misrepresentation, fraud, exercising unauthorized discretion, trading errors, covering up trading errors, forging client signatures, falsifying employment applications, and churning accounts to maximize commissions. However, I have never, not once, seen anyone terminated because of crude sexist remarks, even when they have been made to the same individual over an extended period of time. I recall that at one Christmas party a broker in his late sixties asked a woman in her twenties to dance with him and then inquired, "Do you make love the way you dance?" He had been making unwelcome advances toward her for months, and she had formally complained about his behavior on a number of occasions. In the end, nothing happened.

Our society seems to send and receive mixed signals over the issue of sexual harassment. Bill Clinton's affair with Monica Lewinsky was problematical for some, but his many supporters —almost all of whom were vocal supporters of women's rights—repeatedly minimized the scandal by saying "It's only sex" and "It's time to move on." A few months after Arnold Schwarzenegger's term as Governor of California ended in 2011, news broke that he had fathered the child of his long-term, live-in nanny years before, in 1998. Without missing a beat, he returned to Hollywood, as popular as ever. He starred in a series of movies and ultimately began hosting *Celebrity Apprentice* on television. This show, of course, was created by Donald Trump, elected President after being caught on a live mic bragging about the benefits of fame that allowed him to "do anything he wanted" with women including "grabbing them by the pussy."

While Clinton, Schwarzenegger and Trump were behaving badly, women won countless victories in court that solidified the legislative success they had achieved decades earlier. The financial penalties imposed upon Wall Street firms were severe, and the damage done to their reputations, if anything, was worse. Major Wall Street firms rewrote their policy manuals and re-engineered many components of hiring, training, evaluation, and compensation. Diversity became so prominent a watchword that it seemed like Goldman Sachs, Morgan Stanley, Merrill Lynch and the rest were about to become charter members of the Rainbow Coalition.

Surprisingly enough, Wall Street became gay-friendly long before the Supreme Court legalized same-sex marriage, offering health insurance and all other benefits to domestic partners—regardless of gender. Morgan Stanley has hosted an LGBT leadership summit called "Out on the Street" for the past six years. Goldman Sachs maintains an Office of Global Leadership and Diversity that is involved in a multitude of programs supporting women and minority employees. Similar efforts are common at every major Wall Street firm. Wall Street at the highest corporate level has been out in front of the push toward diversity. I remember hearing as early as 1973 how important it was to develop a more diverse workforce. As a manager—and this goes back over thirty-five years—part of my bonus was dependent upon minority recruiting.

Wall Street's highly vocal support of diversity was no doubt influenced by the wave of discrimination lawsuits brought by women and minorities over the last twenty years, but much of this attitudinal change was sincere. Wall Street executives are not monsters. They are by and large good people who want the best for their customers, their employees and their shareholders. It is perplexing then that despite all the legislative reforms, legal settlements, and court decisions that have been handed down, sex discrimination still plays a role in the career pathways of women on Wall Street, albeit less extensively than in years past; and sexual harassment likewise is omnipresent, perhaps less overt and egregious than before.

The prohibition era did not end the consumption of alcohol or the occurrence of alcoholism. Posted speed limits didn't stop people from driving too fast, and truancy laws didn't eradicate class cutting. Today we live in an age of relative enlightenment, our language often holding up common ideals of empowerment, tolerance, and individual human rights. Why then have bias in the workplace and sexual harassment remained such a staple part of life on Wall Street? Can it really be nothing more than "Boys will be boys?"

I think not. Most likely high-T and alpha male behavior would not be that visible or pervasive unless most of the power and influence were also in the hands of men. This is especially true on Wall Street. Even today, almost 80 percent of first year investment bankers are male. Wall Street veteran Sallie Krawcheck opined that today's numbers are not much different from the time she started in the late 1980s. Beyond Wall Street, little more than 5 percent of the CEOs in Fortune 500 companies are women. Facts don't lie. Looking back twenty-five or fifty years, yes, there has been a sea change in workplace behavior and corporate policies regarding diversity and discrimination. But if it can be said that power corrupts, and if most of that power is held by men, the struggle for genuine equality is likely to be protracted.

Panning for Gold

• • •

HAVE YOU EVER HAD OCCASION to call upon a plumber or an electrician for a "fix it" job or home improvement project? Sometimes telephone calls are returned days later, other times not at all. Occasionally a worker will walk off a job in midstream, or not show up in the first place. Waiting lists can extend for months. Such behavior is perhaps rooted in tradition. My father, who was a builder, discovered that his carpenters, just like their fathers, did not work during deer hunting season, and he had to adjust his schedule accordingly.

The Wealth Management business works a little differently than that. Imagine a financial advisor receiving a call like this: "I was given your name by my accountant, and I'd like to see if you could look over my portfolio and make some suggestions. No rush—any time in the next few weeks is fine." The response would be predictable and immediate— "Don't worry. I'll be right over!"

Wealth Management can be a very lucrative business. It is also highly competitive. A valid case could be made that the business is saturated with so-called wealth managers, all in hot pursuit of a relatively static and limited number of wealthy investors. You can find these advisors camped out on the banks of the Money River, a metaphorical creation of novelist Kurt Vonnegut in *God Bless You, Mr. Rosewater*:

"The Money River, where the wealth of the nation flows. We were born on the banks of it-and so were most of the mediocre people we grew up with, went to private schools with, sailed and played tennis with. We can slurp from that mighty river to our hearts' content. And we can even take slurping lessons, so we can slurp more efficiently."

"Slurping lessons?"

"From lawyers! From tax consultants! We're born close enough to the river to drown ourselves and the next ten generations in wealth, simply using dippers and buckets. But we still hire the experts to teach us the use of aqueducts, dams, reservoirs, siphons, bucket brigades, and the Archimedes' screw. And our teachers in turn become rich, and their children become buyers of lessons in slurping."

Cerulli Associates is a highly regarded consulting firm specializing in research and analytics for large-scale asset managers in the financial services industry. These "asset managers" could be portfolio managers, financial planners, investment advisors, insurance agents, or dinosaurs (stockbrokers). They could work for large firms like Goldman Sachs or Morgan Stanley, banks like J.P. Morgan or Wells Fargo, or independently as registered investment advisors. Cerulli estimates there are approximately two million households in America that have investable assets of more than $1 million, exclusive of home, autos and personal possessions, and there are approximately six hundred thousand professionals who hope to help them manage their affairs. Do the math. For every individual hoping to make his bones in the investment business, there are only three households with more than $1 million in investable assets. Most of us are well aware of what is referred to as income inequality, and we think of it as the widening gulf not just between rich and poor but also between rich and middle-class Americans, whose sense of well-being has eroded slowly over time. On the other hand, the affluent—let's say those with over $1 million in investable assets—have seen their numbers grow steadily as well, but growing faster still is the number of financial advisors, or as Vonnegut would say, the slurpers who have taken up residence on the banks of the Money River.

There has always been a Money River, but fifty years ago it had little resemblance to the river of today. It was more like the Roe River near Great Falls, Montana; the Roe holds the Guinness Book of World Records for being the shortest river in the United States. Little more than two hundred feet in length, it is easy to find, identify and explore. If you are interested in going to Great Falls to see it for yourself, you can stay at any of three nearby motels where rooms go for as little as sixty dollars a night.

The Money River today is long, serpentine and complex, and its inhabitants (wealthy investors) own a huge variety of financial products that were not even in existence a few generations ago. When I started out at Merrill Lynch, the firm produced an endless supply of educational brochures and pamphlets and provided them without charge to any customer or prospect who was interested (and probably some that were not). The most requested of these was Louis Engel's *How to Buy Stocks*. If that sounds like pretty basic stuff, it's because it was. Common stocks, of course, are still found in the Money River, but so are options, structured notes, hedge funds, limited partnerships, exchange-traded funds, financial futures, options on futures, separately managed accounts, collateralized debt obligations, private equity funds, and more. Even money market funds didn't exist in 1972. This may be a case of the tail wagging the dog, but it is no wonder that the role of the financial advisor has changed so radically during the past fifty years. The Money River became almost unrecognizable.

How it changed requires a little financial history. Most investors today own mutual funds. They are found in all corporate 401-K retirement plans and have become a staple of individually managed portfolios as well. As commonplace as they may seem today, mutual funds have had a relatively short history, first appearing in the United States in 1924 when Massachusetts Financial Services launched what was to become its signature fund, the Massachusetts Investors Trust. The initial offering was a private one, and it provided MFS with the grand total of $50,000; the money was spread among forty-five stocks, all of which were purchased as odd lots. Four years later, the fund was opened to the public at large.

MFS Investors Trust grew gradually over the years, as did the mutual fund industry in general, but at first, this growth was slow and steady. There were about one hundred funds in existence by 1950, and another 150-plus available for trading by 1970. Since then, the industry has exploded. Investors now can choose among ten thousand mutual funds and an equal number of hedge funds. Roughly speaking, for every fund that existed in 1970, there are one hundred today. During the early years of the Wall Street dinosaur, life was simple, and change was slow. After 1970, something happened that changed that dynamic.

That something was the money market mutual fund, a product conceived by Bruce Bent and Henry Brown. Their brainchild, The Reserve Fund, was first introduced in 1971. Space travel actually pre-dates the money market mutual fund. What is looked upon as an omnipresent, everyday convenience by Millennials and GenXers is in truth a relatively novel invention first experienced when Baby Boomers reached adulthood.

There are two reasons behind this. The first is a rather obscure piece of legislation (Regulation Q) that was part of the swirl of New Deal reforms relating to investments and banking. Regulation Q gave the Fed the power to fix deposit rates paid by banks. The idea was that banks paid way too much for deposits during the Roaring 20s, and this made them less able to survive when the stock market crashed, and the Great Depression hit. In a way, Regulation Q was designed to protect the banks from themselves.

When I was a child, I remember that banks paid about 3 or 4 percent interest on their deposits. Schoolchildren were encouraged to open passbook savings accounts and bring a dime to class each week to learn about frugality and the benefits of saving regularly. All you needed to open an account was a signature card and address. It all seems very quaint today. I can only imagine what my friendly neighborhood banker would say if I wanted to recreate that experience for my grandchildren.

In any event, 4 percent interest was fine as long as interest rates in the real economy were stable and reasonably close to 4 percent. However, in the 1960s, things began to change. Financing the Vietnam War and President Johnson's Great Society domestic spending programs forced the federal government to borrow heavily. Inflation bubbled up. When the first wave of Baby Boomers reached adulthood in 1970, they needed to buy houses, cars, and major appliances, and they borrowed money to finance these purchases. The federal government and millions of baby boomers became heavy borrowers simultaneously, forcing interest rates to rise. By January 1, 1970, the ten-year US Treasury paid 7.79 percent. Banks were lending money out at 8 or 9 percent. When lending rates are 5 percent higher than deposit rates, it's a very good deal for the lenders and an equally poor one for the depositors. In quick order, the tipping point was reached.

While banks at the time were prohibited from setting their own deposit rates, there was nothing that prevented a mutual fund from doing so. Brown and Bent's Reserve Fund invested largely in US Treasury Bills and other highly liquid, short-term money market instruments. The fund opened up a new world of investing to the small investor, offering high yields, daily liquidity, and an incredible degree of safety. In the early 70s, Treasury investing was quite difficult for many. Treasury Bills required a $10,000 minimum (versus the Reserve Fund's $1,000), and at the time this sum was out of the reach of most middle-class investors. In 1971, the median price of a new car was $3,700.

You could acquire Treasuries in one of two ways: through a broker or through the Federal Reserve. Most brokers would process Treasury orders only for established customers and charged a fee to do so. The Federal Reserve did not require the payment of a fee, but it did insist that Treasury buyers make their purchases in person at a Federal Reserve Bank. There are twelve of them in the United States. If you lived in Miami or New Orleans, you'd have to travel to Atlanta to do business at the bank. Even if you happened to reside in a city that had its own Federal Reserve Bank (as I did), there was nothing convenient about making a transaction. Virtually every step of the process was manual, and long, slowly moving queues of investors seemed to be everywhere in view. In many ways, purchasing a U.S. Treasury Bill was as tedious a process as obtaining a passport.

The Reserve Fund and all of the iterations of money market mutual funds that followed it transformed the investment landscape. Fidelity Investments was the first to link the concept of check writing with a money market fund. Compared with low-yielding passbook savings accounts and certificates of deposit, Fidelity's Daily Income Trust offered the high yields, safety, and low costs common to all money funds, but its check-writing feature gave investors a level of liquidity that attracted them like a magnet. FDIT, launched in 1974, was an instant success. Other mutual fund companies soon followed Fidelity, and a tremendous amount of money began to flow from banks to the mutual fund industry. I then heard the imposing word economists used to describe this movement of money out of the banking system—"disintermediation." You could just as easily call it a revolution. Over thirty money market funds were in existence by the end of 1975; within the next ten years, about 150 became active. In 1973, the Reserve Fund held $150 million in assets; ten years later, money market funds had custody of nearly $200 billion.

Brokerage firms began to offer their own money market funds, out of necessity as much as anything else. Until these funds made their appearance, wire house customers had no convenient way to invest short-term cash. It sounds hard to believe today, but brokerage firms profited handsomely from the "free credit balances" of their retail customers. Here's how it worked: if you sold some securities and wanted to keep the cash handy for a future purchase, the money simply sat in your account, just like cash in your wallet. Some firms paid one percent interest but only if these funds were subsequently reinvested in other stocks and bonds. Other firms paid nothing. The interest that full-service firms like Merrill, E.F. Hutton, and Dean Witter had earned from free credit balances was enormous, but in short order, the pipeline was shut off. Money market funds proved to be a game changer throughout the industry. All of the leading brokers had to make money funds available to their clients, not just to keep them happy, but simply to keep them on the books.

Interestingly, brokers at full-service firms were far from eager to embrace the change. Remember, the 1970s was still the age of the dinosaur.

Money fund transactions were processed manually, one at a time, and every purchase or sale was completed without any sort of fee. Many investors opened money market accounts with traditional brokers and did no commission business, choosing only to buy or sell shares in money market funds. These clients who did no "business" aggravated dinosaur brokers to no end. Within a few years, as much as a third of each firm's daily order flow was tied to money fund purchases or sales, causing endless frustration among sales and operations personnel. Handling these transactions was tedious, time-consuming—and expensive. Many of Wall Street's dinosaurs were short-sighted, unable to envision the long-term benefits that money market funds could bring to their practices.

Merrill Lynch's Cash Management Account, introduced in the late 1970s, changed the rules of the game even more. Its architect was Tom Chrystie, and Chrystie was fortunate enough to have the support of Merrill's CEO Don Regan in selling his idea to the firm's Executive Committee and Board of Directors. THE CMA account was controversial from the start, and Regan and Chrystie got a good deal of pushback within Merrill. The CMA account was no doubt innovative, but it was also complicated, foreign to the firm's brokers, and quite costly to implement. Initial test marketing proved to be unimpressive. There was a widespread sentiment among Merrill executives that it should be dropped altogether. Regan decided to forge ahead. He was reported to have said at a top-level meeting, "There's been a vote taken here today, and it's one to nothing. I'm the one."

The CMA account was rolled out nationally in 1978. The account combined many elements of the Reserve Fund and Fidelity's Daily Income Trust with a few added wrinkles. In essence, the account allowed investors to combine a traditional stock and bond brokerage account with a money market fund. Funds could be accessed either through check writing or a Visa card. The account's optional margin feature allowed customers to utilize a credit line tied to the value of their holdings. Most important, the account had a daily, overnight sweep feature that captured all available cash (including proceeds from sales and dividends from common stocks) and automatically invested it in the CMA Money Fund. At the time, the fund offered a tempting double-digit rate of return. By the end of 1978, the prime rate was 11.75 percent, on its way to 18 percent a few years later. Billions flowed into Merrill Lynch and all the other brokers that soon introduced look-alike products. Although banks by now had been able to offer competitive CD rates and had been doing so for several years, the CMA created a real buzz. *Forbes* lauded it as one of the most innovative financial products of the 20th century. The *New York Times* said in 1982 that the account represented "the leading edge of the revolution that is transforming Wall Street." Even the dinosaurs began to warm to the idea. They couldn't help but notice how the CMA and other so-called central asset accounts were bringing in new money and new clients. For the first time in my memory, prospective customers began to create lunch-hour traffic jams in the offices of discount firms like Fidelity as well as full-service firms like Merrill Lynch.

As the Money River had begun to change, so did the folks who occupied its banks. Retail brokers who had, in the past, spoken only about stocks and bonds with their clients were now engaging in conversations encompassing money market instruments, the Fed, and inflation. Their business cards used to read "Investment Broker" or "Account Executive." New job titles began to proliferate—Investment Consultant or Financial Advisor being the most common.

Where brokerage firms had formerly dealt with the risk capital of a relatively modest number of stock market aficionados, they were now dealing on a vastly wider scale, trying to reach a market of millions of middle-class and affluent investors and savers who wanted to beat inflation but didn't know how to do it. Even in the late 70s and early 80s, when high interest rates and inflation caused severe damage to both stock and bond prices, money kept pouring in, new accounts were established, and lasting relationships were formed. When the inflation cycle peaked in 1982, both the equity and fixed income markets went on a tear, and business got even better. Many of the folks who had only wanted to open money market accounts stayed on as customers when rates dropped, taking advantage of other products and services.

One of these was single-premium deferred annuities. They came in two different flavors: 1) A fixed annuity that resembled a certificate of deposit with a guaranteed rate of interest and 2) A variable annuity whose return was tied to a mutual fund. Both were investment contracts issued by insurance companies, and whatever their differences, they shared a few things in common—they were opaque, hard to explain, and loaded with fees. In fairness, they did offer a conservative investor approaching retirement some real advantages (like tax deferral and guaranteed lifetime income) that the usual menu of stocks, bonds, and mutual funds did not.

Wire houses jumped all over this. In the late-1970s, tens of thousands of dinosaurs began to get their insurance licenses (required for all annuities) along with Series 6 securities licenses (necessary for variable annuity sales). Most firms hired a small army of insurance agents as internal specialists, who were expected to drum up business by educating retail brokers and holding seminars for their prospects and customers. The seminars were ordinarily hyped by offering a steak dinner at a high-end restaurant, although while traveling in the mid-1980s, I saw a few that were held at Po' Folks in Georgia and Florida for the early (4:30 pm) dinner crowd. Po' Folks went bankrupt in 1988, but the tradition of promoting business with free meals lives on today.

Dinosaurs were carefully instructed never to utter the word "annuity" when introducing the subject in conversation. Studies showed that most investors reacted negatively to the word, thinking immediately of an expensive, complicated insurance contract. This was understandable, since annuities were indeed expensive, complicated insurance contracts. Nevertheless, when the subject was broached, they were referred to as concepts, opportunities, retirement income vehicles, or perhaps tax-advantaged investment instruments. Whatever the case, sales of annuities surged during this time, and not just because of the lure of a free meal. They proved to be very effective in helping dinosaurs pan for gold even if the stock market was temporarily stumbling.

Limited partnerships and tax shelters also started to appear at this time. In terms of expense and complexity, they made annuities look like

Series E bonds. Wall Street is creative if nothing else, and it offered up a virtually unlimited variety of such investments. Limited partnerships invested in office buildings, warehouses, hotels, mobile home parks, apartments, oil wells, and natural gas pipelines; in addition, one could choose among aircraft, bus, railcar and equipment leasing deals, or cargo ships, oil tankers, and motion pictures. There were even partnerships that invested in horse breeding and rare coins.

Some did well, especially the more conservative, real estate income deals that focused on mature projects with established tenants, but over time many limited partnerships met with unintended results. Some of the stories were darkly comic—like the wind-down of Bruce McNall's Athena Funds. McNall was riding high in the 1980s, a boy wonder who held controlling stakes in the Los Angeles Kings and Toronto Argonauts by the time he was forty. His pursuit of wealth had started early, when he was eight years old and wandered into a rare coin shop in Arcadia, California. He was astounded that two- thousand-year-old coins were selling for $1 each. *Sports Illustrated's* Richard Hoffer wrote about what followed:

> At 15, with inventory he had built through his own mail-order business in ancient coins, McNall opened a numismatic shop. At 16, having sold out to enroll at UCLA and study ancient history, he had $60,000, a Jaguar XK-E, one apartment near campus and a grander one a little farther away. At 20, cajoled back into business by some of his professors and their wealthy friends, he opened a new coin shop, this time on Rodeo Drive. He appraised a coin collection belonging to J. Paul Getty and told Getty it was "junk," after which he became Getty's adviser on numismatics.

Years later, while he was selling collectibles to the Louvre, hanging out with Tom Hanks, Kurt Russell, and John Candy, and breeding thoroughbred horses, McNall signed on with Merrill Lynch as General Partner of the Athena Funds, whose partnerships were designed to invest in rare coins. McNall's was responsible for the coin collection; as General Partner, he would decide what to buy and when to sell. Merrill's investors would put up all the money; McNall would get a piece on the back end when all the coins were sold.

At least that was how it was supposed to work. A Merrill Lynch audit revealed that the coins—oops—weren't where they were supposed to be. McNall had taken them out of the partnership and pledged them as collateral to obtain a personal bank loan. It turned out that years of shady dealings and overspending had taken their toll, and by the early 1990s, his empire was about to implode. In 1993 it did. He defaulted on a $90 million loan to Bank of America, was successfully prosecuted for fraud and conspiracy, and ended up serving nearly five years in prison. After his release, he was on national television promoting a book he had just written about his experiences. It was aptly titled *Fun While it Lasted: My Rise and Fall in the Land of Fame and Fortune.*

Merrill made all the Athena investors whole, but the reputational damage suffered by the firm and its advisors did not easily disappear. The McNall-Athena saga was perhaps the most gossip-worthy of the limited partnership flameouts, but at $30 million it was hardly the biggest. Prudential Bache ended up paying a record $2 billion in fines and restitution for its role in a massive fraud during the 1980s. Customer losses were exponentially greater than that. Prudential Bache's Direct Investment Group, the one responsible for limited partnership sales, was guilty of skimming and taking kickbacks from partnerships it had put on its sales platform. False claims about the safety of the investments were made repeatedly, and hundreds of thousands of investors, many of them retirees of moderate means, lost their life savings as a result. Prudential's advisors felt betrayed and blindsided, as they were fed misleading information first—and then passed it on to their customers as gospel. Dinosaur advisors had looked upon partnerships as a way of elevating their practices by reaching a more affluent audience with more sophisticated products, but in the end, Wall Street's rush to bring products to market coupled with poor risk management doomed the effort.

In the 1970s there was talk of so-called financial supermarkets becoming dominant in the industry, pushing aside the smaller, old-school stock and bond firms that had dominated Wall Street trading for generations. I remember that Merrill Lynch for a short time got involved in title insurance, executive relocation services, and small business commercial lending. Several commercial banks similarly experimented with different business models and did so with great success. Norwest Bank of Minnesota, formerly a mid-size regional bank, grew to be the fourteenth largest bank in the U.S. by the early 1990s. Even though its banking footprint was still limited to the upper Midwest, it operated loan offices and mortgage offices—as many as fourteen hundred—in virtually every state in the country. Norwest also owned and operated insurance companies, a discount brokerage firm, and a number of mutual funds.

As these changes took place, the industry continued to consolidate, and names that used to be on the tip of my tongue years ago—Hornblower Weeks, Clark Dodge, DuPont Walston, and many more—simply disappeared. Wall Street began to attract a new set of players, and they were big. GE (Kidder Peabody) and American Express (Shearson, Lehman, and E.F. Hutton) come to mind immediately. Even Sears Roebuck got in the business, acquiring both Allstate Insurance and Dean Witter. Sears' acquisition of Dean Witter was thought to be highly amusing by everyone except the retail brokers who worked at Dean Witter. The memory of it still brings a smile to my face. I recall that Sears established Dean Witter kiosks in its stores, perhaps situating shell-shocked brokers somewhere between the lingerie and sporting goods departments. There were jokes about Craftsman mutual funds or Kenmore tax-free municipal bonds—ones that you could take back and replace if they broke down. Humor aside, it was clear that the lines in the sand that used to separate banks, brokerage firms and insurance companies had begun to blur.

It wasn't an easy process for the industry to reinvent itself. For example, when Merrill was rolling out its CMA account nationally, it was taken to court by the banking industry in every state where it attempted to do business. The banks claimed, understandably, that the CMA Money Fund constituted a deposit account, something that brokerage firms were prohibited from offering under Glass–Steagall. Merrill fought back strenuously. Leaving no stone unturned, the firm partnered with Bank One of Ohio to issue and clear all of the checks connected with its CMA.

As commission rates continued to fall, new strategies emerged. By the 1990s, what we used to call stock brokerage firms began to sell insurance, produce financial plans, and issue mortgages. Some firms got involved in real estate brokerage, others in commercial real estate development. New, complex, opaque products were introduced, requiring retail advisors to become more knowledgeable and aware of their nuances. Alliances were created with third-party money managers; these so-called "private accounts" were priced on a flat-fee basis, and no commission charge attached to individual trades. Pretty soon fee-based platforms appeared everywhere, pushing dinosaur brokers closer and closer to extinction.

In the 80s and 90s, corporations began to grant stock options more and more freely. Formerly doled out exclusively to upper management, options soon made their way down through the food chain. Some companies even granted them to all full-time employees. Winning a corporate stock option plan was tantamount to Indiana Jones' finding the Holy Grail. Apart from substantial transaction fees, these plans opened the door to lucrative ancillary business like large Rule 144 sales for a company's top executives.

Usually, things worked out well for all parties concerned, but I remember one case where a Gloucester, MA-based sports marketing firm (Cyrk) got its name in the paper when it probably wished it hadn't. It turns out the company had earlier placed O.J. Simpson on its Board; while he was awaiting trial for murder in 1995, he exercised some options to defray his legal expenses. All such sales are a matter of public record, and this one got some tongues wagging in Boston. How can one describe it? Strange, awkward, cringeworthy? Yes, yes, yes. But unexpected things do happen when panning for gold.

For many years most Wall Street firms wanted nothing to do with the College for Financial Planning and the Certified Financial Planner

(CFP®) designation, or any other professional designation for that matter. The consensus was easy to explain: business was good, quite good, so why shake things up, especially when doing so might lead to future liability and litigation? Companies that maintained tuition reimbursement programs for their employees would not pay for CFP® courses, nor would they permit their brokers to put the designation on their business cards. Ultimately, the industry woke up and saw that the real danger was in failing to embrace enhanced training and education for their advisors. There was no upside in standing still while the world was changing. Today most firms actively encourage their advisors to earn the CFP® designation—and others as well. Some mandate it.

Investing was never a poor man's sport, but in the age of the dinosaur, you didn't have to be exceptionally wealthy to be a highly coveted customer. All that was required was a speculative temperament, a desire to trade, and perhaps a margin account to spice things up. There was only one defining difference between A clients and B or C clients: good customers traded a lot, and bad customers didn't. Large, inactive accounts were referred to dismissively—"big positions, no commissions." The entire game plan of retail brokers in the 70s and much of the 80s consisted of buying a stock, waiting until it (hopefully) went up in price, selling it, and then trying to do it again. Top producers were those that built big equity positions; that is, they loaded up on the same stock in nearly all of the accounts they managed. Many of their customers, even the most affluent ones, would have portfolios consisting of oversized positions in three or four stocks—and nothing else. Big producers would have a big day when they could blow out a big position and replace it with another.

Technological advances allowed discount brokers like Schwab to lower their commissions steadily as time went on, contributing to an internal price war within the discount space. Traditional wire houses obviously had to adapt to a new world order, and for a time they were able to do so successfully. There were several reasons for this. Discounters had very limited services, resources, and product offerings in the 1970s. They had a mere handful of branch offices, they were largely unknown, and of course, their customers had to conduct business over the telephone until online trading was introduced in the 1990s. It was not until that point that their growth became exponential, and they were able to carve out a large share of the market. The discounters were disruptive, to be sure, but it took them a great deal of time to gain traction in the marketplace.

Full-service brokers placed more and more focus on asset gathering. At Merrill, the AAA acronym (asset gathering, asset allocation and asset management) came to embody the core of its business strategy. Rookie brokers who completed their training were focused almost exclusively on increasing their assets under management (AUM), and traditional transactional trading was de-emphasized. Much of my training had been focused on building and managing stock portfolios; I was taught how to analyze an annual report, examine a proxy statement, and interpret a prospectus. I was also required to create model portfolios for various investment objectives and periodically make formal presentations to my peers and mentors. This process is foreign to today's advisors, who are encouraged to farm out equity investing to independent third-party managers or use cookie-cutter portfolios created by in-house or third-party research. By the mid to late 90s, the transition from commission-based transactions to fee-based advice had gained momentum and represented a sea change in the way investors connected with the investment industry.

Seeking to distance itself from the world of eye-shades, ticker tapes, and the casino-like atmosphere of the exchange floor, Wall Street's image-makers began to lay it on pretty thick. Financial advisors began to call themselves "private wealth advisors" or "managing directors." Full-service firms no longer advertise specific stock recommendations, municipal bond new issues, industry reports or market forecasts. Instead, they describe themselves in flowery, almost poetic terms designed to create a level of comfort among their potential customers. The following was taken from UBS' website:

With deep expertise and resources for addressing complex wealth challenges, the UBS Private Wealth Management division and its

distinguished team of Private Wealth Advisors offer perspective
and insights into what affluent clients need and expect—industry-
leading innovation, global solutions and an exceptional level of
service and execution unmatched by any other wealth management firm. UBS Private Wealth Management Advisors are committed to serving an exclusive community of multigenerational
families, entrepreneurs and corporate executives.

It's not much different on Merrill Lynch's website:

We start by understanding your concerns and priorities and then
form a strategy to help you pursue your goals—even as they change
over time. The result is a lasting relationship and an approach that
reflects your unique values. You'll benefit from a dedicated one-
on-one relationship with someone who brings understanding, pas-
sion and a fresh perspective to your situation.

From individuals and families to business owners and executives, our private wealth advisors are experienced in working with
substantial wealth. Uniquely qualified to guide you in accessing
specific wealth management solutions personalized to your individual needs.

All of this sounds a lot different from the business I became a part of in
1972, and it is. I have used two words to describe the world I entered in
the age of the dinosaur: "entrepreneurial" was one, and "feral" was the
other. Unlike today, when many advisors work on teams (some so large
they could be considered branch offices), we all worked solo, both literally
and figuratively. Retail brokers could come and go as they pleased, buy the
securities they liked, sell the ones they didn't, pick and choose whom to
seek out as clients and define our own sales territories. If it was necessary
to negotiate commissions, we could do that as well.

All successful dinosaur brokers had to build their businesses from
scratch, and generally, this meant they had to summon up the courage to

make at least one hundred cold calls a day. This was spelled out in highly specific detail when I first applied to work at Merrill. The first two or three years were going to be a crucible. The rewards could be astonishing, but I would have to be strong enough to endure the constant rejection I would inevitably face. My wife would have to be told that the job was going to be all-consuming, and there would be evenings and weekends when the demands of my work would keep me away from the family. Vacations were pretty much out of the question.

Until Day 1 at Merrill, I had no idea how the business worked, but it didn't take long to find out. I am sure there are not too many undergraduate or graduate students who aspire to be telemarketers or cold callers as an entry-level position in their chosen field. If I had been offered a chance to begin my working career by cold calling small businesses to pitch any of the following—typewriters, paper, filing cabinets, forklifts—I am sure my arrogance would have led me to turn down the opportunity. However, the idea of latching on to a major investment firm and having my business card read "Member NYSE," well, that was an entirely different matter. The draw was irresistible.

Smaller firms didn't have formal developmental programs; instead, as soon as their trainees passed their licensing exams, these firms assigned their rookies to an established producer who served as their mentor and counselor. This business model was accurately depicted in the movie *Boiler Room*, where Giovanni Ribisi would cold call furiously all day, hoping to land a live prospect that he could hand off to his big producer coach, played by Vin Diesel. Ribisi would be able to go it alone only after Diesel was able to open twenty-five accounts.

The other extreme, more common today at larger wire houses, involves lengthy developmental programs often lasting two to three years. Trainees study online, attend workshops and seminars, are given attentive and personalized coaching by full-time managers, and earn advanced certifications. Often, they are initially assigned to successful, established teams, where they can learn the business from the ground up, assisting senior advisors preparing for periodic client reviews or presentations for major prospects. On occasion, they will sit in on such meetings, like auditing a class in college.

Whatever the approach, the cold call is not entirely dead. This is somewhat amazing since I have never met anyone who likes to make cold calls, nor have I encountered someone who enjoys receiving them. They are in fact quite painful for both the caller and the recipient. Yet, in spite a national Do Not Call registry that has made telemarketing more difficult than in the past, the cold call still endures. Morgan Stanley recently posted the following on one of its online recruiting ads:

TO SUCCEED YOU'LL NEED THE RIGHT COMBINATION OF PERSONAL ATTRIBUTES

Drive. As a Financial Advisor, you are entirely responsible for yourself and your income. It is a highly competitive business, and there is a lot of competition. You need to be organized, focused, and highly disciplined.

Ambition. You need to really, really want to succeed. This is not a 40-hour-a-week, punch the clock job. You'll work many hours, struggle through slow periods, and face tough challenges while building your business. You'll get there eventually, but you must be the kind of person that doesn't give up.

Accountability. There are no shortcuts to success in this business, and you'll need to be demanding of yourself. But there's something else – you are responsible for treating your clients properly, disclosing what they need to hear, and doing your absolute best to help them. Not only is this the right thing to do, it's essential to your own success.

Confidence. Can you make at least 100 cold calls a day? Do you believe in your abilities enough to withstand rejection, and challenges to your opinions? Do you genuinely like helping people, talking with them, engaging in conversation that may not result in immediate tangible benefit?

Can you make at least hundred cold calls a day? This is another way of saying, "Are you man enough?" Yes, I can, and yes, I am. Early on, we were encouraged to keep track of our outgoing calls on a legal pad—a check mark for every call, and a circle around the check for every time a prospect was engaged in conversation. If someone was genuinely interested, we'd fill in the circle. Screeners and secretaries were the bane of our existence, and their presence made this numbers game almost impossible. For every hundred cold calls, you might reach twenty or twenty-five people and identify two or three legitimate prospects; perhaps, at some point, you could persuade one of these people to open an account—or perhaps not. The whole process involved very long odds. There are many more people in the business who want to tell investors what to do with their money than there are investors who are interested in listening to them.

Cold calls notwithstanding, the investment business has changed greatly, and this has influenced the rules of engagement between investor and financial advisor. This change has given rise to an industry within an industry. Camped on a tributary of the Money River, one can now find an army of practice management consultants and software developers whose mission is to help advisors compete more effectively in a world built on relationships rather than transactions.

One such individual is Don Connelly. Drawing on a lifetime of experience in the industry that included E.F. Hutton, Oppenheimer, and Putnam, his firm provides guidance and coaching to financial advisors via online training modules, webinars, workshops, and keynote speaking engagements. His client list resembles a Who's Who of banks, brokerage firms, and insurance companies. He knows all about dinosaurs—he was one himself. His job is to help financial advisors grow their businesses and operate successfully in a world where pricing, regulation, and technology have all experienced dramatic changes.

His observations are arresting. The big wire houses are not growing. Dinosaurs are aging out of the business, and the heightened regulatory and compliance burdens have pushed many of them out of the business earlier than they had planned. Big producers in the dinosaur mold are looked upon as loose cannons if not outright liabilities. We live in a litigious society, and brokerage firms don't want to be sued for securities losses any more than they do for sexual harassment or discrimination.

Putting aside the disheartened dinosaurs who are leaving the business, there has been no real organic growth experienced by wire house advisors. Major firms don't talk about certain metrics publicly, but it is generally accepted that advisors at the leading wire houses are having a terrible time bringing in new clients, especially Millennials and GenXers. Talk seems to settle on less than one net new household per advisor per year. Another trend is clear: the average age of wire house advisors is increasing, and the number of their active accounts is not. Assets under management have been able to grow meaningfully only because the long-term rise in equity and fixed income prices has masked the reality of stagnant performance in attracting new customers.

Absent change, the current wire house model may find itself at a large competitive disadvantage. In recent years, many advisors have gone independent, and that trend is accelerating. Today, more advisors work independently than for large banks and brokerage firms. Connelly points out that whether the advisor is independent or an employee, he faces the same challenge, namely building and strengthening enduring relationships with his clients. The way he looks at it, dinosaurs used to "give away" advice (research) and charge for transactions. More and more, the modern advisor is giving away trades and charging for advice.

Transactional pricing is a race to the bottom. Even the discount firms are well aware of this. In 2017 Fidelity went to $4.95 a trade, a rate that was immediately matched by Schwab. Can $2 or $1 be far behind? Discounters like Schwab and Fidelity are engaged in a price war, hoping to attract new clients who will take advantage of other products and services that each firm may offer. Cheap trades are just a door opener.

Connelly is convinced that investors want and need advice and are willing to pay for it. Perhaps even more important to them is the strength of the personal relationship they have with their advisor. Investors are not terribly interested in numbers, alphas, downside capture, inverse correlations, statistics and jargon. They want results, certainly, but they also need more—someone who communicates effectively, listens, and cares.

Rob Knapp's career path is similar to that of Don Connelly; he began as a retail broker, rose to a senior executive position at a national investment firm (in his case Merrill Lynch), and much later struck out on his own. He is now an author, speaker, coach, and founder of the Supernova Consulting Group. Supernova's mission is simple: to enhance the quality and effectiveness of a financial advisor's practice, and as a corollary, to strengthen the relationships he has with his clients.

Knapp experienced an epiphany of sorts years ago when he reviewed one client survey after another and discovered that above all else clients valued frequent personal contact from their financial advisors—even more than investment results and performance. It was a generally accepted axiom you had to get bigger to grow, and for years the focus of the industry was on opening new accounts and then opening more new accounts. I remember being told in explicit terms that even after I became established in my career, the need for adding new accounts would never disappear—ever. It was assumed that attrition was unavoidable.

Knapp was a maverick of sorts, and the Supernova system that he espouses illustrates that. He learned to grow you have to get better, not bigger. He found that many senior advisors had been handling upwards of five hundred accounts, and couldn't possibly keep up with the service demands and challenges that this naked fact presented. Their clients were dissatisfied, and turnover was disturbingly frequent.

It took years of trial and error until Supernova was formally launched in 1994 while Knapp was still at Merrill. The system required a big leap of faith: advisors who bought in agreed to cull their books dramatically, ultimately capping the number of households in their universe to less than one hundred. A structured system was put in place whereby every client would be guaranteed the following as a bare minimum: a monthly telephone call, a quarterly portfolio review, and a semi-annual face-to-face meeting. Additionally, each client would be provided with a detailed financial plan and receive periodic updates. Knapp also made a bold service guaranty—all phone calls returned within one hour and all service requests resolved within one day. Knapp felt that reliable scheduling was essential to the success of the program, and to back that up he had his advisors turn this task over to their assistants. The results were astonishing: many advisors were able to dramatically enhance their business, some by 50-100 percent. With fewer clients to serve, they were able to give their very best customers the attention they desired. Service quality increased, as did the level of client satisfaction, and attrition practically disappeared.

Bill Good comes from a different gene pool. Like Connelly and Knapp, he wakes up every morning to help financial advisors become more successful. While he has mellowed somewhat over the years, he still has traces of dinosaur blood running through his veins. He calls his primary product the Gorilla CRM System for Financial Advisors. His latest book is titled *Hot Prospects*. He promotes scripted cold calling almost as aggressively as he did forty years ago. Taking exception to today's conventional wisdom, he does not discourage his followers from opening lots of small accounts—thinking that one never knows which of them may become large in the future. He knows how hard it is to build a book and says upfront that his firm's "ideal client is someone who has survived a few years in the industry." Unlike Connelly and Knapp, Good relies much more heavily on CRM software as a practice management tool and is a strong believer in maintaining constant contact with prospects and clients via email. Does Gorilla Marketing work? Certainly, it can—if you work it.

In this business, it is not only hard to do well; it is hard to become mediocre. Attrition among advisors during their first five years in the business is substantial. Most advisors are highly motivated, intelligent, and well trained, but they are often paddling upstream as they pan for gold. Apart from that, Schwab, Fidelity, and other discount firms have taken a huge market share from old-line firms and continue to do so. GenXers and especially Millennials are likely to continue to be attracted to so-called robo advisors. Finally, there is the issue of performance. The embarrassing fact is that that most money managers and publicly traded mutual funds have consistently failed to outperform indexes like the S&P 500.

Given these forces, it is understandable why it is so hard to make the grade as a financial advisor today. Besides, the competition is intense, with hundreds of thousands of advisors holding active licenses. In the end, I still find this field filled with promise. We may have too many advisors, but we don't have too many good ones. We never will.

Sometime around 1980, I was reviewing an employment application. On the surface, it looked promising. I saw that the individual had graduated from Bowdoin College, and he indicated that he was currently President of a company in the seafood-processing business. This piqued my interest; he was only in his mid-twenties. After I interviewed him, I learned how deceiving initial impressions could be. First, he had a pronounced lisp, a serious issue in a job where verbal communication skills are key. His company consisted of one person, himself, and one asset, a small boat. His business involved picking up fish scraps at one end of a harbor and unloading them on another dock. I wasn't curious enough to ask why he did this, but I did want to know if he was making any money in his venture. He said he wasn't. He had persevered for three years, but something beyond his control forced him to look for another job. I asked him what that was. He responded, "The boat thunk."

This misfit, of course, was an exception. But it is remarkable how many advisors don't make it in the business, despite their talents, intelligence, and acquired skills. I remember speaking to a group of advisors in Philadelphia in 1987. Several kept asking me what I did to become successful. I told them the truth: up at 5:30, in the office by 7:00, read the *Wall Street Journal*, listen to a research call, spend much of the day speaking and/or meeting with prospects and clients, inhale lunch at my desk, work on portfolio reviews, and return home to examine research I hadn't had the chance to peruse during the day. I explained I did this every day and had been doing it for years. Incredulous, they persisted, "Yes, but what did you really do?" I repeated my answer a few times, never quite convincing those in attendance that I didn't have a shortcut. And I didn't. Yes, I was a good communicator, unafraid to make decisions, and knowledgeable about the financial markets, but so were many others. I did work extraordinarily hard, and I tried to live my life by three simple rules: show up every day, try my best, and do the right thing. Like Connelly, Knapp, and Good, it only took me twenty-five years to become an overnight success.

Crash

• • •

IF I BELIEVED EVERYTHING I read, I could quickly convince myself that I have lived through hundreds if not thousands of market crashes. We live in a time when virtually every event is broadcast as "breaking news," innocuous comments spark immediate outrage, and information is routinely exaggerated. In the financial markets, relatively modest price movements are commonly described by both print and television media with highly dramatic language. Where else but on Wall Street can you hear words like *crater*, *pummel*, *collapse*, or *swoon* virtually every day?

Hyperbole aside, so-called "crashes" do not occur every week or every month, but when they do take place, the pain is deep and real. Perhaps that is why they are so unforgettable. In my own experience, the Crash of 1987 stands out above all because stocks declined 20 percent in one day, the largest one-day drop in the history of the NYSE. Apart from this dubious distinction, the 1987 market break was unique in other respects as well. There was no recession or trouble present in the economy before, during, or after October 19—Black Monday. Ravi Batra penned a bestseller at the time called *The Great Depression of 1990*. The depression never occurred, and the book has been out of print for years. The '87 crash was described by market analyst Bob Farrell as a "financial accident," meaning its root causes could be found within the financial markets themselves, not the economy at large. Here, a combination of high interest rates on bonds, low dividend yields on stocks, excessive leverage and speculation, and computerized program trading coalesced at precisely the wrong time and produced a meltdown of epic proportions. Interestingly enough, the Dow Jones Industrial Average managed to post a gain for the year, as it did in 1986 and again in 1988. No one remembers that—but everyone recalls the crash.

The real Great Crash, the mother of all crashes, occurred in 1929. It was a seminal event in American and world history, much like Pearl Harbor or the 9/11 terrorist attacks. Unlike 1987, which was pretty much a one-day bear market, the 1929 debacle marked a high-water mark for stocks that was not exceeded until 1954. At its worst, the Dow posted a decline of 89 percent, when it reached the incredible level of 41.22—its low for the twentieth century.

Much has been written about the crash, especially about its causes and consequences. There is no need to rehash this debate here. Because the crash was ultimately followed by a seemingly endless bear market and a catastrophic worldwide depression, many people link the two as if they were joined at the hip, convinced that the Great Depression was the inevitable byproduct of the crash. It's certainly plausible enough. The 1929 crash caused immediate panic, widespread bank failures, and a credit contraction. Yet one could argue that if safety nets like FDIC insurance had existed, there never would have been a run on the banking system in the first place. Remember too, this was a world without unemployment insurance, Social Security, Medicare, Medicaid, and other entitlement programs we take for granted today. There was no SEC to regulate the securities industry or to protect investors. If you had a bank account or a brokerage account, and that firm went out of business, you lost everything. So I think while it is fair to say that the 1929 crash may have been the catalyst for the hard times that followed (in a way the first domino that tipped over), there were many other factors at play which caused the US as well as the world's economies to spiral into the abyss, and equally important, to stay there.

An understanding of history may not enable us to control the future, but it can certainly assist in contingency planning. In this regard, it makes sense to take a close look at the 1929 market decline and the debacle that followed. There are lessons to be learned. The Great Crash shook the nation's confidence to its core, especially since it came on the heels of the Roaring 20s, a period of unmatched prosperity and optimism. The United States, after having emerged victorious and relatively unscathed in World War I, became a preeminent world power. Our population, which stood at ninety-two million in 1910, increased to a hundred six million by 1920 and one hundred twenty-three million by 1930. Only in 1918 did the US actually lose population, and that was by a minuscule 0.06 percent. This was largely the result of having over three million American men mobilized into wartime service (and out of their bedrooms); within a year, population growth returned to its previous norm.

Our postwar economic and population booms were not experienced by the war's other combatants. During World War I, American combat deaths approximated fifty thousand; by comparison, it is believed that seventeen million soldiers from other combatant nations were killed in action. Europe was devastated after the war: Germany humiliated and broken, England nearly bankrupt. Germany and France lost about 4 percent of their populations, and in 1920, both countries had fewer citizens than in 1910. Russia devolved into a Bolshevik state where economic hardship and political oppression quickly overwhelmed the idealism of its revolution. Birth rates throughout Europe collapsed in the 1920s, and the local economies struggled throughout. The Roaring 20s in the United States was a time of disillusionment and despair throughout the European continent.

The American bull market of the 1920s became a self-fulfilling prophecy, fueled by the optimism and nationalistic pride that defined America at that time. Our growth, success, and newly found status as a world power stood in stark contrast to the defeatism on display in Europe. "The Lost Generation" is a phrase coined by American Gertrude Stein, but in truth, it was more descriptive of the prevailing sentiment of society in Europe than it was for the U.S. In America, this was a time of high expectations and supreme confidence. The League of Nations made its home in New York; Babe Ruth became the sports world's first megastar; Hollywood emerged as an entertainment hotbed, and Charles Lindbergh (an American, of course) became the first person to successfully cross the Atlantic Ocean in an airplane. Sears Roebuck and its catalog revolutionized retailing. The mass production automobile, the radio and a national telephone network were all transformational in their influence on how the average American lived.

Throughout the 20s, the market was on fire. Millions of Americans invested in stocks for the first time, eager to cash in on the economy's boom. Between 1921 and the 1929 peak, the Dow Jones appreciated nearly 600 percent, practically doubling in the last twelve months before the market peaked in September. This bull market was a feeding frenzy of epic proportions, fueled by speculation and aggressive margin buying.

Until the market peaked in September and then violently crashed in the following month, the American public remained highly enthusiastic and supremely upbeat about prospects for the financial markets. Investors certainly put their money where their mouths were, and borrowed heavily to invest even more capital. At the market peak, the total amount of margin loans actually exceeded the total amount of hard currency in circulation. Although his words were to haunt him later, the noted economist Irving Fisher announced in the summer of 1929 that in spite of all of the decade's gains and historically high valuations, "stocks prices have reached what looks like a permanently high plateau."

To give you an idea of how stretched stock valuations were, consider RCA. Originally founded as the Radio Corporation of America, RCA was the quintessential growth stock of its era. Traders fondly referred to it as "Radio," and they didn't have to stop and explain what they were talking about. In the 1920s, the company was active in motion pictures, music and broadcasting. RCA produced feature films and owned movie theatres around the country; they established a network of radio stations and manufactured radios for consumers to purchase. In the 1950s, the company became a power in television broadcasting as well by following the same script. NBC, the National Broadcasting Company, was an RCA subsidiary. In addition to owning a number of its local network affiliates, RCA became a dominant manufacturer of television sets. This was a good company in 1929, but also one that grew consistently for generations afterward. My point is this: RCA was so overvalued in 1929 that if an investor bought the stock at its pre-crash peak, he would have had to wait until 1986 (when GE bought the company) to break even. That's fifty-seven years!

After the market break in 1929, there was a bounce, then another swoon followed by a partial recovery, and finally a long, numbing slide into oblivion in 1932. Stock prices did begin a protracted and frustrating quasi-recovery at that time, but as we have seen before, they didn't reach their 1929 levels for another twenty-five years. The economy soon slid into depression, unemployment ultimately peaking at 25 percent. The country was shell-shocked. President Herbert Hoover cheerfully announced that "recovery is just around the corner," but he was probably just trying to talk the market up. As it turned out, he could not have been more wrong. Investors who had not been wiped out by the crash faced another calamity when banks and brokerage firms routinely failed. Farmers were devastated by low crop prices and often lost their farms to foreclosure. In the southern plains, Armageddon had come. Wind erosion and a severe drought wrought havoc on a vast region that became known as the Dust Bowl. Years of dust storms created an environmental catastrophe and hundreds of thousands of refugees. One of the 1920s most popular songs was "Makin' Whoopee." In the 1930s, it was "Brother, Can You Spare a Dime?"

The effect on the nation's psyche was profound. Perhaps there were some Americans who could admit (if pushed) that the 1920s bull market would not last forever, or that at some point there would be a pause—at the very least, a pause—in its upward march. A crash was believed to be out of the question. The probability of bank failures, massive bankruptcies, or a depression of historic proportions were all given a near-zero chance of occurring, at least during the Hoover administration.

When credit dried up and the economy went into free fall, the collective response of the American people was initially one of denial. Denial was followed by anger, and over time, a portion of this anger was directed against Wall Street. The Street's bankers and brokers, who should never be confused with idealistic good Samaritans to begin with, were nevertheless made the scapegoats for everything that had gone wrong with the stock market in 1929 and for the terrible aftershocks that followed.

Franklin Delano Roosevelt was elected president in an overwhelming landslide victory in 1932. His campaign was short on specifics, relying more on his innate optimism and personal charm, but FDR's language and tone quickly changed on the day of his inauguration. Invoking a biblical narrative (The Cleansing of the Temple), Roosevelt said, "Practices of the unscrupulous money changers stand indicted in the court of public opinion, rejected by the hearts and minds of men." He went on to say, "The money changers have fled from high seats in the temple of our civilization. We may now restore that temple to the ancient truths. The measure of the restoration lies in the extent to which we apply social values more than mere monetary profit." The money changers of his time, of course, were banks and brokerage firms.

As if the crash of 1929 wasn't enough, the years that followed almost defy description. The financial system was under tremendous stress, and as the Great Depression deepened, there was a classic run on banks everywhere. In mid-February 1933, Michigan became the first state to close its commercial banks. Within weeks, Delaware became the forty-eighth and last. On March 4, the day that Delaware acted, the New York Stock Exchange voluntarily shut down. It was also the same day that Roosevelt was inaugurated as President.

Roosevelt quickly declared a national bank holiday. The first piece of New Deal legislation was the Emergency Banking Act, and it quickly sailed through Congress. It authorized the Federal Reserve to supply immediate liquidity throughout the banking system by buying "good" assets (performing loans and bonds). Banks that were hemorrhaging cash now had liquidity. Deposits may not have been insured, but at least they were considered to be safe. Banks and the New York Stock Exchange opened on March 15 and remained open throughout the depression.

My point is this: the Crash of 1929 and the depression that followed it have had a powerful and enduring influence on the securities industry that is still evident today. Almost instantly, government's attitude toward financial services turned 180 degrees. Laissez-faire was out, and regulation was in. A raft of legislation was passed during FDR's administrations: the Securities Act of 1933, the Securities Exchange Act of 1934, the Glass–Steagall Act, and the Investment Company Act of 1940. All this legislation had a primary purpose: to protect the investing public. One might ask, "To protect the public from what?" The answer is clear. The legislation was directed against the greedy, shady, scheming crowd that ran Wall Street. The individual that put a bull's-eye on Wall Street was a little-known attorney named Ferdinand Pecora.

Pecora became the fourth Chief Counsel for the US Senate Banking Committee's investigation of the 1929 crash. The first two were fired, and the third resigned, all within a year's time. The committee was totally ineffective, and not much was expected of Pecora when he assumed his new duties. He was hired primarily to provide a summary and final report. Pecora, however, was a firebrand, intensely progressive and idealistic, and the hearings that he conducted immediately captured the attention of the nation in the same way that the Watergate hearings did some fifty years later. Their influence became so pervasive that they are generally referred to as the Pecora hearings. The hearings lasted only ten days, but Wall Street was never the same afterward.

Pecora called the titans of Wall Street to his hearings in Washington; among those present were Richard Whitney, J.P. Morgan Jr., and Charles Mitchell. All three, as well as several other prominent bankers who testified, were hammered relentlessly by Pecora. Shock and outrage greeted the news that Morgan, one of the wealthiest men in the country, paid no income taxes in 1931 and 1932. This was a man who raised horses and hunted fox on his New Jersey estate and had a 330-foot boat custom built to his specifications. Mitchell, the President of National City Bank (now Citibank), was forced to admit that he sold his shares of National City—to his wife!—simply to create a tax loss. This transaction allowed him to escape paying income taxes in a year his salary was more than $1 million—a staggering amount of money at the time. Mitchell was then forced to admit that he bought the shares back from her shortly thereafter, which was legal at the time but a sham if there ever was one. He resigned from his post within days.

Whitney, the President of the NYSE, was his imperious self, and he managed to survive Pecora's grilling in somewhat better shape than Mitchell and Morgan, but as his personal misdeeds became public knowledge in the years that followed, he ultimately found himself bankrupt, expelled from the NYSE, and imprisoned in Sing Sing, where he served a sentence of nearly four years.

Throughout the hearings, a wide variety of shady trading practices and occurrences of self-dealing were uncovered. After the session concluded, Herbert Hoover, just days removed from office, said, "These men are not bankers, they are banksters who rob the poor, drive the innocent to poverty and do infinite injury to those who honestly work and strive." Hoover was stunned by the revelations; the Senate Banking Committee had only begun its investigation because Hoover had originally suspected a conspiracy of short selling by "bear raiders" had been the primary cause of the Crash. Instead, he found out that bad behavior was systemic throughout the Street, and that the public face of Wall Street executives was not much more than a charade.

The die was thus cast. The crash and the depression were traumatic effects that changed a generation for good. Many people alive today can remember parents or grandparents whose thrift could seem almost pathological. The immediate shock gave way, in the face of severe suffering and economic loss, to resignation, anger and a renewed interest among the intellectual classes in socialism. (On the other side were conservatives who believed Roosevelt's socialist tweaks to the American system made him the Antichrist.) An investigative commission was assembled, just as similar bodies were convened after Kennedy's assassination or the terrorist attacks on September 11. The Pecora commission exposed wrongdoing, and within a matter of months, Congress was busy piecing together legislation that for the first time got the US government deeply involved in the business of regulating Wall Street. This sequence of events—crash, outrage, investigation, and regulation—has repeated itself many times since 1929.

The scope of regulation has grown immensely in modern times. Some pieces of legislation are known by their acronyms, like ERISA or SIPC. Other laws are referred to by the names of their congressional sponsors, such as Dodd–Frank or Sarbanes–Oxley. Still others use shorthand; a piece of legislation whose official title is "Uniting and Strengthening America by Providing Appropriate Tools Required to Intercept and Obstruct Terrorism Act of 2001" is better known as the Patriot Act. Of course, there is the plain vanilla method as well: "The Securities Acts Amendments of 1975" or "The Foreign Corrupt Practices Act." Whatever form financial legislation has taken over the past seventy-five years, one thing is quite clear: there has been a lot of it. Increased regulation is one of the great legacies of the Crash of 1929.

One might ask, "What about the repeal of significant parts of the Glass–Steagall Act?" Did this not represent a total about-face? Glass–Steagall, of course, was part of the Banking Act of 1933, and it created a "Chinese Wall" of sorts between insurance, brokerage, merchant banking and commercial banking. The prevailing thinking at the time was that a separation of commercial and investment banking functions would result in greater transparency, less risk, and a healthier financial climate.

In truth, Glass–Steagall saw its influence erode gradually over the years. Loopholes present within the act itself allowed Wall Street firms to circumvent many of its goals. Then, in the 1970s, the creation of the money market mutual fund proved to be a bonanza for investment firms that were now able to offer retail investors high-yield deposit accounts with check-writing privileges. These central asset accounts certainly looked and smelled like bank accounts, even if they technically were not. They revolutionized the financial services industry. The repeal of the last vestiges of Glass–Steagall in 1999 did not represent a trend reversal of decades of increasing rules and regulations, but simply a recognition of conditions that had changed over the years. Post-repeal, brokerage firms and banks may have been able to compete directly with each other, but they were both heavily regulated.

Some observers maintain that if Glass–Steagall had not been repealed, we would today have a greater number of smaller banks, that no bank would have been too big to fail, that the credit crisis would never have occurred, and that taxpayers would not have been stuck with the bills for bailing out our financial system. To me, this seems like twisted logic. A credit bubble is a credit bubble whether it is being financed by five large banks or five hundred small ones. History has been witness to innumerable bubbles, but very few were created or kept afloat by a cabal of enormous multinational banks. In fact, none of them was. They were all sustained by greed and unbridled optimism.

Whatever the case, extreme price volatility has been a defining feature of the stock market since 1929. This has puzzled many observers. One might think that increasing exchange volume would have led to greater financial market liquidity, and as a result, less volatility. That has been far from the case, especially during event-driven breaks that often turn into massive panic attacks. These jarring price declines seem to be occurring with numbing regularity in recent years. Even more puzzling to the public are flash crashes. They appear out of the blue and often have no connection with specific news or events. Every time one takes place, investor confidence takes a hit.

Stock market crashes have been occurring with greater cross-border impact as well. Global financial markets are interconnected, as is the global economy. Often bad news in one country can create a global disruption. The Russian financial crisis in 1998 is a good case in point. In that year Russia defaulted, and the value of the ruble plummeted in currency exchange markets. This led to panic selling in some so-called emerging market nations like Thailand and Brazil, and it affected more than currency exchange. Stock markets were in free fall as well, and the meltdown soon became epic.

The crisis became particularly acute in the United States with the near failure of a highly regarded hedge fund, Long Term Capital Management. Two of its principals, Robert Merton and Myron Scholes, were renowned economists and Nobel Laureates. Wall Street banks were in fact so comfortable with LTCM that they ended up lending the firm fifty times its equity to work its magic in the markets. That's equivalent to financing a home purchase with a two percent down payment, perhaps worse, when you consider that the collateral (futures on rubles?) proved to be quite illiquid as the crisis unfolded. Total loans to LTCM were north of $125 billion; the notional value of the securities in its portfolio over $1 trillion. Yet while LTCM was adding layer upon layer of debt to its balance sheet, the firm's equity was never much more than $5 billion!

Unable to meet its margin calls, the fund was doomed. It was bailed out by a consortium of Wall Street firms—and a little help from the Federal Reserve, which provided much of the liquidity to finance the bailout. The bailout was a function of financial necessity; if LTCM was allowed to implode, it would have taken half of Wall Street with it. Merrill Lynch, Goldman Sachs, Morgan Stanley and several other major firms then took over the operations of LTCM, slowly and carefully unwinding its positions and shutting the fund down. Interestingly enough, Lehman Brothers was one of the few that declined to participate; as we know, it collapsed during the credit crisis in 2008 after it too had overleveraged its balance sheet and needed a financial rescue to survive. Their rescue never came. How ironic.

We've seen a number of market meltdowns since LTCM. The dot-com selloff that began in March 2000 is probably best known to the average investor since all things internet quickly became so entrenched in our daily lives. It was the most "normal" of modern-day crashes. This was a classic bubble, which built momentum over the years and then turned without warning or a specific catalyst. While there may not have been a sudden, violent drop in prices, losses were prodigious. Many firms failed completely; others that managed to survive or even prosper until this day saw astonishing share price declines. Cisco shareholders suffered a top to bottom loss of 80 percent; Amazon 90 percent; Apple dropped 50 percent in just one day in September 2000.

The terrorist attacks of September 11, 2001, triggered a short but severe market break. A wave of panic selling began when stock exchanges opened for trading on September 17, and fell nearly 15 percent in just four days. Airline and other travel-related companies were particularly hard hit, with price declines of 50 percent or more quite commonplace. This was obviously an event-driven crash, and the market responded in predictable fashion. Just as it had after John Kennedy's assassination or the Japanese attack on Pearl Harbor, stock prices went into freefall but managed to stabilize in a matter of days. Even after the failure of Lehman Brothers in September 2008 and all of the chaos that ensued, some measure of calm was restored in the weeks that followed. (Full confidence followed much later; after all, the Lehman bankruptcy alone destroyed nearly $700 billion in wealth.)

It is not surprising that when the country suffers a national tragedy like those mentioned above, an immediate and severe reaction in the stock market follows. That makes perfect sense. Presidential Commissions were established to investigate Pearl Harbor, the Kennedy assassination, and September 11. They were not formed to determine why the stock market declined in reaction to them.

In the last few years, the game has changed; the advent of electronic exchanges, globalization of markets, and high-frequency trading have made possible an entirely new kind of crash—the "flash crash"—so called because it appears unexpectedly, does its damage, and then disappears just as quickly, like a flash of lightning. Most investors are aware of the phrase "flash crash," yet I am entirely confident that very few if any have any clear idea how such declines occur and what if anything can or should be done about them. More than six years after the first flash crash, the SEC continues to review the subject, deliberating over possible changes in market rules, regulations, and sanctions.

Stanley Kubrick's *2001: A Space Odyssey* was released in 1968, but its influence endures today. In the story line an onboard computer named HAL takes over control of the mission, and in a memorable scene, HAL refuses to open the pod bay door and allow the movie's central character, astronaut Dr. David Bowman, to gain reentry to the spaceship. HAL said, "I'm sorry Dave. I can't do that. The mission is too important for me to allow you to jeopardize it." The asylum wasn't taken over by the inmates but by a machine.

Described often as the result of glitches, malfunctions, computer errors, programming mistakes and/or snafus, flash crashes have become reasonably common and troublesome features of modern stock market activity. We'll be taking a much closer look at high-frequency trading later in the *Death of the Dinosaur*, but I am introducing the subject here because its connection with contemporary flash crashes is so strong. HFT and flash crashes are joined at the hip.

The August 24, 2010, flash crash was the most spectacular in a series of flash crashes. It is hard—extremely hard—for anyone to decipher and intelligently explain how these bizarre events unfold and how they end. This is true even for people like me, who have spent their lifetimes in the industry. On this day, the Dow Jones Industrial Average plunged a thousand points and then recovered the bulk of the loss in a matter of minutes. There was no news to account for the strange and frightening price swing. This report from the British daily, *The Guardian*, may clarify the matter:

> There was a frenzy of speculation about what might have caused the rout, from explanations ranging from fat fingered trading to a cyber-attack...Within days, officials in the US were blaming big bets by a trader on Chicago's derivative exchange." [The order had been placed on behalf of a Waddell and Reed mutual fund.] "At 3:23 pm the mutual fund had used an automated algorithm trading strategy to sell contracts known as e-minis... It sparked selling by other traders, including high frequency traders."
>
> The official report by the Securities and Exchange Commission and the Commodities Futures Trading Commission outlined a 'hot potato' effect as the HFTs started buying and then reselling the e-mini contracts. Some orders were executed as 'irrational prices' as low as one penny or as high as $100,000 before share prices returned to their pre-crash levels in just twenty minutes.

On second thought, perhaps this explains nothing—or everything. Can big bets on e-mini contracts, which even most Wall Street insiders could not accurately define, really cause a cataclysmic market crash? Can most investors, even sophisticated ones, give an example of an automated algorithm trading strategy? Is that what modern investing is all about? Apparently, at least on one day, it was.

There are two kinds of flash crashes. Large flash crashes like the one in 2010 affect the entire stock market, and so-called mini flash crashes refer to activity confined to a single stock. Do not think for a minute that a mini flash crash refers to a more modest or restrained drop in price. While the larger market flash crash may affect many more investors and garner far more publicity, mini flash crashes can be just as lethal. What happened on May 17, 2013, was astonishing. One minute before the NYSE closed on that day, shares of Anadarko Petroleum that had been trading at $90 suddenly dropped over 99 percent to $0.01—yes, a penny a share. Twenty-six trades quickly took place at this price before the stock immediately snapped back to close at $90.38. The explanation was that a last-minute sell order for one hundred fifty thousand shares of Anadarko was entered by mistake; a prior sell order for four hundred thousand shares was never canceled. Somehow, that is supposed to explain a 99 percent drop in price and a loss in market value of over $40 billion. This is hard to accept, let alone comprehend.

In response to the Anadarko and several other similar mini-crashes, in September 2016 the SEC fined Bank of America more than $15 million over what it termed inadequate risk controls. It was revealed that between 2012 and 2014, the bank's Merrill Lynch unit had given several large customers "direct market access," i.e., the ability to place orders directly without going through ML as an intermediary. The attraction for such an arrangement, of course, is speed of execution. SEC Rule 15c3-5 required brokerage firms "to implement risk management controls and supervisory procedures reasonably designed to manage the financial, regulatory, and other risks of this business activity." It was never made clear what was reasonable and what wasn't.

The action in Anadarko was perhaps the most spectacular of similar flash crashes cited in the disciplinary action against Bank of America, but the fact remains it was not unique. The New York Stock exchange canceled all the bogus trades. Merrill Lynch spokesman Bill Halldin stoically said, "We continue to enhance our programs with new technologies and controls." SEC Enforcement Director Andrew Ceresney couldn't have been more understated when he issued a statement acknowledging that mini (single stock) flash crashes "can undermine investor confidence in the markets."

The SEC's sanction against Bank of America may have put this particular matter to rest, but it and other disciplinary actions it has taken have done very little to remove the risk of such market disruptions in the future. We now live in a world where electronic trading dominates; where algorithms are substituted for human judgment; where machines have become even if by accident more powerful than the engineers who created them. Many trades, if not most, are now executed directly by machines. The NYSE and its specialist system have lost influence as well as relevance. Despite well-meaning legislation and regulatory oversight, danger abounds. HFT currently accounts for more than half of a typical day's trading volume. As a result, the risk of future, random flash crashes—both mini and maxi—has grown.

When the Kansas City Board of Trade closed its trading floor a few years ago, Alec Liu wrote, "the announcement signaled another step into virtualization for the stock market, which has gone from being a real-life place where people shout orders at each other to bundles of high-speed wires and giant servers, a market built on speed and efficiency and ones and zeros." It is inarguable that technology has transformed the financial markets in a positive way—but fully automated electronic trading systems have often had dire unintended consequences. Wall Street needs to address this issue, fix what's broken, and effectively regulate what isn't. One more flash crash is one too many.

Never Again

• • •

I WILL NEVER FORGET THE first time I saw a prospectus for a new issue of common stock. On the front cover, the following message appeared in large, boldface type: "Neither the Securities and Exchange Commission nor any state securities commission has approved or disapproved of the securities or passed upon the accuracy or the adequacy of the disclosures in the prospectus and any contrary representation is a criminal offense." Immediately thereafter was an exhortation to turn to a specific page for a discussion of risk factors, and following that, a declaration that the investment in question was neither FDIC insured nor bank guaranteed and might lose value. For a neophyte, this was pretty ominous stuff. Many an inexperienced client would comment that they would never buy something that wasn't "SEC approved," as if that would somehow be equivalent to the *Good Housekeeping* seal of approval.

Warnings like this appear on financial documents all the time. Every time a mutual fund ad shouts out "Five stars rated by Morningstar!" or "#1 growth fund last three years!" you will always find the disclaimer that reads, "past results are not indicative of future performance." Similarly, whenever a company is in the market to raise equity or issue debt, one will come across the ever-present announcement:

This communication shall not constitute an offer to sell or the solicitation of an offer to buy securities nor shall there be any sale of these securities in any state

*in which such solicitation or sale would be unlawful prior to registration or quali-
fication of these securities under the laws of any such state.*

The Securities and Exchange Commission is an all-powerful government agency that is responsible for oversight of the securities industry.
Its presence is felt everywhere. The SEC oversees mandatory disclosures
by public companies (Corporation Finance Division) as well as mutual
funds (Investment Management Division). The agency also watches over
FINRA, the industry's self-regulatory organization created after the 2008
credit crisis. Its enforcement division has significant power to investigate
violations and can refer egregious offenses to federal and state attorneys
for criminal prosecution. When SEC examiners show up for an audit,
often unannounced, heartbeats begin to race.

Today, the securities industry is one of the most heavily regulated in
the country, but surprisingly enough, it was one of the least regulated until
relatively recent times. During the 1800s, multiple stock exchanges were
established, and the NYSE, not much more than a tiny club at its founding, had become a major financial institution. Communications enhance-
ments proceeded throughout the century: first the telegraph, followed
by the ticker tape, then the telephone, and lastly transatlantic cables. All
of these enabled the exchanges, especially the NYSE, to broaden their
reach and influence. As stock ownership became more widespread, volume
increased. Initially, the exchange priced its securities once a week, then
once daily, and later twice a day. Ultimately, technology and the swelling
number of investors combined to augur the emergence of a continuous
auction market, giving nearly real-time quotes since the ticker rarely ran
more than a few minutes behind actual transactions taking place on the
floor. Numbers are very fuzzy, but it has been estimated that at least one
million Americans owned stock at the turn of the century.

As the industry matured, it somehow managed to avoid regulation at
both the federal and state level. Apparently, the feeling that case law would
serve as an adequate deterrent to questionable and/or criminal behavior
was widespread. This is especially surprising since the 1800s saw more

than their fair share of stock market crashes and banking panics. In recent times, such events like the dot-com bust in 2000 and the 2008 credit crisis have led immediately to widespread outrage, demands for investigations, and the issuance of more powerful and expansive regulations, e.g. Sarbanes–Oxley and Dodd–Frank. I can only speculate as to why the call for regulating the securities industry was so muted until the twentieth century. Railroads were regulated in 1887 with the passage of the Interstate Commerce Act and the creation of the ICC. The IRS was established in the mid-1800s, and the forerunner of the Bureau of Alcohol, Tobacco and Firearms (ATF) appeared as early as 1791, when Congress authorized the taxation of imported spirits. Animal cruelty laws were passed by the New York legislature as early as 1828. The NYSE traveled free and easy for a very long time.

Regulation of the securities industry came much later, and it came grudgingly. The first state to pass legislation in this realm was Kansas in 1911. Other states, mostly in the Midwest and West, soon followed. It is generally believed that these states took the lead because they felt inherently distrustful toward Wall Street and needed some layer of protection from the ogres in New York City. Even then brokers were demonized. An early stockbroker joke, like the one that appeared in Fred Schwed's 1940 book, *Where are the Customers' Yachts?* makes this point all too clearly:

Once in the dear dead days beyond recall, an out-of-town visitor was being shown the wonders of the New York financial district. When the party arrived at the Battery, one of his guides indicated some handsome ships riding at anchor. He said, "Look, those are the bankers' and brokers' yachts." "Where are the customers' yachts?" asked the naïve visitor.

The first state securities laws are commonly referred to as "blue-sky laws." They were created to protect investors from highly speculative if not outright fraudulent investments. The term "blue sky" is attributed to

U.S. Supreme Court Justice Joseph McKenna, who wrote about "speculative schemes which have no more basis than so many feet of blue sky." Most of the states that enacted blue-sky laws enacted measures covering the licensing of firms as well as their agents. Sometimes a state would deny registration of certain securities; in other words, securities that were not "blue skied" couldn't be sold in that state. Usually, this prohibition applied to flimsy offerings involving wildcat drilling or speculative gold mining, but occasionally perfectly good securities were passed over without any real thought or justification. Often this happened to foreign securities that in many cases were issued by blue-chip multi-national corporations. Imagine purchasing a stock like Louis Vuitton or Volkswagen and waking up to a trade confirmation that practically shouted out in bold letters "Possible Blue Sky Violation."

In any event, early securities regulation was haphazard and ineffective. Many states, even by the 1930s, had no mechanism with which they could effectively oversee investment firms and their sales representatives. Some states that did pass blue-sky regulations had no departments or divisions of government exclusively dedicated to enforcement of their own blue-sky laws; instead, early state securities regulators often operated as unofficial subsidiaries of state railroad commissions. Licensing was not required in some states, and in others where it was, the requirements varied from state to state.

By 1933, every state except Nevada had enacted some form of securities legislation. The concept of oversight had gained traction and acceptance over the years, but reform was generally resisted by Wall Street insiders. They felt the NYSE could best regulate itself—thank you very much. They reasoned that the investment world would be far better off without interference from different government commissions, rules, and regulations. After all, this was the age of laissez-faire, was it not? Revealingly, John Hanna wrote in the 1934 *California Law Review* (the same year that the Securities and Exchange Act became law), "Much of the extreme exasperation with the law which is current in financial circles relates to the application of the law to particular critics themselves. The disclosures of salaries, bonuses and other advantages of insiders, which the Act requires, are exceedingly distasteful."

Charlie Mitchell certainly would have agreed. We've already seen that Mitchell, the President of National City Bank (the forerunner of today's Citicorp) had to resign in disgrace from his position in 1933 after Senate hearings brought to light he had sold National City stock to his wife in a sham transaction—only to repurchase the shares a few days later. Noteworthy is that the trade took place in 1929, and the paper loss on the trade enabled Mitchell to avoid paying any federal income taxes that year. However, were it not for the mostly forgotten Senate hearings conducted by New York attorney Ferdinand Pecora, Mitchell's actions would have remained undetected. As it was, it took four years for the sham to be brought to light.

Today, of course, a prearranged transaction like this, with or without a family member involved, would be problematic enough. The fact that it was initiated by an executive who was the bank's largest individual shareholder is almost beyond belief. The availability of information on executive and director compensation is today considered an essential element by analysts and investors in assessing corporate governance; and, of course, it is mandated by the SEC.

The securities legislation that Congress passed in Roosevelt's first term as President represented a complete break with the hands-off policy of the past—and for good reason. The Great Depression was a global catastrophe. There are no other words to describe it. While I was in college I remember reading an account of a man who was making a decent living as a car salesman. One day he went to work and discovered the dealership where he worked had gone out of business. Frightened, he went to his bank to withdraw cash, only to discover the bank had failed. He went home and told his wife he had just lost his job and the family's nest egg.

Within days he was forced to sell his car to get money for groceries. His experience was not entirely unique.

After the Crash of 1929 and the ensuing Great Depression, a consensus formed: when and if the nation could recover, this must never happen again. As the economy withered, this conviction grew stronger. The Securities Act of 1933 and the Securities Exchange Act of 1934 were both game changers, critically important acts of Congress that transformed the securities industry. Reading about early federal securities legislation, however, may be about as interesting as memorizing the sixty-three clauses of the Magna Carta. Being mindful of that, I will make a few brief points. Taken together, the '33 and '34 acts provided the federal government and a newly created government agency, the Securities and Exchange Commission, broad authority to regulate the stock market and brokerage firms. Companies had to file public financial statements for the first time—registration statements for new issues and quarterly and annual reports for seasoned ones. Misleading statements, fraud, misrepresentation and the like were identified as crimes. Investors were given the power to sue for losses. The SEC was created to enforce securities laws and was given broad authority over the trading of secondary issues on the nation's various stock exchanges.

It has been said that both the '33 and the '34 acts would never have been signed into law had it not been for the stock market crash in 1929. That's a fair assumption. Even though the Crash of 1929 was not solely responsible for the calamity that followed, many Americans believed that it was. The crash and the depression were thought to be inseparable events, and that absent the crash, we would have been spared all the pain that ensued. Reinventing history like this can be dangerous since there have been any number of sudden, severe market crashes that did not foreshadow a broad-based economic collapse. In fact, many were aberrations, brief moments of panic bookended by years of prosperity.

Nevertheless, a consistent pattern of behavior has emerged since the 1930s when the stock market has experienced unexpected volatility and weakness. In such cases, outrage and finger- pointing have often followed, predictably followed by a swift political reaction. After the 1987 crash, regulators created "circuit breakers" (temporary trading halts) that were designed to calm things down during fast market conditions. In 2002, Sarbanes–Oxley followed a series of securities scandals that occurred shortly before, the most spectacular of which was the bankruptcy of Enron—if not the largest, certainly the most infamous corporate failure in U.S. history. Dodd–Frank similarly came upon the heels of the collapse of the stock market in 2008-9 and the severe recession that followed it.

What is most surprising is that it took so long after the 1929 crash for the '33 and '34 acts to pass. The crash itself will forever be regarded as a seminal event in American history, but so will the Great Depression. When Franklin Roosevelt was inaugurated in March 1933, the economy was in ruins and had been for some time. Thousands of banks had failed; many others that had remained solvent simply closed their doors in what was the last in a series of banking panics that had transpired since the crash. There were more than four thousand bank failures in 1933 alone. By March, every state in the country had closed its banks, declared some sort of banking holiday, or limited the amount of cash depositors could withdraw. The crisis didn't end until Roosevelt himself was able to restore calm. In a national radio address, he told the American public that he was going to declare a three-day national banking holiday, authorize the Federal Reserve Bank to provide additional liquidity (currency) throughout the system, and slowly permit the nation's banks to begin functioning normally. It must be pointed out that when FDR announced the banking holiday, it was a moot point since almost all of the banks in the country were closed anyway. In spite of that irony, his talk had a profound, almost magical effect. The

Great Depression continued for years, but the banking crisis ended abruptly.

Once the Acts of '33 and '34 passed, it quickly became clear that prodigious changes had taken place in the area of financial regulation; almost overnight, a vast amount of power had become vested in the federal government. As time went on the scope of regulation increased no matter who was president, what political party held power, or whether the nation was at war or peace. Even during the 80s and 90s, as Glass–Steagall was losing traction, and even after its ultimate repeal in 1999, the brokerage industry was more heavily regulated than it had been twenty-five or fifty years earlier.

To be sure, many would argue this point and claim that the repeal of Glass–Steagall meant turning back the clock to laissez-faire capitalism—where the gloves come off, rules go out the window, and a giant financial scrum takes place. Not so. At its core, Glass–Steagall simply prohibited commercial banks from acting as investment banks (underwriting securities) and prevented brokerage firms from becoming banks (taking deposits). Regulatory oversight of these two industries didn't stop with the disappearance of Glass–Steagall; in many ways, it increased. To my mind, it has increased because all of the crashes, flash crashes, frauds, scams, bubbles, and busts of the twentieth century served as catalysts for change and reform. What can one say about the market crash of 1987, a sudden one-day decline of 20 percent, wiping out billions of dollars in equity for reasons that even today are not entirely clear? That it was an accident? That bad things happen? Water under the bridge?

Long-term investors who happened to get trapped in the crash of '87 or the mini-crash of '89 or any of the flash crashes that followed were victims of a dysfunctional market. Volatility of this magnitude, especially when it is unrelated to any fundamental condition in the economy at large, is a cancer upon society. It is perfectly understandable why every market debacle is followed by a groundswell of support for reform. Investors want answers; if they can't get answers, they want action.

Not all such reforms have been effective. One reason is very simple: people with criminal intent don't obey the law. Clergymen read the Bible, politicians run for office, and criminals break the law. All the statutes in the world pertaining to churning an account for commissions or unauthorized trading or misrepresentation or fraud have not and will not prevent this behavior from occurring to some degree.

Dating back to 1933, there has been an ongoing debate regarding financial regulation and oversight. On these issues, Democrats and Republicans have publicly, at least, been polar opposites: Democrats favoring more regulation and Republicans less. It is probably not entirely coincidental that much of the reaching legislation affecting the industry was passed during the terms of Presidents Roosevelt, Carter, Clinton and Obama—all Democrats. But regulation didn't disappear during the Republican administrations from Eisenhower to George W. Bush. (In fact, it was Bush who signed off on Sarbanes–Oxley.) It just grew more slowly. If there is a reversal under Trump, it will mark a severe break with the past.

Consensus has been almost impossible to achieve in this area, no doubt because opinions about Wall Street and what it really stands for are often strong and deeply entrenched. Sometimes I think these feelings are immutable (whether as a result of social environment or fixed personality factors I leave to you to decide). In the early 1980s, I was responsible for running Merrill Lynch's Vermont office, and several of the brokers there arranged for me to have dinner with Bernie Sanders. Sanders was then in his late 30s and had just been elected mayor in Burlington; he had achieved national notoriety because he identified himself as a socialist, and there was a running joke at the time about the People's Republic of Burlington. Whatever the case, I was happy to meet him, and when we met, I told him so. I said that in spite of our differences, I believed we'd get along just fine. He looked at me, almost expressionless, and said softly and matter-of-factly, "I doubt it." Clearly, he didn't think highly of Wall Street then, and it seems obvious that he has not warmed up to it since. Given the frequency of the industry's self-inflicted wounds over the past several decades, one can hardly blame him.

The administrations of Bill Clinton, George W. Bush, and Barack Obama were witness to a steady increase of regulations affecting dozens of industries, and the banking and investment industries were no exception. The repeal of Glass–Steagall was not much more than an acceptance of reality and gave formal recognition to changes that had already taken place in the financial services arena; in no way did it represent a break with the past, something that would signal a return to laissez-faire. The two most significant financial reform packages since the 1930s—Sarbanes–Oxley (2002) and Dodd–Frank (2010)—represented the most far-reaching pieces of regulatory legislation since FDR's New Deal. They both became law *after* Glass–Steagall was repealed.

Securities regulation was originally focused on one thing—protecting the investor—in much the same way banking regulations were designed to safeguard the interests of depositors. Recent years have seen extreme volatility, and as a result, the scope of regulation has become much tighter and more extensive. During the credit crisis of 2008-9, a number of financial institutions failed, and others came perilously close as credit dried up and the banking system teetered on the edge. Many of the regulations that were later embodied in Dodd–Frank were enacted not only to defend investors and depositors but also to protect these institutions from their own mistakes and blind ambition.

A plethora of bailout packages followed the credit crisis. Today the federal government's rescue of Wall Street is looked upon as a betrayal by millions who connect the dots this way: fat cats got saved, and the little guy got sold down the river. There was an absolute furor over bonuses paid by many of the firms that accepted bailout money, at one point leading the Democratic majority in Congress to propose a 90 percent tax on bonuses paid by banks. Their trial balloon went nowhere, but at the very least it revealed the level of outrage that was present throughout society. Lost somewhere in the fury was the recognition that if the banks weren't allowed to fail, their depositors would remain solvent. Absent bailout legislation, they would have become victims. Due to massive dilution, shareholders of AIG, Fannie Mae, and the rest were in no way beneficiaries of TARP and other bailout measures, but their policyholders and depositors certainly were.

There is very little consensus on the subject of regulation, whether we have too much or too little, if we have just the right amount, or whether it is entirely effective. It is almost a given that if one opportunity to make money is closed off, the "creativity" of Wall Street will invent another. There are many moving parts in our economy and within the financial markets, and it is very difficult to regulate one part of the nation's business without adversely impacting another. This point was made recently by Tom Allen, a former five-term congressman from Maine whose terms of service wrapped around two important votes, the repeal of Glass–Steagall and the passage of Sarbanes–Oxley. When he slowly said, "It is *so hard* to regulate," he meant every word, and he couldn't be more correct.

I crossed paths with Allen forty years ago in Portland, Maine, where he was then practicing law. He was, and is, extremely affable, thoughtful, nuanced, and honest; these are characteristics a cynic would say are rare among politicians. Much more recently, I asked him where we would be without Dodd–Frank, and he disarmingly said, "I don't know." His point was simply that it was probably a mistake to speculate on what might have been (for example, what would have happened if Germany developed an atomic weapon before the United States did). He recognizes the bill's shortcomings but believes that they in no way invalidate its accomplishments. Are banks better capitalized today? Yes. Did Dodd–Frank shut down a certain type of detrimental activity? Yes. To him, it is obvious that the industry was simply not capable of adequately regulating itself, and government intervention was both necessary and justifiable.

We spoke a bit about the 2008 Credit Crisis. In September, AIG Insurance was on the verge of bankruptcy and was rescued through an emergency loan of $85 billion from the Federal Reserve. This occurred one day after the Lehman bankruptcy when Treasury Secretary Paulson announced there would be no further bailouts. Fed Chairman Ben Bernanke was furious with AIG, saying at a Senate hearing:

"If there's a single episode in this entire 18 months that has made me more angry, I can't think of one, than AIG," he said. "AIG exploited a huge gap in the regulatory system. There was no oversight of the financial products division. This was a hedge fund, basically, that was attached to a large and stable insurance company, made huge numbers of irresponsible bets, took huge losses. There was no regulatory oversight because there was a gap in the system."

In spite of the enormity of the loss, the taxpayer-funded rescue, and the subsequent brouhaha over bonuses paid to AIG executives, there was no clarion call for regulation of the insurance industry at the federal level, nor was a cry for reform issued in the years after the crisis passed. Unlike banks and brokerage firms, insurance companies were regulated at the state level. They still are. In fairness, the states have done a reasonably good job, and in those infrequent cases where an insurance company has actually failed, state reinsurance funds have been able to protect policyholders. Throughout the drama, AIG policyholders were paid on all claims; it was the shareholders who suffered a virtual wipeout. But Bernanke's point is well taken—AIG got itself into trouble by raiding the depositors' piggy bank and speculating with their money.

Untold thousands of hours have been spent crafting legislation designed to prevent legitimate investors from becoming innocent victims. The intent of financial reform is to level the playing field, protect investors and depositors from fraud and misappropriation of funds, and to give all an equal opportunity to succeed. In a way, these principles are basic to almost all of the country's landmark social legislation: civil rights, gender equality, and the rest. However, putting aside the best intentions of our lawmakers, it is next to impossible to accurately predict how successfully such rules and regulations might function when they are given a chance to operate in the real world. Much of the legislative process is trial and error; otherwise, no law would ever be repealed or amended.

Many of the most well-meaning, sincere efforts to right past wrongs have failed to do so. In some instances, reform legislation has overreached, subjecting financial institutions and their customers to distracting, unnecessary intrusions that cost all parties time and money. Purchasing a home today typically involves the receipt of two goliath-sized bundles of documents: a mortgage application package from a lending institution and a binder of miscellaneous closing documents. Each of these along with its accompanying disclosures ordinarily approaches a hundred pages in length. Such documents are always saved and never read, much like my Uncle Phil's collection of *National Geographic* magazines.

The compliance burden that has been placed on banks and brokerage firms is staggering, and for the smaller firms practically unbearable. Tom Reilly knows this from personal experience. His Massachusetts-based boutique firm Fernwood Investment Advisors manages about $300 million. Reilly founded Fernwood in 2000 and by 2007 gave up his broker-dealer license because of the time and money demands mandated by regulatory compliance. Since then Fernwood has operated exclusively as a registered investment advisor, managing money for a fee. As a result, he is unable to earn transactional fees or sell financial products.

Even as an RIA, Reilly operates in a rigid, stifling environment. Fernwood pays a compliance consultant who works on average two full days a week—keep in mind that this is a firm that has at best a half-dozen employees. Reilly himself spends fifteen–twenty hours a month on compliance. All of his employees, including receptionists and administrative assistants, are subject to a high level of individual scrutiny. Tiny odd lot trades in an employee's personal IRA account require preapproval from the firm's compliance officer. Privacy policies must be sent to each client annually. A seemingly endless stream of forms and documents need to be filed quarterly and/or annually because all RIA firms that manage over $100 million in assets must be federally registered. Bear in mind that someone managing a $100 million pool of assets is not running a $100 million business except in an extraordinarily literal sense. Since advisors typically charge a management fee of approximately 1 percent of assets, the annual revenue generated from such a practice would likely be only $1 million, and while $1 million may not be chopped liver, neither does it represent a staggering sum of capital. By comparison, the average stand-alone Chick-Fil-A franchise has annual sales in excess of $3 million.

Federally registered advisors are subject to periodic SEC audits, and Fernwood had one in 2013. Three SEC staffers showed up on a Friday afternoon, unannounced of course. Reilly observed that they were all young and inexperienced, and in his opinion, they didn't have a particularly strong working knowledge of how the RIA business worked. They stayed for fifty days examining books and records and asking questions of him and all of his other employees. One rudderless day followed another until the examination mercifully drew to an end. Reilly, never losing his sense of humor, colorfully referred to the audit process as a Petri dish of bacteria. Without question, he understands the need for regulation and its role in protecting the individual investor, but he also feels that the costs of regulatory overreach—both in time and money—are insufferably high.

I know of another individual who after decades of industry experience decided to start a small RIA in Florida. He registered his LLC in 2016, a process that took close to five months due to a few rather picayune errors of omission on his application, like failing to include a zip code with a mailing address. Each shortcoming was brought to his attention after four or five weeks had elapsed. The application could not be amended; every rejection required an entirely new do-over, with a new submission called for on FINRA's cumbersome electronic portal. The state of Florida also required a fresh set of fingerprints, even though the individual in question had been fingerprinted on numerous prior occasions throughout his career. The state's Office of Financial Regulation mandated that the prints be transmitted electronically by one of the state's authorized agents—and they were, but a few weeks later they were rejected for being illegible. It took a few more weeks to get past the fingerprints. In the end, the business did not go live until very late in 2016 and realized its first dollar of revenue in 2017. Nevertheless, Florida's regulators insisted that a formal 2016 income statement be submitted as follows:

Revenue 0

Expenses 0

Net Income 0

Additionally, the state mandated that the financial statements be filed with a footnote attesting that they had been prepared on an accrual basis, in accordance with GAAP, and bear the signature of a notary. The applicant facetiously asked, "Since the numbers were 0-0-0, was it absolutely necessary to provide a notarized statement rather than a simple explanation?" The answer was a resounding "yes." I wonder what the notary thought.

It is no different for small and medium-sized banks, as Jim Kuhlman would attest. Kuhlman is the president of Premier Community Bank, which operates in Southwest Florida in the Venice-Sarasota-Bradenton area. When I asked him what challenges Dodd–Frank presented in terms of time, money, and human resources, he softly answered, "Oh my God…" before his voice trailed off. He asked me if I had seen a copy of Dodd–Frank while holding his hands about a foot apart. I said I hadn't and told him he was the first person I had met who had done so. It turns out that this piece of legislation runs twenty-three hundred pages.

Kuhlman is a pragmatist who knows that Dodd–Frank is the law of the land and also recognizes the benefits of many parts of the legislation. He pointed out how bank examiners had been justifiably slammed for laxness, especially in the years leading up to the credit crisis of 2008. During the real estate boom, banks and mortgage companies were cranking out loan after loan to unqualified borrowers, often fudging documentation or waiving certain requirements altogether. They learned the hard way that is not a very good idea to lend money to someone who can't pay you back. He fully supports the need for intelligent regulation, but he feels, as many do, that the scale of Sarbanes–Oxley is often over the top and its reach excessive.

Mike Holmes has a little experience with Sarbanes–Oxley and Dodd–Frank as well. After a successful banking career, he retired to his native Florida in the early 2000s, and he became involved with a very small start-up bank near Tampa, Central Bank. It has remained a very small bank and still has only one branch office. In spite of its small size, the bank retains a full-time compliance officer on the deposit side and contracts with several consultants to monitor the loan side of their business. Since SOX and Dodd–Frank, he estimates that the cost of compliance for small banks has quadrupled.

Earlier, Kuhlman had a similar experience at Florida Shores Bank, where he served as president from 2006 to 2014. When he successfully sold the bank in 2014, he estimated that the hard costs of compliance ran around $1 million annually, a 1000 percent increase in eight years. This is an colossal nut for any small business to absorb. Even at the time of its sale, Florida Shores had only $400 million in total assets, an impressive number by ordinary standards, but in the world of banking, modest. Compare this with (regional) Synovus Bank's $30 billion, or Wells Fargo's $2 trillion.

Dodd–Frank is philosophically aligned with the Patriot Act, the Banking Secrecy Act, and a host of other regulations and mandates designed to ferret out wrongdoing like money laundering and terror financing. The war on financial skullduggery has been far from successful. John Cassara, an expert in trade-based money laundering, knows how creative the criminal mind can be. Citing an actual example, he described how money launderers exchanged currency for gold jewelry, melted it down, recast it into nuts and bolts, painted everything battleship gray, and then arranged to "sell" the nuts and bolts to co-conspirators in another country. Somehow the bad guys were caught, but in most cases—Cassara believes perhaps 98 percent of the time—money launderers of this type are successful. They can move money out of the country without detection by over- and under-invoicing; and in the process, they can circumvent the banking system entirely.

The last twenty years have seen a veritable explosion in new and more far-reaching financial regulations. Sarbanes–Oxley followed several enormous accounting frauds that resulted in corporate bankruptcies, WorldCom and Enron. Until the credit crisis, these were the two largest corporate failures in American history. Sarbanes–Oxley addressed accounting transparency, records retention and financial disclosure; in addition, it created new, higher standards of behavior for executives and directors of public companies. Dodd–Frank, which came on the heels of the credit crisis and a number of new, record-setting bankruptcies, represented an even more sweeping attempt at Wall Street reform. The industry's self-regulatory organization grew in size through the combination of NYSE and NASDAQ internal compliance divisions. This new SRO is called FINRA, or the Financial Industry Regulatory Authority. FINRA may be an SRO, but it is not omnipotent—ultimate power lies with the SEC. The Consumer Finance Protection Board (CFPB) was authorized by Dodd–Frank, and it came into being in 2011. Its priorities are loans, credit cards, and mortgages. Another landmark piece of legislation, the Housing Economic Recovery Act, was an emergency response to the housing crisis and the Great Recession of 2008-9 that it spawned.

It has been many years since the credit crisis ended, but only since the election of Donald Trump has there been serious talk of rolling back business regulations. Frankly, that talk has been centered more on manufacturers than on banks and brokers. I would guess that regulatory relaxation in the financial services realm will be modest in future years if it occurs at all. Trump must deal with firebrand Senators Elizabeth Warren and Bernard Sanders as well as the millions of passionate progressives they represent. He also has to worry about his base—white, blue-collar workers—that oddly enough would be harmed if an agency like the Consumer Protection Finance Bureau were disbanded. This is a situation to watch closely.

It is almost as hard to gauge the effectiveness of all of the Wall Street reforms as it was to craft the rules and regulations in the first place. On balance, Sarbanes–Oxley, Dodd–Frank and the rest can be looked on as successes. As a result of these measures, accounting and auditing standards were tightened, and investors and depositors were able to receive greater protection. Most importantly, the entire banking system was made more secure by the imposition of more conservative net capital requirements. Was there overreach? Yes. Can all of the costs of compliance be justified? No. Did tightened lending standards in a perverse way impede the housing recovery? Yes, because millions of would-be homeowners couldn't get a loan unless they had impeccable credit and a large down payment.

In the end, however, all of the elements of regulatory reform have created more good than harm. This is especially true in banking. In 2016, only one bank failed, compared with 140 liquidations in 2009. During the Great Recession, depositors were anxious and fearful that their money wasn't safe. Many put their cash in gold, which more than doubled in price within a few years' time. To my knowledge, it was the only asset class to show a positive return during this period. Today there is absolutely no talk of a banking crisis and for good reason. Securities firms are in much better shape as well, though it must be pointed out that many of those operations are no longer independent. Prudential Securities, Merrill Lynch, A.G. Edwards, Bear Stearns and Paine Webber are just a few of the companies that lost their former identity during the credit crisis.

Regulatory reform, however, has not put a dent in greed or gullibility. This is especially true in the securities industry, where opportunities for cheating, fraud, scamming, and insider trading present themselves on countless occasions. Prosecutors have been quite aggressive recently in attacking the nexus of wrongdoing, especially with respect to insider trading. The industry itself has spent enormous amounts of time and money in attempting to clean up its own act and restore its image and reputation. Let's not forget the thousands of pages of new government regulations issued during the past few decades that have made the term *laissez-faire* almost obsolete. But unfortunately, when it comes to turning bad people into good people, there is no easy fix.

Going Over to the Dark Side

• • •

HISTORY MAKES IT CLEAR THAT it is hard—extremely hard—to control the behavior of people who do bad things, and it is even harder to catch them when they do. This is especially true for white-collar crimes. Consider the case of Bernie Madoff, who ran a multi-billion-dollar Ponzi scheme for over twenty years without detection. There was no whistleblower. Madoff's charade was discovered only because his investors panicked during the 2008-9 credit crisis, and they all wanted out at the same time. Unable to meet their requests for redemption, he meekly gave up and turned himself in. Otherwise, he'd still be in business today.

Most investment scandals, however, do not involve behavior as brazen and sociopathic as Madoff's, or anything close to it. People change as they go through life, and on Wall Street, the constant temptation of wealth and power can prove to be irresistible. One of the more infamous bad guys, Charles Keating, was for a very long time a good guy. Keating was a devout Catholic. During World War II, he served in the US Navy as a fighter pilot. After graduating from the University of Cincinnati, where he was a champion swimmer, he went to law school and subsequently started a law practice with his brother and a mutual friend. In 1969, Richard Nixon appointed him to serve on *The President's Commission on Obscenity and Pornography*. He appeared to have a brilliant future but ended up as the leading figure in one of the biggest financial scandals of recent times.

While in his thirties, Keating became friendly with Carl Lindner, a very wealthy local businessman. Lindner soon became Keating's largest client, then his only client. Within a few years, Keating left his law partners and joined Lindner as Executive Vice President of American Financial, an insurance and investment company that Lindner ran. He was now making good money, and many noted his value system and personality seemed to change—for the worse—as he achieved more success. He earned a reputation for being something of a bully at work.

When Lindner acquired a smaller firm, which he often did, it was Keating's job to oversee the subsequent "restructuring," a euphemism for downsizing. In the mid-1970s, he was named in several stockholder lawsuits and ultimately entered into a settlement agreement with the SEC after being charged with fraud for filing false financial statements with the agency. This settlement, like virtually all SEC settlements, was reached without "admitting or denying guilt." Nevertheless, Keating's reputation was damaged—if not scorched.

He moved West at the age of fifty-three for a fresh start, in a sense to go it alone. Almost. He became Chairman of American Continental Homes, a struggling homebuilder that had been a subsidiary of American Financial. In the process, he also became the company's largest stockholder. For a brief while, he became involved politically with John Connally's failed 1980 campaign for President. Later, Ronald Reagan seriously considered Keating for an ambassadorial post in the Bahamas but decided to go in another direction when Keating's SEC troubles were brought to his attention. Keating was stung but soldiered on. He orchestrated a tremendous turnaround at American Continental, and within a few years the company produced profits in the millions, assets in the billions, and was the proud owner of three corporate jets and a helicopter. As tough and ruthless as he had become in business, he maintained his charitable predisposition and close connection to the Catholic Church. Keating gave millions to various Catholic charities. Like many scammers, he cared deeply about his public image and reputation. Perhaps this was just narcissism, or possibly it illustrated that Heating's persona was more nuanced than generally believed.

In 1984, American Continental acquired Lincoln Savings and Loan for only $50 million. It was a small, sleepy, conservatively run bank that managed to survive the recessions that were sandwiched around 1980, and by 1983 it was producing a small profit. Keating immediately replaced management personnel at the bank, and he also effected a radical change in its mission and strategy. The bank began to operate like a modern-day hedge fund, forsaking its traditional investments in home mortgages and personal loans and instead concentrating on raw land purchases, real estate development projects and junk bonds. Part of this was made possible by the earlier deregulation of the savings and loan industry, but most of it was a by-product of Keating's single-minded pursuit of winning at all costs. For a while, his strategy worked, at least on the surface, as Lincoln's assets ballooned 500 percent in five years. Keating's aggressive expansion—in hindsight, one could say irresponsible and reckless, but nevertheless legal—was not sustainable. Many of the investments soured, and bank examiners started poking around as early as 1986.

The end was just a few years away. The bank was hemorrhaging cash, and Keating was desperate to stop the bleeding. Any vestige of moral or even partially defensible behavior went out the window. Bank managers and tellers enthusiastically offered depositors higher-yielding Lincoln "certificates" without mentioning they carried no FDIC insurance. Their pitches were carefully scripted, and depositors were given total assurance about the safety of these new investments. If there is a better example of the concept of moral hazard in the workplace, I cannot think of one. Thousands lost their life savings when the bank finally imploded. Before the bank failed, Keating himself went to Washington to enlist the support of five US senators, including American icons John Glenn and John McCain, to whose campaigns he had contributed generously in the past. He was hopeful he could use his influence to have them intervene in a Federal Home Loan Bank investigation. They didn't but were tarnished anyway and soon became known as the "Keating Five."

When American Continental went bankrupt in 1989, bank regulators took control of Lincoln Savings and Loan. The cost to American taxpayers was $3.4 billion. Soon afterward, Keating was personally indicted for fraud and racketeering. He was found guilty and spent almost five years in jail before having his conviction overturned. The government was hell-bent on retrying the case, but Keating was able to strike a plea bargain with the Justice Department just before the retrial was about to begin. Along the way, Keating was forced to declare bankruptcy, as his personal assets had been wiped out by government fines, restitution paid to Lincoln's victims and his own legal fees. He often claimed he was the victim of a "witch hunt" and while he was incarcerated described himself as a political prisoner. He and his wife Mary separated after nearly fifty years of marriage. His last years were spent quietly in Phoenix, where he lived with his daughter Mary and her husband, Olympic swimming medalist Gary Hall. He passed away several years ago at the age of ninety. For someone whose life started out on such a promising note, Keating ended up running off the rails, losing his wife, money, and reputation.

Michael Binstein and Charles Bowden wrote in their book *Trust Me: Charles Keating and the Missing Billions*:

> Charlie Keating built things, and, at some level that haunts anyone who looks over his records, he thought his schemes would work. He did not simply rob a bank. He broke a bank with his dreams. If he is simply a thief, why did he put the money into deals and projects instead of into his own pocket? If he is just a hardworking businessman simply trying to make a profit and create jobs, why the need for jets, fancy meals, big paychecks to his family? If he is such a devout communicant of his faith, why did he peddle hundreds of millions of dollars' worth of junk bonds to old people when he knew his empire was in serious jeopardy?

The story of Charles Keating and Lincoln Savings and Loan speaks to the moral imperfections that exist in all of us. You may remember when Rosie Ruiz popped out from a subway station a few miles from the finish line at the New York Marathon. After having "won" the race, she got to bask in the glory of her first-place finish for perhaps one day before her fraud was revealed. She could have chosen to train like everyone else, i.e., to start at the starting line, finish at the finish line, and walk away with self-respect and a genuine sense of accomplishment. Instead, Ruiz chose to take a shortcut. So did Keating. Throughout his business career, Keating was conflicted, and at the end of it, lost his way entirely.

And so did Martha Stewart, a wealthy celebrity and entrepreneur, who got caught up in an entirely avoidable insider trading case in 2001 and ultimately went to jail for a year. For those who don't remember the sad details, Stewart's broker told her that her friend (and also his client), Sam Waksal, was selling stock in his company, ImClone Systems. Since he was the CEO, that was good enough for Stewart, who immediately sold 3928 shares (her entire position). Shortly afterward, ImClone announced that the FDA had failed to approve one of the company's new drugs, and the stock dropped 16 percent. By selling before the announcement, Stewart avoided a $46,000 loss. Obviously, the transaction looked somewhat suspicious, and regulators jumped on it. They requested a meeting with Stewart, and she obliged. This was her chance to come clean.

Knowing that a large stockholder sold stock in his own company does not necessarily constitute a crime. Stewart did not serve on the Board of Imclone and knew nothing of its internal operations. Who knows what went through her mind just before she decided to sell her small position? When she was later questioned about the incident, Stewart could have been disingenuous or truthful (or perhaps both) and said something like: "Oh my! Yes, my broker told me that Sam was selling, so I figured I'd better get out too. Is that wrong? I'm very sorry. What do I need to do to make things right?" Instead, she chose to cover up, to deny, and to lie to the SEC. Ironically, the government dropped the insider trading charges against her, and she ended up being prosecuted (and convicted) for obstruction of justice.

The lure of wealth can be irresistibly tempting, and the securities industry creates temptation like no other. At its core, the business is filled with overwhelming conflicts of interest, many of which are inescapable. Do investment bankers during an initial public offering serve two masters—the customers who end up buying into an IPO, or the company going public? Shareholders want the best (lowest) price possible, but the subject company is hoping to extract the highest. Retail brokers, at least in the age of the dinosaur, charged commissions on every trade. Where exactly does suitability stop and churning begin? What about corporate executives who can put some small level of spin on a story to make an earnings miss appear to be a minor hiccup? Is this fraud? Or is it a rosy, optimistic representation of the company's performance? Does anyone question why the college savings plans sold by full-service firms contain fully loaded mutual funds? The reason is simple: it's legal, and thus far there has not been an uprising of customers who have objected. In fact, during the 70s, full-service firms put a ½ percent load on money market fund purchases—until anemic sales forced them to stop the practice. Some called it price gouging, and others called it a ½ percent sales charge. There is a measure of truth in both.

Recently, the Department of Labor made several proposals that touch on the role of today's financial advisor: what it is, and what it should be. Consider the following statement, lifted verbatim from the DOL's 2016 own final ruling concerning fiduciaries, retirement plans, and financial advisors.

Many advisers do put their customers' best interest first and there are many good practices in the industry. But the balance of research and evidence indicates the aggregate harm from the cases in which consumers receive bad advice based on conflicts of interest is large.

The DOL's ruling, as you might expect, is laborious to read. It is over two hundred pages in length, and while providing very little in the way of specifics, its intent is clear. With respect to participant-directed retirement accounts like IRAs and 401 plans, broker-dealers and advisors would be held to a "fiduciary standard" of behavior, meaning that they must act in the best interests of their customers, as opposed making certain their recommendations were "suitable and appropriate." To many, they sound like the same thing, but the new DOL regulations caused a great deal of consternation for investment firms and clients alike. Imagine being told about this, and then asking your own advisor, "What does this mean? Weren't you always acting in my best interests?"

Financial advisors, even dinosaurs, have always been required to know their customers, record and update their personal financial information, identify their investment objectives, understand their temperament and risk tolerance, and make recommendations suitable and consistent with their goals. Fiduciary standards go a bit farther along this continuum. Are there lower-cost alternatives available to the client? Is the client receiving regular, periodic updates and information regarding his retirement plan investments? Is this communication being documented? Is the compensation received by the advisor disclosed? Is it fair? These questions lead not to answers but more questions: If lower cost is better, is lowest cost best? What constitutes regular, periodic communication? What level of specificity is required when documenting verbal communication between advisor and client? How can one know if the level of compensation received by an advisor is fair?

While the Trump administration has indicated it will move to roll back part or all of these regulations, the ruling has nevertheless thrown the industry into a tizzy. Fearful of stepping out of bounds, some large firms decided to take preemptive measures early on. Merrill Lynch Wealth Management went so far as to announce it would prohibit all commission-based trading in retirement accounts—unless those accounts were moved to its Bank of America discount platform, Merrill Edge. (Picture a customer who wants to trade individual stocks in an IRA account being told he can't, at least if he wants to consult with his advisor.) At Merrill Edge, the only contact between the customer and the company is a call center whose representatives are prohibited from giving advice.

Other firms decided to permit some continuation of the status quo, but one can rest assured that these accounts will receive the rapt attention of internal compliance, with virtually every trade questioned and scrutinized. In a situation like this, an advisor will be put on the defensive and made to feel as if he has behaved inappropriately, even if his intentions and actions were entirely selfless and proper. Many veterans have simply been leaving the business in frustration if not outright disgust.

One can see very clearly how difficult it is to align the interests of advisors and investors. In recent years, the growth in different products and services did more than give investors greater choice; it also increased the opportunities for conflicts of interest. The case of Drexel Burnham, Mike Milken and the junk bond mania of the 1980s is a good case in point. Milken, like Keating, was vilified, prosecuted and jailed. While the legal case against Milken's specific offenses was clear-cut, and his punishment at least partially justified, the man himself was—and is—far more layered and complex. Milken was no Attila the Hun, an innately bad man turned monster through an insatiable lust for land, wealth and power. He was talented, exceptionally bright, and creative; and he was always philanthropically active, well before his fall from grace. Yet like many highly successful Wall Street professionals, he became blinded by his success, almost obsessed by it, and it cost him his good name, freedom, and a great deal of money. In the last twenty years, he has tried mightily to rehabilitate his image, and even though he has been partially successful in doing so, most people who lived through the junk bond era remember him as a slimeball. That's the painful truth. At the end of the day, his wounds were self-inflicted.

Milken grew up in the tony town of Encino, California. He completed his undergraduate work at University of California (Berkeley) with high honors and graduated Phi Beta Kappa. His M.B.A. was earned at the prestigious Wharton School at the University of Pennsylvania. His professors at Penn helped him land his first job on Wall Street with Drexel, at the time known as Drexel Firestone, and after a 1973 merger, Drexel Burnham. Milken stayed on with the merged firm. He was so highly thought of he was named head of Drexel's convertible bond unit—at the age of twenty-seven.

I suppose there has always been high-yield debt, i.e., bonds that pay a great deal more in interest than other IOUs. It was Milken, however, who legitimized high yield as an asset class, and because of his outsize influence, he became known as the Junk Bond King. At Drexel Burnham, the junk-bond label was worn like a badge of honor—junk-bond financing and secondary market trading combined to lift Drexel into the top tier of Wall Street investment firms during the 1980s.

The high-yield debt unit at Drexel was seeded with $2 million in 1973. Milken was a brilliant trader and in no time was able to attract an ever-increasing number of investors. Soon he had $20 million, then $200 million, then much, much more. He was making a fortune and within five years convinced Drexel to move his unit back to California. Why not? It was now the most profitable part of Drexel, and Milken was the firm's most valuable employee. Some people felt his earnings were obscene. Wrong. They were more than obscene. Before he was forty, he became one of the wealthiest people in America. In 1987 alone, he earned over $500 million.

He was an original thinker. In short order, he demonstrated that high-yield debt could perform an important and functional role in the economy. Before Milken rose to prominence, high-yield was regarded as garbage by all serious, sophisticated investors—something to be avoided at all costs. Milken showed the world that high-yield could be used as a legitimate financing vehicle in mergers and acquisitions. In the late 1970s, stocks had been mired in a bear market for years, and equity valuations were as low as they had been since the Depression. In an environment of undervalued stocks, companies became attracted to the idea of buying other companies; and to do that, of course, they needed money.

In a so-called leveraged buyout, an acquirer uses a small amount of equity and a large amount of debt to raise enough money to buy the assets of its "target company." Milken had the resources and the complete confidence of corporate raiders, who combed the countryside for companies that might be vulnerable to a successful takeover. The key ingredients: a low stock price, an underperforming business, unhappy shareholders looking for an exit, and overhead that could easily be cut. Virtually all of the deals were hostile, that is totally unexpected and unwanted, and of course, the target companies fought back strongly to preserve their independence. Nevertheless, the takeover attempts were largely effective. ABC Buyout Partners would announce that it would be making an all-cash offer to buy XYZ Manufacturing and immediately flash a letter from Milken and Drexel Burnham that it was "highly confident" it would be able to finance the transaction. Those two words—highly confident—were all it took.

After the transaction closed, ABC Buyouts Partners would have control of the target company's Board, and almost immediately begin to downsize, restructure, and cut costs. Many factories were closed, and jobs were lost, an unfortunate development to be sure. In the end, however, XYZ would be recast into a leaner, meaner, more profitable business, one that could be resold at a much higher price. From the eyes of Drexel and the corporate raiders, at least, this was an ideal outcome. The ends fully justified the means, a somewhat twisted example of folks helping folks.

It was also perfectly legal. Yet after fifteen years of riding high, being the toast of the town, finding himself on the covers of *Business Week* and *Forbes*, Milken found himself in a world of trouble. An ambitious US Attorney, Rudy Giuliani, became heavily involved in prosecuting corruption on Wall Street, and he felt that the world of junk bonds was at its nexus. Corporate financiers/raiders like T. Boone Pickens, Carl Icahn, and Ron Perelman all did business with Milken, and their names soon became feared throughout corporate America. By far the most notorious of these men was Ivan Boesky, whom Giuliani successfully singled out and charged with insider trading. Boesky agreed to testify against Milken in return for leniency and was ultimately sent away for several years. Along with Boesky, Princeton/Newport Partners, a well-respected investment management firm, was targeted by Giuliani and raided by federal agents. Seizing documents and tape recordings, Giuliani felt that there was a high level of collusion between Drexel and Princeton Newport. He brought charges of racketeering and insider trading against the firm, both of which would have given its principals (if convicted) huge fines and long jail sentences. Instead, five Princeton Newport executives each served a few months in jail, and paid fines averaging in the six figures.

It was apparent that Giuliani had his eye on Milken, and he went after him with a vengeance. Some of the tape recordings that had been uncovered earlier revealed incriminating conversations between a senior Drexel trader and Princeton Newport, and since the trader reported directly to Milken, the government connected the dots and charged Milken with insider trading. He was given a total of ninety-six indictments on these and other charges, but Milken claimed innocence from Day 1. He fought Giuliani for three years, but time was against him; the tide had begun to ebb. The junk bond market started going sour in 1986, and after the 1987 stock market crash, it entered into a death spiral. The government's case against Milken was ultimately settled, and Milken admitted guilt on several acts of securities fraud and stock manipulation. He was threatened with much more if he didn't cooperate. Facing overwhelming odds, he folded; by 1990, Drexel Burnham was bankrupt.

The racketeering charges (RICO) sought against Milken did not stick, nor did any charges of insider trading. Milken received a ten-year sentence, served less than three, and paid a fine of $600 million. He was still a phenomenally wealthy man when he emerged from jail, and today is worth over $2 billion. Giuliani rode his successful prosecution of Milken into politics and was elected Mayor of New York in 1994. Six years later, after both had experienced cancer scares, they met in New York to discuss health, wellness, nutrition and exercise. This still strikes me as an odd moment in history, much like the meeting between Richard Nixon and Elvis Presley. Years later, just after Donald Trump was elected President, Giuliani said that Milken would be an "excellent candidate" for a Presidential pardon.

Mention Milken's name, even today, and most people will wince, assigning him to a scrap bag of Wall Street's worst dirtballs, schemers, and criminal masterminds. He was none of these, but neither was he one of God's messengers. Milken was guilty of wrongdoing. Trading at Drexel was far from transparent. Drexel employees often ended up with especially lucrative investments under strange or suspicious circumstances. So did favored customers, and sometimes Milken entered into prearranged trades with them. This type of transaction, a way of manipulating the market, is a clear violation of ethical standards in the industry.

There are countless examples of lives on Wall Street—just like that of Milken—that suddenly take an unexpected detour. Milken, Keating, and many others were leading purposeful lives, and a combination of circumstances conspired to push each of them off track. For Keating, it was the savings and loan crisis that sent him scrambling to raise capital from unsuspecting depositors in a desperate and misguided effort to save his empire. Remember, S&L bank failures were spreading throughout the industry, not just at Lincoln Savings and Loan. Before the fraudulent sale of uninsured certificates, Keating's bank was over-leveraged, poorly run, and probably doomed to collapse anyway. However, that was the case with hundreds of other banks during the 1980s. What made Lincoln Savings unique was its leader Charles Keating, who orchestrated a fraud in order to save his bank.

Milken's fall from grace was a little more complex, as early success may have bred a sense of grandiosity and self-importance. One can speculate that Milken was so committed to the enduring value of junk-bond financing and activist investing that almost anything he and Drexel did, even "minor" indiscretions, could in some way be explained away if not fully justified. Let's not forget though that Milken's modus operandi was not held up to scrutiny until the high-yield market started to roll over in the mid-1980s. The crash of 1987 sealed its fate—and Milken's with it.

At the turn of the century, corporate scandals became even more spectacular. Think about Ken Lay, Jeff Skilling, and Enron. The Enron bankruptcy in 2001 was an unmitigated disaster, and more than any other event or trend was the catalyst behind the passage of Sarbanes–Oxley in 2002. Even today it is not entirely clear what Lay and Skilling knew and what they didn't know. Without doubt, they suffered from Milken disease, where hubris takes control of one's thought processes. At the very least both men were guilty of poor oversight and worse judgment, and they blindly put Enron into so much debt that if the company ever ran into trouble, it would have no way to wiggle out. They spent shareholder money as if it were their private piggy bank. They naïvely believed that the business of energy trading could become a sustainable one; it didn't, ultimately proving to be not much more than smoke and mirrors. As Enron's stock surged in the late 1990s, they became spin doctors. When it started to sour, they spun some more.

Skilling and Lay were both convicted entirely on circumstantial evidence and the testimony of other Enron executives who perpetrated the accounting fraud and agreed to cooperate with the Justice Department. The off-balance sheets partnerships that sunk Enron were secret creations of Andy Fastow, the company's Chief Financial Officer. He and his co-conspirators somehow convinced Enron's leadership and Board to fund the partnerships—without having the debt appear on the company's balance sheet. In hindsight, this was a ridiculous, indefensible tactic, but as we know, there are no do-overs in life. Think about this. Fastow makes a Board presentation, and all Board members sign off on it, as does Enron's accounting firm and outside counsel. Does it not stand to reason that the CEO and president would follow suit?

Fastow formed several partnerships in this way, and each time after they were funded, he quickly arranged to have tens of millions of dollars wired out to himself and his collaborators; Skilling and Lay received nothing. In fact, there are sources within Enron who claimed that when Skilling asked Fastow if he was earning significant compensation from the arrangement, Fastow dismissed the question. He reportedly told Skilling the amount he received was a fraction of his base salary at Enron, something in the low six-figure range.

When the government got involved in prosecuting Enron, they put the squeeze on Fastow. He cooperated, and he fingered Skilling, Lay, and others; in the end, he received a six-year jail sentence. His wife, who also worked as Enron's assistant treasurer, served one year. Andrew Fastow is now on the speaker circuit, talking about corporate fraud and ethics at major universities throughout the country. Lay died before he was sent away. Skilling, in 2017, was still in prison. He hopes to be released in a few years.

I have witnessed many former co-workers whose lives have gone astray. They were not celebrities, and they were responsible for financial damages in the millions of dollars, not billions. It doesn't matter—their stories had similar endings. I recall how two individuals, both talented, promising young men with big personalities, ended up with gambling debts and then concocted Ponzi schemes as a way of putting their lives back on track. While the schemes were active, they continued to work their "day jobs" as if their lives were proceeding normally. Nobody suspected a thing. The crash of 1987 did them both in, just as it had Bernie Madoff; when their victims panicked and asked to pull out, they didn't have the cash to pay all of them at once. Enter the SEC and the FBI. Both men went to federal prison, and both were banned from the securities industry for life.

It's probably not news to anyone that people have been corrupted by the lure of wealth and power. That's been the case since the dawn of time. Equally interesting though is that the prospect of wealth doesn't necessarily make good people do bad things; sometimes it just encourages good people to do stupid things. The biggest investment mania of my lifetime, the mother of all bubbles, was the dot-com feeding frenzy in the 1990s. It lasted perhaps six years. Billions of dollars were made and subsequently lost; lives were transformed and then shattered. The dot-com era holds many life lessons for all of us. Hopefully, some of them will be taken to heart.

Dot Com

• • •

WHEN I GRADUATED FROM HIGH school in 1965, the Dow Jones Industrial Average was trading near 1,000. Seventeen years later, after a furious rally, it found itself at approximately the same level. Five presidents, two oil embargos, and four recessions later, the stock market made no progress. Basically, between 1965 and 1982 no one made much money, and investors of all stripes became exhausted and discouraged. One can't blame them. Seventeen years is an awfully long time to break even.

All of us who entered the securities industry in the 1960s and 70s came to believe that this was normal and that all the stories we had heard from veteran brokers, traders, and analysts about bull markets of bygone years were either hallucinations or fantasies. Even though stocks were trading at historically cheap levels, my contemporaries and I had become so conditioned to losing we just stopped hoping. I didn't know what a bull market was, and I really didn't believe one was possible.

Ironically, the bottom may have been put in when *Business Week* ran a not so exquisitely timed cover story in 1979 entitle "The Death of Equities." To this magazine's everlasting embarrassment, stocks soon afterward embarked on a jagged, irregular but sustained advance, and in the 1980s began to make real progress for the first time in twenty years. In fairness, neither *Business Week* nor I had could have imagined what the future had in store. No one has tomorrow's newspaper. In 1979, two of the thirty stocks that comprised this widely followed index were Chrysler and Esmark (formerly Swift, best known as a meatpacker). They were

147

replaced by IBM and Merck, both considered dazzling growth stocks then but rightly considered mature corporations today. That's the way it is in the world and especially in the stock market, where change is a constant.

Most bull markets have their own unique characteristics and their true believers, enthusiastic investors who feel that the good times will never end because—well, because—this time it's different! Technological advances and productivity increases have been the fuel for much of America's historic economic growth and stock market gains. Just think about the influence of railroads, the telegraph, automobiles and air transport, the Industrial Revolution and automation, health care, or radio and television. It was no different when something called the internet first appeared. Its importance was immediately apparent.

In its early stages, in the 1980s, however, the bull market was not driven by technology at all but by a welcome change in fundamentals. Interest rates and inflation, both of which had been suffocatingly high, began to come back to earth, and corporate earnings started to rise. Yes, the market's upward trajectory was interrupted by a violent stock market crash in 1987, but the damage it caused was relatively short-lived. As we've seen, the market closed out 1987 with a small, positive return, and rallied further in 1988. Ronald Reagan left office a hero and passed the torch to his Vice President, George H.W. Bush. All seemed well in the world. For the next half-dozen years or so, continued progress was made. When Bush was succeeded by Bill Clinton, peace, prosperity, economic recovery, rising employment, and a continued drop in interest rates continued apace, and the Dow easily surpassed 3,000.

Between 1985 and 2000, the Dow "suffered" only one year of negative returns, a minus 4.3 percent in 1990. That was sandwiched between a plus 26.9 percent in 1989 and a plus 20.6 percent in 1991. Looking at the early 80s as a starting point, the Dow had managed to quadruple in twelve years. If the bull market had ended then, it would have qualified as one of history's most substantial and enduring—but 1995 was no market top. If anything, it turned out to be a launch point. The dot-com era was about to begin.

In 1991, the World Wide Web was just a concept. In that year, there was just one live website and no public awareness of communicating via something called the internet. Even by the end of 1995, only fifteen million people on the planet used the internet. But by the summer of 2000, a little more than four years later, three hundred fifty million were connected online. Today, well over three billion souls are plugged in. The development of the internet was, like the railroad and the telephone before it, a true game-changer in the history of communications and had a profound influence on almost every level of activity in society—government, business, leisure, and education. I suppose one might include money laundering and terrorist financing as well.

Everyday language changed. A hard drive, formerly a twelve-hour trek in an automobile, was now more commonly thought of as a device. Drivers were not necessarily people who drove cars and trucks; instead, they became known as the files that enabled hardware devices to communicate with a computer's operating system. An application, formerly something filled out by hand to apply for college admission or a job, soon became the term used to describe a software program that ran on a computer or smartphone. Computers didn't get sick, but they did become infected with viruses. Viruses were removed by technicians, not treated with drugs. Websites were once inhabited by spiders; now they were designed by software engineers. All manner of living was revolutionized; communication became instantaneous, the footprint of the world shrunk, and globalization accelerated. And the stock market, especially technology and internet-related stocks, went on a tear the likes of which most of us had never imagined possible. The NASDAQ index rose an astonishing 500 percent between June 1995 and March 2000. The big boys of the dot-com era—Cisco, Intel, Microsoft, and EMC—appeared to possess supernatural powers and sold at astronomical valuations. At one point the market capitalization of Microsoft was more than double that of the entire stock market in Korea.

In any event, as the dot-com bubble gained momentum, all caution was thrown to the wind. One of the major factors behind this sea change in enthusiasm was the introduction of online stock trading. In some ways, one could argue that Charles Schwab's influence upon the rapid growth of the internet was comparable to that of Amazon. Trading on the internet was cheap, fast, private and effortless. Hundreds of thousands of investors now fancied themselves as day traders; many quit their jobs altogether, confident that they would be able to support themselves just by taking a seat in front of their computers and jumping in (and out) of an attractive stock *du jour.* Why work? This was too easy.

Venture capital and private equity funds specializing in technology and internet-related stocks exploded. Biotechnology also got a fair amount of attention, but a disproportionate amount of energy was focused on all things internet. Thousands of companies were looking for seed capital, and they found what they needed with ease. First venture capitalists, then Wall Street investors provided countless billions to these dazzling new startups. The attraction seemed magnetic. Sadly, few of the companies that were successfully funded and ultimately went on to go public made money, but in the beginning, it didn't seem to matter. When it was all over, of course, it did.

People who should have known better were looking at metrics like eye-balls and users—anything but revenue and profit. The ride was dizzying. The dot-com era ushered in a world of young people, suddenly very rich, on the covers of *Time* and *Newsweek* and *Forbes.* One of them, a neighbor of mine in Wellesley, Massachusetts, built a gargantuan home complete with an indoor pool and a regulation basketball court. When he discovered that his sunroom turned out to be a little too small for a treasured oriental rug, he kept the rug and rebuilt the sunroom.

The internet era was unique in a number of ways. One of its most distinguishing characteristics was that dot-com companies were typically started by one or two people—let's call them visionaries—who had an innovative idea or concept but didn't possess much personal wealth. Remember that many of the early dot-com entrepreneurs were extremely young; in fact, Steve Jobs, Bill Gates, and Mark Zuckerberg were all college dropouts. Many would-be entrepreneurs needed access to "other people's money." Those that bootstrapped their own companies, like Gates, had to be extremely patient. He founded Microsoft in 1975; at the end of 1976, the company's total revenues were only $16,000.

Gates and Microsoft, of course, were an exception; using other people's money was the rule. This was a far different scenario than the old days of *laissez-faire* capitalism; in 1893, Richard Sears and Alvah Roebuck put their own money into a small mail-order watch company in Chicago, one that later grew into America's iconic retailer, Sears Roebuck. Sam Walton did much the same thing when he bought a five-and-ten in Bentonville, Arkansas, in 1950 and renamed it Walmart. Thousands of first-generation Americans in the early 1900s began businesses by borrowing money from Uncle Joe or Aunt Minnie. Private equity as a formal asset class did not exist.

The dot-com bubble wouldn't have happened without venture capital. Serial entrepreneur Judy George knows the landscape well, having interfaced directly with leading private equity firms like Bain and Bessemer for the past thirty years. She notes that risk capital today performs the same function that it did in the 80s and 90s; the difference between the two eras is in the appetite for risk. Venture capitalists have become less adventurous. In the 90s, many of the leading business schools were focused on entrepreneurial studies, and MBAs by the truckload were committed to getting active in some aspect of the bull market in technology stocks; it mattered little whether their careers led them to venture capital, investment banking and IPOs, research and analysis, or an executive position within a promising startup itself. This field was sizzling, and there was a sense of urgency to get involved and get a deal done.

In the 1990s, VCs would look at anything, and we know from the miserable history of many of the investments they made that they put money in almost everything. George observed that young entrepreneurs without money of their own, a Rolodex, reputation or track record were often enough able to secure seed funding for their dot-com startups. Today, you would need to cobble together a financial syndicate of family, friends, and neighbors, and if that proved insufficient, perhaps turn to Plan B—the credit cards in your wallet. Venture capitalists expect today's entrepreneur to have a history of success and money of their own to put in a deal, usually at least 10 percent, sometimes as much as a third. This means if the VCs go in for $10 million in an initial round of investment (called the A round), the founder(s) would be expected to co-invest at least $1 million.

The numbers surrounding ownership percentages are pretty linear. If you put in 10 percent, you are earmarked for 10 percent ownership, never more. VCs want control, and it is unheard of for a syndicate of venture capital firms to end up with a minority stock position, i.e., 49 percent or less. Generally speaking, if VCs own 90 percent of a company's stock, they will control 90 percent of the Board seats. And they will exercise control, total control, in fact, if the company goes three months or more without making its numbers or hitting its major benchmarks. At times like this, the relationships between the VCs and company management can get strained or even toxic. It is funny in a way to picture these very same VCs trying to put their own fund together, raising money from institutions and ultra-high-net-worth investors, traveling around the country for months on end, making pitch after pitch on bended knee; but after they've raised the money and are ready to invest it, they will take on an entirely new persona. Now they have become the smartest guys in the room. They have the checkbook.

The web (no pun intended) of relationships between a startup's founders, its executives, venture capitalists, independent angel investors, and Wall Street investment bankers and research analysts was the financial engine behind the internet's explosive growth. These relationships often became mangled battlegrounds. Unlike Sam Walton, dot-com entrepreneurs and founders almost always ended up owning a minority position in their companies; the VCs had control of the Board and overall decision-making. As you might imagine, founders and VCs often did not see eye to eye on operational issues and frequently had differing long-term agendas as well. VCs, unlike many founders, did not share a sense of calling, or sentimentality, or any sort of emotional connection with the company in question. They were simply looking to monetize their investment.

Wall Street played its own peculiar role. In the dot-com era, the goal of most startups was to go public, and many well-known investment firms were eager to oblige them. Morgan Stanley, Alex Brown, and Smith Barney were especially active in the IPO arena; Paine Webber, Merrill Lynch and others were occasional players as well. First, one needed to determine when a company was "ready" to go public. In hindsight, this would seem to be a laughable proposition since the vast majority of dot-com era IPOs ended up as total wipeouts. For every eBay or MapQuest there were hundreds of busts like furniture.com and pets.com; but in the midst of the feeding frenzy, optimism reigned supreme, and on Wall Street, the number one priority was getting deals done and getting them done now.

Investment bankers kept their ears close to the ground, building networks, connecting with partners in major VC firms, combing the countryside for information, calling upon promising internet startups, meeting with founders and executives—all with the hope of building and fortifying relationships with key people in the internet space. Without having these relationships in place, there was no chance of moving forward and bringing a deal to fruition. Of course, the most promising companies, those with the most buzz, knew that they had Wall Street bankers salivating and played their hands as coolly as James Bond at a blackjack table in Monte Carlo. This was the ultimate mating dance.

What an incredible, lucrative business this was, at least at first. The deals themselves, i.e., the IPOs, were often surprisingly modest in size and as a result generated equally humdrum fees. You might have a company with perhaps twenty million shares outstanding, held by VCs and insiders, but the IPO itself could be composed of only three or four million shares. Sometimes insiders were cashing out a portion of their holdings; sometimes the companies would sell new, previously unissued shares directly to the public; sometimes it was a combination of both. Insiders were prohibited by law from selling their own shares (founders' stock) to the public within a few years of acquiring them, and besides, even if this were legal, it wouldn't pass the smell test

Small deals like this created a scarcity mentality. Every investor wanted a piece of the pie, but there weren't enough pieces to go around. Virtually every dot-com offering was assumed to be hot, often white-hot, and it was not at all unusual for a new issue, initially priced at $15 or $20, to start trading at $50 or $75 or more. Cobalt Networks, priced at $22 in 1999, traded as high as $154 on Day 1, a few hours after underwriters released its shares. The company was ultimately acquired by Sun Microsystems, but Sun sadly ended up winding down Cobalt's operations in 2003 and abandoning its product line altogether. That's how most of these stories ended.

Conflicts abounded. Once a dot-com was taken public, it was understood that its stock would be followed by the underwriting firm's research analysts. Would it surprise anyone that most of the research opinions issued were positive? Wall Street has many words for such positive endorsements—buy, aggressive buy, emphasis list, overweight, focus list, alpha list, and conviction buy being some of the most common. There was never much doubt why almost every IPO was followed by a ringing recommendation from the firm that originated and managed the deal; it would have been suicidal to do otherwise. In those rare cases when a strong buy was not forthcoming, analysts often spoke in code. Recommendations like neutral, hold, and market perform had a hidden meaning: dump it. Issuing an outright sell recommendation was out of the question.

There were other complexities defining the relationship between Wall Street bankers and their dot-com clients. IPOs were looked upon as door openers, not one-off transactions. Ideally, they could and would lead to many different kinds of future business alliances. After every IPO there would be directors, executives, and founders sitting on large and (on paper) valuable blocks of stock. Where would they keep their accounts? What about the venture capital firms that ordinarily held even larger quantities of these securities? Or think about the company itself, which may have raised $100 million, often much more? It would now need to invest those funds in liquid securities. Where would it go? There would be other needs as well. Who would administer the company's stock option plan? Who would set up and handle a 401-K? Could this business possibly be given to a company whose analyst had just issued a negative research report? The answer to this question is self-evident.

Conflicts also appeared at the retail brokerage level. In many ways, this represented a total role reversal for dinosaur brokers of the 70s and 80s. Such dinosaurs used to be the hunters; they now became the hunted. Hard-to-get prospects and hard-to-please customers suddenly became rabid in their hot pursuit of the next IPO—and if that weren't available for some reason, any IPO would do. Only retail brokers could provide that access. Active customers practically begged for internet IPOs, as did non-customers, investment advisors, relatives, college classmates, neighbors, and members of the local PTA. Total strangers would call in clamoring for stocks like Palm Pilot; when it came public a few weeks before the bubble peaked, the *Los Angeles Times* reported that it was "arguably the most anticipated initial public offering in years. Shares of Palm Inc. were almost impossible for even the most wealthy and well-connected investors to buy. That's because just a sliver of the company's shares—about 4.1 %—were sold to the public." It soared on the first day of trading and crashed soon after.

When IPO stock was available, it was now the dinosaurs who assumed control. Some became masters of manipulation. "Well, Mr. Jones, you must realize that new issues like this that are in such high demand can only be parceled out to our very best customers. You understand that, don't you? Perhaps you might consider consolidating all of your other investment accounts with me here at XYZ Securities. If you could do that, I'm sure that we could better accommodate you in the future."

Sometimes investors would try these tactics themselves and beat the dinosaurs to the punch. "Could you pick up a thousand shares of Priceline for me when it goes public next week? No? What if I were to move my personal accounts to you and direct all the trading from my family foundation as well? Perhaps I could bring in the corporation's account too. Would that help?" This type of smarmy behavior occurred all the time and created a toxic atmosphere. Deceitful conduct like this knew practically no limit. Sometimes CEOs of private dot-com companies would let it be known that they expected certain investment banks to "take care of them" when doling out shares of hot IPOs. One might have naïvely pretended that this was a way to establish an effective working relationship, but in truth it wasn't much different than a mobster expecting a payoff—or in the vernacular, getting one's palm greased. Let's call it extort.com.

In the 1990s, everyone made money, and everyone was a genius; compare this to the 1970s when brokers were often regarded as little more than aggressive, cold-calling cretins. It was amazing how a change in venue and expectations could transform lemons into lemonade. As IPO after IPO soared and as the NASDAQ index skyrocketed, one-time dinosaurs were now the toast of the town, invited to charity celebrations, regattas, museum openings, hospital dedications, and other prestigious events. They were quoted in the media and fêted at galas. In the 1990s, for the first time in at least a generation, retail financial advisors began to receive the most treasured of all compliments: the unsolicited referral.

Making money in the dot-com era seemed to be easy, too easy. Imagine you are an eager college graduate or M.B.A. in your twenties. You have just joined a promising startup and have been given something called restricted stock or stock options; imagine, too, that your level of comprehension about these subjects is pretty much limited to the following: "If our company does well, you will make a lot of money on this stuff." *Business Week* was quick to pick up on this as a sign of the times, running a 1999 cover story blurbed "How This Kid made $60 Million in 18 Months: Digg.com's Kevin Rose leads a new Brat Pack of Silicon Valley Entrepreneurs." It all appeared to be so effortless, but in the end, it became evident that it was easier to make money than it was to keep it. Digg.com was once valued at $175 million, but in 2010 its assets were sold for only $500,000. Countless dot-com companies fared much worse; they just closed their doors and abandoned ship. In those cases, stockholders lost everything, and landlords were left holding worthless leases.

Hundreds of thousands of young professionals went on a round-trip journey from rags to riches to rags. My son was one of them. After receiving his M.B.A. in the mid-1990s, he joined a small strategy consulting firm that began to advise clients in the areas of e-commerce and internet-based marketing. He called me one day to say that he thought his firm might be sold. He phoned a few weeks later and revealed that yes, everything was on track, and when the acquisition took place, he would be getting stock in the new, merged firm. He felt the amount would be pretty substantial, and he was understandably excited, at least for a few more weeks until the NASDAQ index peaked in March 2000 and reality set in. The merger never took place. A few months later he found himself jobless in San Francisco. He ultimately made his way back to Massachusetts to pick up the pieces, and yes, like many young adults with similar experiences in that era, he moved in with Dad.

Most Americans looked upon the dot-com bubble era as a strange and somewhat bewildering episode in our nation's recent past. After the bubble finally burst, aftershocks were felt most heavily in technology-focused communities like Silicon Valley, Boston, and Seattle. Wall Street obviously was punished as well. Still, for the vast majority of Americans living between the coasts, life continued without much interruption. Compared to the credit crisis of 2008, the dot-com bust, for all of its attendant publicity, had very little impact on working-class America living in the heartland. In truth, it was looked upon as some sort of biblical plague affecting young, self-absorbed intellectual elites. It wasn't part of the real world.

That perception was pretty accurate, and it was never pointed out with more mastery than in the 2002 documentary film, *Startup.com*. The film offers a revealing, largely unscripted look at the cradle-to-grave experience of a 90s startup, govWorks Inc., that was cofounded by two former high school friends, Tom Herman and Kaleil Tuzman. Herman was the creative force and nerdy, inspirational engineer; Tuzman, who fancied himself as the operational and financial expert, quit his job at Goldman Sachs to join Herman in what would later prove to be a quixotic venture. *Startup.com* was co-directed by Jehame Nejaim, who was Herman's roommate at Harvard, and veteran filmmaker Chris Hegedus. In its own way, it was as cringeworthy as a pilfered sex tape, offering up countless awkward scenes and uncomfortable conversations. I recommend it highly.

GovWorks was designed to be a website portal that would facilitate online tax and licensing payments to local governments. The company managed to raise $60 million from VCs in 1998 and went bankrupt in 2001. If the company had been quicker to market, it may have had a chance to survive, but poor execution and wasteful overspending—both all too common qualities in this era—sealed the company's fate. GovWorks hired indiscriminately, taking their headcount up to 250 in little more than a year. They held an expensive retreat for their employees—really not much more than a pep rally—when the company was just a few months old. Tuzman, Herman, and other managers argued for days about the company's mission and name.

When Kaleil and Tom visited Boston's Highland Capital to make a pitch for funding, Bob Higgins (yes, that Bob Higgins, Highland's co-founder and legendary venture capitalist) appeared on screen and made a *Shark Tank* "take it or leave it" investment offer, known as a term sheet, on the spot. Flabbergasted, they begged for time and tried to crunch some numbers on their laptop, but their computer quickly froze up in classic fashion. They then tried to call their lawyer and childishly expressed self-righteous anger when they couldn't immediately speak to him. When Higgins returned to seal the deal, they appeared reluctant to accept it with open arms and began to pepper him with questions. Higgins withdrew the offer altogether—one of the best decisions he ever made, and probably the best investment he never made.

When the company started performing poorly, govWorks began to retrench and lay off its workers. Soon thereafter, Kaleil and Tom appeared on screen together, and in a highly uncomfortable and dramatic moment, Kaleil proceeded to fire Tom. The conversation appeared to be scripted, almost as if it were lifted out of a dreadful cable reality show. Perhaps it was. In any event, I felt like a voyeur, strangely fascinated by the interchange and at the same time embarrassed because I couldn't stop myself from watching it. Kaleil took great pains to explain that the separation was necessary for the well-being of the company; he then went on to say that he loved Tom. As they parted company, they hugged each other. The camera followed Tom out of the office, down the elevator and onto the street. The first thing he did after he exited the building was call his law-yer and talk about retaliation. When this scene was being shown at the screening I attended, members of the audience were audibly groaning in emotional pain.

GovWorks continued in a death spiral after Herman left the company. It ended up laying off all 250 employees and burned through every dol-lar of capital it had raised. Tuzman and Herman remained friends for a while and tried to make a comeback with another business venture called Recognition Group. They formed this company to advise failing enter-prises (like govWorks) how to restructure their operations and become healthy and viable. David Segal of the *Washington Post* likened this to "get-ting tips on quitting cigarettes from the Marlboro Man."

Occasionally a few resourceful dot-com entrepreneurs were able to avoid the misfortune experienced at govWorks. Les Yetton, an industry veteran who has been active in the world of startups and private equity for decades, told me about one such company named Softricity that suffered a near-death experience in 2000 but ultimately managed to resuscitate itself. In 2007, Microsoft bought the company for over $200 million. Its pathway to success, however, was long, circuitous, and terribly painful for the firm's original investors and employees.

Softricity was the second iteration of Softwarewow.com, the brain-child of creative founders Stuart Schaefer and David Greschler. Bringing in industry pros like Harry Ruda as CEO and Yetton as sales and business development chief, Softwarewow.com quickly raised millions in equity; as was common during those times, they also managed to spend all of it almost as fast. The company was originally conceived as a web portal like Infoseek, Lycos, Excite, and Yahoo; the idea was that the technology enabled clients to try out different software applications without downloading or purchas-ing them. This portal was in a sense a centralized location where one could test drive software created by a variety of different developers.

Going back twenty years in time, Yetton's memory of what trans-pired was crystal clear, and his words were quite haunting. It was a time of excess everywhere, "especially among VCs, and there was an abundance of free-flowing cash. Businesses got funded that never should have gotten funded. There wasn't much information available, at least not like today." As strange as it sounds, printed magazines like *Network World* and *PC Magazine* served as the primary pipeline for disseminating information about events and developments in the high-tech world.

There was a sense of urgency, a feeling that any delay in funding a dot-com business would result in a lost opportunity. There was a frightening lack of attention to the nuts and bolts of planning and budgeting. Pet.com, one of the era's most notable failures, went out of business within a year after its debut as a public company. It had spent lavishly on marketing and costly national TV ads that included a Super Bowl spot. In its only year of operations, it took in only $1 of revenue for every $20 it spent on advertising. Pets.com offered free shipping on everything, even heavy bags of dogfood, and lost money on almost every order.

Compared to Pets.com, I guess you could say softwarewow.com was a success of sorts, but when the dot-com bubble collapsed, it became apparent that Sofwarewow.com was at the end of the road; it was never able to monetize the web portal piece of technology it had originally created. The VC-controlled Board gave management an ultimatum: you have one quarter to figure out how to transition the company and make it viable, or we are going to shut it down. Difficult times ensued. Headcount went from eighty to thirteen. Relationships between the company's investors and its management, once backslapping and collegial, became adversarial and defensive.

It was at this point that Softwarewow.com changed its name to Softricity and created an entirely different business strategy, developed new products, and began the difficult process of raising the additional money it needed for a second life. This time its focus was on what is called remote virtual computing. The early 2000s represented the formative years of cloud computing, where companies like VMWare and Citrix were beginning to gain attention. Softricity's software allowed a customer to run, for example, hundreds or even thousands of copies of Microsoft Office—or any number of other programs—without their having to purchase individual licenses and install the software directly on multiple desktops. Virtualization proved to be a viable business concept from the start. Within a few years, Softricity's headcount had risen to a hundred, and for good reason: they were selling real products to real customers. The company's sale to Microsoft in 2007 was clearly a win, in a way a just reward for so much perseverance and commitment. Still, this was no overnight success. Ten long years had passed since the early days of Softwarewow.com, years that saw most of its workers lose their jobs and the original investors witness their seed capital go up in smoke.

We must remember that there are two storylines at work here: one is the development of the internet in the 1990s, and the other is the internet stock market bubble of the same era. The part of the story owned by Wall Street had no happy ending. Enormous amounts of capital, both human and financial, were sacrificed. Losses were compounded by poor planning, naïveté, and greed. Ridiculous business decisions were made by people, many of them educated at elite universities, who should have known better. In the end, most of the wounds suffered were self-inflicted. Yes, some individual investors were taken in by Wall Street's hype, but they too must bear some responsibility for looking at the world through an unfiltered, rose-colored lens.

The NASDAQ index peaked in March 2000 at 5048; on September 10, 2001 (the day before terrorists attacked the World Trade Center), the same index stood at 1695, a decline of 67 percent. The subsequent drop in internet-related stocks was far worse, with many companies liquidating their assets for pennies, and investors suffering total losses. As bad as this experience was, it was just an opening act for events that soon followed: September 11, a spate of massive corporate frauds and scandals in 2002, and after a brief respite, the credit crisis of 2008 and the Great Recession that followed. It took fifteen years or more for the markets to regain levels that were last achieved in 2000. Apart from the investment losses, millions lost jobs in failed startups. Still, let's not lose sight of the fact that despite everything—the lost jobs, the failed companies, and an epic stock market bust—the internet has revolutionized the way people live and communicate. The dot-com 90s were a time of great creativity and excitement. Some dreams were broken, but more were fulfilled. And for investors, there was a valuable lesson to be learned: "Hold onto your wallet."

Mortgage Meltdown

• • •

THE BANKRUPTCY OF LEHMAN BROTHERS in 2008 ranks as the largest in US history. It was obvious to some in 2007—and to a few as early as 2005 or 2006—that the end was near. Speculation in real estate, fueled by loose and irresponsible lending practices, had long since reached excessive levels, but it was not until Lehman gave up the ghost and announced on Sunday evening, September 15, it would be filing for bankruptcy on Monday morning that reality set in. The financial markets entered full-blown panic mode. Call it what you will—banking crisis, credit crisis, housing crisis—it was made immediately clear that our economy was about to face gigantic difficulties and its greatest challenge since the Great Depression. The downturn that followed became known as the Great Recession. If not for government support systems—Social Security, food stamps, unemployment insurance, Medicare and Medicaid, insured bank accounts, and massive bailouts of the nation's largest financial institutions—who knows? The dark days that followed could have been as dire as the 1930s, perhaps worse. Millions lost their homes and jobs and their faith in the future.

The fall of Lehman was a catastrophe. The psychological damage was profound; worse was the financial wreckage that followed. Lehman's failure took $700 billion out of the economy—permanently. Even on Wall Street, $700 billion is a lot of money. Most of the losses were sustained by financial institutions, because banks, brokerage firms, insurance companies, and credit unions owned securities issued by Lehman; many of those institutions became financially impaired as a result, drawing the immediate attention of the Fed, the FDIC, and the Comptroller of the Currency. Lehman bonds and commercial paper were owned by a large number of money market mutual funds, causing some individual investors to panic, cut and run.

When a failing Bear Stearns was acquired by J.P. Morgan Chase earlier in the year, there was a palpable sense of relief after months of apprehension and uncertainty. Even when Fannie Mae was placed into conservatorship by the government just a few weeks before the Lehman announcement, the markets remained reasonably stable despite the dreadful drumbeat of news. After Lehman's bankruptcy filing, however, all bets were off. The Dow Jones Industrial Average quickly dropped from 11,000 to 6,500 in just six months, a loss of over 40 percent.

Dick Fuld was the CEO of Lehman Brothers. A high energy, Type-A alpha male, Fuld became somewhat reclusive in the years that followed Lehman's bankruptcy. He was vilified by the press, subpoenaed by Congress, and bad-mouthed by former colleagues and subordinates. It was not until 2015 that he made his first voluntary public appearance, and he was as unapologetic as ever. Tom Braithwaite reported for the *Financial Times* on May 28:

> "Wow, I haven't done this for a while," Mr. Fuld said. "This is my first public event since '08. I don't include my wonderful time with Congress," he added. Mr. Fuld showed no sign of contrition over the demise of the bank, which he led from 1994. The crisis was "a perfect storm," he said, "but it starts with the government." It paved the way for unsuitable borrowers to buy homes, caused an interest rate shock, and then unfairly "mandated" the bankruptcy of Lehman while saving competitors.
>
> He acknowledged that all investment banks "had too much leverage" but insisted that Lehman was still solvent when it was placed into bankruptcy...
>
> "Did we try to do everything we possibly could? Did we fall prey to some other agendas? I'll leave it at that.

"There's so much I'd love to say," he went on. "Dah dah dah dah dah. Enough said on that." He reached for a glass by the stage and took a sip. "No, this is not scotch or rum."

...Fuld pointed to Barack Obama's administration and said: "We need new leadership. Everything's 'great'," he added. "Why the hell does it not feel better? Why has the belly of America been ripped out?

He went on to say, "enjoy the ride — no regrets"..."Look in the mirror, 'this is about you and me. Are we OK? Let's enjoy the ride.'"

While it is not entirely clear what Mr. Fuld was driving at, he did make one point quite definitively—"Don't blame me and don't blame Lehman." And while he may not be quite the victim he makes himself out to be, he is right about one thing: The Dick Fulds and Lehmans of the world were not solely or even primarily responsible for the chaos of the times. We can't forget about the investors who recklessly took on debt to finance their real estate purchases, the banks and mortgage companies that blindly made this capital available to them, the real estate appraisers who signed off on ridiculously high valuations, the credit agencies that put investment-grade ratings on mortgage securities that were anything but, or the loan originators who knowingly accepted and processed loan applications that contained phony and incomplete information. At times the relationship between so-called investors (known charitably as flippers), their attorneys and their funding sources had the look of a criminal enterprise. Sometimes it was more than a look. It was not unheard of, especially in the most speculative markets like Florida, Nevada, and California, for bank presidents and any number of co-conspirators to be sent off to jail after their fraudulent behavior was uncovered and successfully prosecuted.

Wall Street, of course, did play a significant role in the credit crisis, but it is not particularly well understood by the public. First is the recognition that (as Fuld himself admitted) the investment banks had "too much leverage." Lehman Brothers was not the only firm that was knee deep in debt; so was Merrill Lynch, Wachovia, Countrywide, Washington Mutual, Goldman, Morgan Stanley, AIG, Fannie Mae or virtually any other major financial firm that comes to mind. Many of these companies were levered at twenty-five times equity, some even more. Think of it this way. If you had a net worth of $100,000, would you feel comfortable owing a creditor $2,500,000? And would you feel at all secure if your collateral was declining in value with mind-numbing speed? Probably not.

Wall Street's investment banks took on mountains of debt for one reason: to make more money. Consider this—if you can borrow $1 billion, put it to work, and for argument's sake realize a 10 percent return on those funds, why not borrow $3 billion and make three times as much? Or $25 billion? Why not indeed? Keep in mind that it is much easier for investment banks to borrow money than it is for consumers to apply for a car loan or a mortgage. Firms like Lehman could raise money effortlessly by selling commercial paper, bonds and preferred stock to various government entities, institutional clients and other banks. They did it all the time and if necessary could have been in the market raising capital every day of the week.

Major Wall Street investment banks had successfully financed their operations in this way for decades. They had made so much money that they began to develop an arrogance that bordered on the delusional. Was there any reason for them to believe in 2003 or 2004 that the housing market would collapse, pushing values down by 50 percent or more? Absolutely not. Would it make sense, after seeing all your competitors expanding their balance sheets, taking on more debt, and making more money as a result, for you to retrench and play small-ball? Again, a unanimous verdict—no chance.

Instead, the nation's banks chose to practice what came naturally to them. In the early 2000s, they levered up their balance sheets to maximize profits and began to deal in higher-risk securities with wider spreads and higher margins of profit. The Volcker rule, part of 2010's Dodd-Frank financial reform legislation, was designed to prevent large banks from using their capital to trade in such risky, complex derivatives (especially exposed to subprime mortgages). Amazingly, the rule was never aggressively implemented after the passage of Dodd–Frank. For years after the financial crisis, banks received exemption after exemption.

On the surface, Wall Street's part in the housing crisis seems simple enough: its investment banks were a key if not the key funding source for the credit boom of the early 2000s. Mortgages were funded and placed into pools, and these pools were then packaged and resold to institutional investors. By 2006, the housing market began to cool, and soon afterward it rolled over and collapsed. Innumerable mortgages went underwater, and the boom turned into a bust. As housing values declined, and as the economy worsened, homeowners had to face the possibility of foreclosure. Many lost their homes. It took several years for the economy to stabilize and begin to recover.

There was another side to this equation. Banks that owned the mortgages in question were underwater as well. Granted, there was not and is not a great deal of sympathy for mortgage lenders who end up with losses by making bad loans, but their fate was as large a part of the financial crisis as was that of the nation's suffering homeowners. Credit was becoming harder and harder to get well before Lehman went under, but after that company went bankrupt, it dried up altogether. The secondary market in subprime mortgages reflected this reality; in a very real sense, there was no market. Banks looking to trade out of these securities were getting bids of thirty cents on the dollar, sometimes less. As investment banks had to mark down the value of their holdings, their condition became ever more precarious. As credit markets froze, the banks at the center of the storm found it almost impossible to raise money to sustain their operations. In the end, it was the Federal Reserve that stepped in to prop up the system, and this support was later bolstered by taxpayer-funded rescues and bailouts. It is more than ironic that the best known of these (TARP, the Troubled Asset Relief Program) provided $700 billion of emergency relief, simply replaced the $700 billion of wealth that was destroyed when Lehman closed its doors.

As we have seen, while Wall Street may have had a featured role in the financial crisis of 2008, it did not play the only part in its creation. To believe so is to accept a myth. Furthermore, the idea that executive officers and directors of the Street's leading financial firms somehow concocted a fraudulent scheme, one that involved their deliberately packaging hundreds of billions of dollars of bad loans and then callously selling them to their best customers, defies common sense. How could any business hope to flourish or even survive if it risked causing irreparable harm to its customers and itself in the process? Merrill, AIG, Lehman and the rest no doubt exercised terrible judgment, employed a dangerous amount of leverage, and bear full responsibility for putting their shareholders—and ultimately the nation's economy—at an unconscionable level of risk. But they did not have a death wish, nor were they led by sociopathic criminals.

At some level, of course, fraud was present during the housing bubble; phony applications, forged signatures, and bogus appraisals undoubtedly played a hand in contributing to the peril society would one day come to face; but let's be clear—the primary cause of the credit crisis was excessive credit. In the same way that an astonishing amount of venture capital paved the way for the dot-com bubble, indulgent lending standards paved the way for the financial crisis of 2008. A seemingly endless supply of credit made it possible for investors to borrow and buy, and borrow and buy some more. The housing bubble started when it was too easy to get financing, and it ended when it became too difficult. There is a reason this episode in history is called a credit crisis rather than a moral crisis.

Borrowers, lenders, developers, speculators, credit agencies, appraisers, and more all played an active part in what was a fool's game, the idea that rising real estate prices could somehow beget even higher prices—in a sense believing that momentum alone could create a self-fulfilling prophecy. As usual, though, it was the Wall Street banks that were singled out for being the primary cause of the credit crisis of 2008 and the Great Recession that followed, just as they had many years ago when the Depression followed the 1929 stock market crash.

In this respect at least, the credit crisis of 2008 was not a one-off, stand-alone affair. In terms of size and significance, it may not have had many equals, but the causes and conditions responsible for its existence have occurred with surprising frequency in recent times. There was another real estate bubble that got underway in the 1970s and 1980s, one that bore an uncanny resemblance to 2008's, and that ended in much the same way—with a spectacular flameout, credit crunch, and recession. It is not talked about often today, and it doesn't have a catchy name, but to anyone who invested in real estate limited partnerships before the Tax Reform Act of 1986, it was as unforgettable as it was devastating.

One can make the case that a root cause for this shakeout was the government itself, especially the tax codes that prevailed at the time. It will no doubt amaze some that the maximum personal tax rate in 1960 was 91 percent, and even though some effort was made during the next few decades to bring it down to a less punishing level, it still stood at 70 percent in 1980. In an environment like this, taxpayers had every motivation to lower their taxes; in fact, they were understandably desperate to do so. And Wall Street being Wall Street, investment banks were falling over each other to accommodate them. In this way, the modern-day tax shelter was born. These creations are best remembered for one primary characteristic—unlike most investments that are designed to produce income, capital gain, or some type of positive return on investment, tax shelters were devised to produce losses. Yes, losses. The code word used at the time was *write-offs*. The larger the write-offs, the greater the tax benefit, and the more attractive the deal.

In what must seem the ultimate catch-22 of financial engineering, the federal government chose to tax all earned income at an exorbitant rate and then allow taxpayers to use any number of offsets (called deductions) to avoid paying tax on the income. The tax code went one step further; it gave additional benefits to certain kinds of investing, especially real estate. If expenses there exceeded income, you could apply the loss against all other earned income like salary, bonus, and/or commission. Real estate offered many such write-offs—mortgage interest, property taxes, closing costs, insurance, property management and the usual line-item deductions for maintenance, legal, accounting, and other administrative expenses. And then there was the biggest boondoggle of them all, accelerated depreciation of real property. Because accelerated depreciation creates a large paper loss on one's tax return, one might be tempted to call it a big loser; but it was really a winner because in those years paper losses produced bankable wealth.

Recently, I was fortunate to speak with Deane Dolben, President of the Dolben Company, whose firm was active in real estate development and syndication before, during, and after the volckerbrick, committed to the belief that a project's ultimate worth was directly correlated with its net operating income—in other words, its ability to produce a positive cash flow. He explained how things changed in 1981 when Congress shortened the depreciation schedule on residential real estate to fifteen years. This meant if you bought a building for $15 million, on average you could write off $1 million a year for fifteen years, potentially getting $10 ½ million in tax benefits (remember, the top tax bracket was 70 percent) from the government of the United States. For real estate investors, this was paradise on earth. Even if the project was break-even or cash flow negative, you could make money on the government's tax subsidies. In a world that had seemingly gone half mad, it was now losses that counted, since losses had become the driving force behind value creation. The more you paid for a building, the more you could write off. Instead of trying to buy low and sell high, many real estate investors were getting bigger returns by buying high and filing their tax returns early.

It's not surprising why so many real estate tax shelters failed; almost all of them had too many fees and too much leverage. Ordinarily, a syndicator would take a fat selling commission himself or pay one to a third party when a prospective investor signed on. There were innumerable other fees: developmental, marketing, legal, accounting, acquisition, and organizational. Often there were also intra-partnership loans made by the general partners (that would have to be repaid), and if anything slipped through the cracks, there was always an additional category— "other."

Investors' equity would typically represent 15-20 percent of the total cost of the transaction, but so did the upfront fees. As they walked away from the closing table with zero equity, tax shelter investors did not have much margin for error.

Like all sizeable developers at the time, the Dolben Company took a close look at getting active in the tax-shelter business. Dolben early on had partnered with Winthrop Financial, a Boston based developer; the two of them collaborated on over a half-dozen deals, and most of these were highly successful. Winthrop had become well known as a leading syndicator not just in Boston, but nationally as well, but by 1984 or so it had also begun to morph from a more traditional real estate developer to an aggressive tax shelter promoter. Winthrop's deals were loaded with fees that some traditionalists would call rapacious. This did not necessarily represent criminal intent but rather a desire to create the highest possible valuation for the properties in question. Using tax shelter math, higher fees would create a higher basis or acquisition cost, and this would make larger depreciation deductions and bigger write-offs possible. The Dolben Company was uncomfortable with the direction Winthrop and many other syndicators were taking at the time, and they soon terminated their relationship with them. Dolben continues to flourish today, but Winthrop began to struggle mightily shortly after the 1986 Tax Reform Act was passed. Many of its properties and partnerships began to fail, and soon thereafter, Winthrop Financial became a sad footnote in financial history.

The Tax Reform Act of 1986 brought a quick end to the tax shelter boom. The repercussions were severe and long-lasting and left the industry shell-shocked. Depreciation was scaled back from fifteen to twenty-seven and a half years, and if that were not enough, taxpayers lost the ability to write off passive losses against ordinary income. The rules of the game had changed abruptly.

Just as the Lehman bankruptcy set in motion a domino effect of other corporate failures, government bailouts, and widespread weakness throughout the economy, the Tax Reform Act had far-reaching consequences. The most obvious aftershock was the decline in property values;

Deane Dolben estimated that the fall-off, approximately 20-30 percent, was almost immediate. The vast majority of highly leveraged real estate tax shelters went south. As loans soured, credit began to contract. "For Sale" signs began to populate the landscape, but not surprisingly, there were fewer and fewer buyers for these properties. Other areas of the economy were affected as well. The high-yield bond market collapsed, and bank failures, especially among savings and loan institutions, became commonplace. Within a few years, the country entered recession.

The parallels between the 1980s tax shelter bubble and the 2008 financial crisis are remarkable. Each had a different catalyst—tax incentives on the one hand, irresponsible lending practices on the other—but in both instances, it was an odd combination of naïveté and greed that coalesced and provided the breeding ground for a feeding frenzy of epic proportions. That's not surprising since at some point all investment bubbles are defined by a collective belief, a mania, really, that this time history will not repeat itself, that this time will be different.

"This time," of course, is never different. In the end, every feeding frenzy turns into a hunger strike, and by the time this change has become evident, the worm has already turned. I've seen this happen in my lifetime with tax shelters, casino gambling, CB radios, and countless "can't miss" investment opportunities in technology stocks like Atari, Commodore, Palm Pilot, and Blackberry. Think about what happened to plasma TVs, and before that, video cassette recorders and video rental companies like Blockbuster Entertainment; or consider the Florida real estate bubble in the 1920s, or the infatuation with railroad stocks seventy-five years before that, or the Dutch tulip mania in 1635. Investment bubbles may not look alike, but the differences among them are mostly cosmetic. Their timing, specific circumstances and narratives may all have unique characteristics, but they all share at least one thing in common—an unhappy ending. Post-mortems always include casualties, victims, and martyrs.

Most investment bubbles are also characterized by extreme human behavior. This was certainly the case during the financial crisis in 2008 and the tax shelter craze that preceded it. During times like this, rational thinking is often displaced by emotion, and sound judgment is almost always blinded by greed or ego—or both. I wonder what Angelo Mozilo of Countrywide, Stan O'Neal at Merrill Lynch, or Bear Stearns' Jimmy Cayne thinks about in his private moments. Each of these individuals was terribly flawed, but none was criminally predisposed or sociopathic. They made poor decisions, and their reputations were irreparably damaged.

Wall Street has no shortage of war stories, especially when it comes to investment disasters involving large losses. The Lehman—Merrill Lynch—Bank of America drama that played out on that fateful Sunday in 2008, and the chaos that followed it, has been retold many times, but it is still worth reviewing. It was the defining moment of my career, not only because of its ability to shock and awe, but because the collateral damage was so extensive and enduring. Business as usual would no longer be a possibility; increased government control and regulatory authority combined to guarantee that the good old freewheeling days of Wall Street would never return.

The Great Recession was broad based, and the economy lost approximately eight million jobs in 2008 and 2009. Contraction in the financial services sector was especially acute; job growth began to falter as early as 2006, and job losses continued well after the recession ended. J.P. Morgan Chase, Bank of America, and Citigroup continued to shed employees in 2011, 2012, and 2013. To make matters worse, what began as a made-in-America phenomenon soon spread internationally. Europe was especially hard hit, and almost a decade later, many of its largest banks are still impaired and undercapitalized.

Bruce Widas had a front row seat to the chaos of the times. In 2007, he was Managing Director (Capital Markets-Fixed Income) at UBS; by the end of 2008, he was on sabbatical. His experience was somewhat unique. During 2007 and 2008, he was given marching orders to reduce headcount in his department—on six different occasions. He had spent years recruiting a talented team of professionals and had forged strong relationships with them, and now he was responsible for laying them off. Before the year was out, he quit. The future looked bleak to him as well, with fewer deals, much lower compensation and more layoffs. He found that he didn't have the stomach for it anymore, and at fifty he left UBS, thinking that perhaps he'd take six to twelve months off and then look for another opportunity. He found out that there wasn't much of a market for fifty-year-old investment bankers. Actually, in 2009 there wasn't much of a market for investment bankers of any age. Widas never came back to Wall Street. He also doesn't miss it.

He has vivid memories of the dark days at UBS. Traders looked at their screens with a sense of disbelief. Mortgage-backed securities that were originally priced at 100 may have traded down to 99½, signaling what most thought to be a bargain; but 99½ was no bargain, nor was 98, nor 96, nor 90. As liquidity dried up, prices kept falling, and falling some more. As the contagion spread, it affected all debt markets. Perfectly good corporate bonds issued by companies like Verizon or GE were crushed. Tax-free bonds couldn't catch a bid, either. It didn't matter if they were general obligations of the issuer or bonds backed by sales taxes or bridge tolls or water and sewer bills or revenue from private colleges and universities. With mortgage-backed securities, conditions became unimaginably extreme as the real economy worsened; homeowners had trouble keeping current on their loans, delinquencies increased, and foreclosures followed. In the derivatives market, the home of the riskiest and most complex mortgage bonds, prices fell to twenty or thirty cents on the dollar, and in many cases entire pools of lower quality mortgages became worthless. Money stopped flowing because credit froze. The only bonds that investors were willing to touch were those issued by the United States Treasury. At one point, the fear factor became so great—it was called a flight to quality—that US Treasury Bills were trading at a premium. In layman's terms, this meant if you invested some money in ninety-day Treasuries, you would end up three months later with less money than you originally invested. Guaranteed!

While this was playing out, Widas had to comply with all of the provisions of Sarbanes–Oxley. SOX legislation had by then been in force for a number of years, and it required executives like him to perform acts of due diligence such as signing off on audits and financial statements of the firm's clients. So, if UBS was doing a deal with AT&T, he would have had to vouch for accuracy in AT&T's income statement, balance sheet, and the rest. This issue of vicarious liability became a nightmare that never went away; starting in 2009, investment banks were routinely sued, often by states and the federal government, sometimes by smaller institutions, pension plans, and foundations, for massive amounts of money. Countless billions were paid in fines and settlements, and several hundred investigations and cases are still pending today.

The economy as a whole suffered much larger losses, with estimated ranging from $5 trillion to $15 trillion and more. Even at $5 trillion, we are talking about a staggering amount of money—total yearly spending of the U.S. government is significantly less than that, and government spending represents about one-quarter of our economy. Yet financial losses like this can only be partially explained in statistical terms; the price that people paid in terms of anxiety, fear, depression, and loss of self-esteem is incalculable. Years later, those feelings and memories remain vivid in many minds.

This subject came up in a recent conversation with Matt Galligan. Galligan, currently President of Real Estate Finance at CIT Financial, pointed out something very interesting. In the real economy, where there are winners and losers, there is rarely an equal number of winners and losers. This imbalance was never greater than during the credit crisis, and he saw this close-up. The winners were sophisticated, ultra-high-net-worth investors (often represented by hedge funds). They were able to profit before the bottom hit by selling securities short, and afterward, by buying up distressed properties and discounted mortgages from highly motivated sellers. But for every hedge fund manager that made millions of dollars trading his way through the credit crisis, there were seemingly millions of other people who lost their jobs or homes or both.

Galligan himself was one of the lucky ones, and he knows it. He had joined the Bank of Ireland in New York City in 2009 and became managing director of their US Property and Finance Group. His group did business the old-fashioned way, funding commercial mortgages; he built a successful team and created a solid book of business. As the credit crisis in the US deepened, it spread globally, and Europe was particularly hard hit. Before long, regulators in Ireland put pressure on Irish banks to repatriate their assets. This is a complicated way of saying they would have to stop doing business in America. Wells Fargo ended up buying the Bank of Ireland's US loan portfolio (at a small premium, no less), but during the months leading up to the sale, Matt had the opportunity to meet with other potential bidders, and one of them was CIT. They got to know each other well—well enough for them to offer Matt and a number of his team members jobs. Matt left the Bank of Ireland on a Friday and joined CIT on Monday, where he is today fully engaged in what he calls the best work experience of his life. He has no real way to explain his good fortune. He feels both humbled and blessed.

Most of us who lived through the financial crisis had starkly different experiences and memories. At the height of the crisis, scarcely a day would pass without yet another revelation of yet another Wall Street horror. Angelo Mozilo, former CEO of Countrywide Mortgage, personally paid a $67 million fine to the SEC, afterward claiming he did "nothing wrong." Stan O'Neal was forced out as CEO by Merrill Lynch's Board for his role in getting the firm heavily involved in subprime mortgages, and he walked away with a $161 million retirement package as a reward. Strangely enough, at the same time, Bank of America, which had purchased Countrywide in 2008 for $4 billion, ended up losing over $40 billion on that company's toxic loan portfolio. And of course, B of A itself received federal bailout money, at least $45 billion worth, plus additional guarantees on loans in excess of $100 billion.

This odd dynamic of bad behavior and big bailouts fostered intense anger and outrage throughout society. When news that AIG was going to pay its executives bonuses shortly after it received billions in emergency funding from the US Treasury, the House of Representatives immediately passed legislation to tax all bank bonuses over $125,000 at a punitive 90 percent rate. The Senate passed a similar resolution, one that would place a 70 percent tax on bonuses paid by any firm that received TARP relief. Neither proposal went anywhere, and even President Barack Obama, no friend of Wall Street, was uncharacteristically quiet and noncommittal about what was clearly an effort to use tax policy to make a political point.

Years later, very little has been forgiven or forgotten. Memories are still raw. This much is clear: Wall Street played a part—an important one, yes—but still only a part in the onset of the financial crisis of 2008 and the Great Recession; yet the clear majority of Americans remain convinced that the Street was the chief culprit, if not the only one. Federal bailout packages, never popular to begin with, inspired intense opposition that grew almost exponentially as time went on. Distrust of all things Wall Street grew to epic levels. A great many Americans were incensed that Wall Street bankers received a taxpayer-funded bailout when they should have gone to jail. The *Occupy Wall Street* movement has already begun to fade from memory, but at the time millions could identify with it in spirit if not in body. They probably still do.

Snakes and Scammers

• • •

THE LATE JOHN HOUSEMAN was featured in a series of memorable TV commercials for the investment firm of Smith Barney during the 1970s and 1980s. He was filmed sitting by himself at an elegant café table set with cut crystal, bone china, and sterling silver place settings—for breakfast no less. He said, "Good investments don't walk up, bite you on the bottom, and say 'we're here.' Finding them takes good, old-fashioned hard work, research, the kind they do at Smith Barney. Smith Barney is among a handful of top investment firms singled out for their work and research." He then paused dramatically, and continued, "Smith Barney. They make money the old-fashioned way. They earn it."

Even if Houseman was being a wee bit biased in his assessment of Smith Barney's unique work ethic, there is no doubt that most investment firms in those days did do business in an old-fashioned way. In little more than the space of a generation, there have been profound changes in virtually every element of the business, from customer acquisition to servicing, back-office technology, pricing, access to information, regulatory oversight, and more. And in very recent times, the advent of internet access and online trading along with the passage of Sarbanes–Oxley and Dodd–Frank legislation have combined to transform the securities industry into something practically unrecognizable when compared to its earlier roots and culture.

As the industry has changed, so has fraud. If Houseman were alive today, he might jokingly say that contemporary scammers "make money the old-fashioned way. They steal it." True enough. But their strategies, tactics, and tools of the trade have certainly changed with the times, and it has become increasingly difficult for compliance professionals and regulators to keep up with the range of truly deviant behavior that has cropped up in recent years. Noteworthy, too, is the fact that this increase in criminal behavior has infected many layers of society, not just financial services.

While most retail investors would applaud the wide net that regulators may cast today—from money laundering to terrorist financing to high-frequency trading and dark pools—they are understandably most concerned with their own well-being. They want to be treated fairly and honestly and to trust the information they obtain and the people who give it to them. They would like to believe that the system is not rigged against the so-called little guy. When they learn of a scandal or particularly egregious act, they would prefer not—repeat, not—to ask someone who works in the industry, "What is it with you guys?" but they just can't help themselves. They've witnessed too much bad behavior. Investors have found it virtually impossible to shake free of the cynicism that has taken hold of their opinions about Wall Street.

Financial fraud, at least in the age of the dinosaur, manifested itself in just a handful of ways. Since fraud can be defined as any act of deliberate misstatement or deceit, it stands to reason that an unsubstantiated, exaggerated statement could be considered a fraudulent one. Issuing a false financial report, making a bogus claim, or guaranteeing any sort of future outcome or investment result are techniques used by con men and scammers, and they all qualify as acts of fraud. Madoff's multi-billion-dollar Ponzi scheme stands apart only because of its size. In every other respect, it was a garden-variety investment scam.

Investment cons are nothing new, but they have begun to appear with increasing frequency in recent years. Oddly enough, fraudulent behavior didn't peak or even plateau when Wall Street dinosaurs began to die off. Instead, it began to increase exponentially. Edward Balleisen wrote in *Fraud: An American History from Barnum to Madoff*: "Since the 1970s, the problem of business fraud has taken a firmer hold on the American imagination. According to *Google Books*, the frequency of the phrases 'corporate fraud' and 'business fraud' in published works has doubled every ten years since 1975. Growth in the number of articles that use one of these phrases in the *New York Times, Wall Street Journal, Washington Post, and Los Angeles Times* reflects a similar exponential curve."

One of AARP's recent studies of consumer fraud revealed how widespread the problem has become. Their work suggests that over 10 percent of our population—that's more than thirty million people—are defrauded in some way every year. Investment fraud is only one of a variety of popular cons: others include advance fee loans (you pay a fee for a loan, but don't get the money) and its twin, the business opportunity scam (you invest in an attractive-looking business that turns out to be an empty shell). Of course, neither can compare with the damage that results from periodic data breaches and identity theft caused by sophisticated computer hackers.

AARP discovered that investment fraud attracts victims who are on balance older, better educated, and more affluent than the population at large; this makes sense since these are the people who live near the Money River. The data also suggested that they are good losers, at least compared to a more broadly based group of fraud victims, and tend to be slightly more fatalistic and accepting after having discovered they have been taken. They send away for free CDs and attend seminars and sales presentations on money-making schemes. In a word, they are players.

Experian carried out a similar study for the Financial Conduct Authority in England and came up with parallel results. Among the findings: "There was very strong representation from the 'Retired with Resources', 'Affluent and Ambitious' and 'Mature and Savvy' segments. For example, the Retired with Resources segment (more likely to be over sixty-five with savings in excess of £10,000) were 3.5 times more likely to be victimized, and the Mature and Savvy segment (more likely to be highly educated, middle-aged males) were 2.5 times more likely to be victimized." Whatever the case, the numbers in England tell the same story as in America—about 10 percent of the adult population falls victim to fraudsters every year. With millions of investors willing to take the bait, and with a plentiful number of con men and women eager to accommodate them, it is hardly surprising that investment fraud has reached epic proportions.

What is remarkable, though, is that Wall Street and its regulators have been fairly ineffective, at least in slowing down the rate of growth of investment fraud. In addition to the efforts of the SEC, securities administrators in each of the fifty states, and the vast internal compliance departments that are found within every major bank and brokerage firm in the country, there is FINRA. The Financial Industry Regulatory Authority was created in 2007 and serves as the successor to the industry's original self-regulatory organization, the NASD. It has a number of important goals and initiatives: to educate and protect investors, to discipline rule breakers, to detect wrongdoing, to arbitrate securities disputes, and to safeguard the public by enforcing regulations. FINRA maintains offices in major money centers throughout the United States and employs hundreds of examiners who work in the field inspecting and reviewing the records, procedures, and operations of broker-dealers and investment advisors. *Broker Check*, FINRA's online tool that enables an investor to view someone's work history and disciplinary record, has proven to be extremely popular; in the last year alone, more than one million inquiries were recorded. Ask any compliance officer on Wall Street about FINRA, and you will hear words like "thorough," "exacting," and "meticulous." You will also hear that there are seemingly limitless numbers of bad guys lying in wait, and they are as hard to discourage as a swarm of locusts. One can only assume that FINRA and the rest of the protectors are simply overwhelmed by insurmountable odds.

In its most rudimentary form, fraud can be best understood as a misstatement of the truth, and its various iterations—exaggerations, charades, fantasies, lies and acts of deceit—all qualify. In my early years on Wall Street, brokers were well-spoken pitchmen, ferreting through research almost daily, brainstorming with co-workers, trying to come up with common stock ideas they could show to prospects and clients. The question, "What do you like?" would be asked everywhere, in the hallway, the elevator, or the men's room. Most outgoing calls involved touting a specific common stock that was believed to be particularly attractive for capital gains or income.

There was nothing necessarily sinister about this practice, if all the rules, regulations, and appropriate standards of ethical behavior were properly observed. That's just the way business was done. However, this business model, being less consultative and more sales oriented, had some built-in challenges and conflicts of interest. The most obvious was that dinosaur brokers were completely dependent upon transactional commissions to stay in business. They did not see themselves as financial planners or portfolio managers or investment advisors. They needed to generate ideas and activity. And so they pitched, and they hyped. Often the line between enthusiasm and fraud could become blurry. There is no foolproof way of determining whether an account is being churned for commissions. Is it active or over-active? Is the broker in question a rogue, or is he roguish? What is the difference between a false claim and an inaccurate recommendation? Is saying "This stock could go to a hundred" fraudulent? No. How about "It should go to a hundred"? Maybe—that's a statement that would need to be qualified. What about "It will definitely go to a hundred"? Yes, that's fraudulent.

Should a dispute between a broker and one of his clients arise, you can see how difficult it would be to establish guilt or innocence, and because of this, it was especially challenging to determine financial damages with any degree of certainty. Situations like this almost always came down to circumstantial evidence, largely because it was the only kind of evidence that was available. Without written records and tape-recorded conversations, without witnesses or some sort of smoking gun, everything else boiled down to "he said-she said." Credibility, both for the accuser and the accused, was key. If a complaint was made by a savvy, middle-aged, male investor, one with a history of active trading, and if the broker in question was thought to be a solid citizen, one who rarely if ever found himself in the cross-hairs of a sales practice complaint, the investment firm in question would vigorously defend itself. If the customer were an elderly, frail widow who suffered losses by trading in speculative stocks, the case would almost always quickly be settled without a trial.

Some instances of fraud, however, are far easier to identify than these. It does not take much imagination to determine exactly what happened after a Ponzi scheme unravels. We know the identity of the scammer and the precise steps he took to set his plan into motion. We also know the names of his victims, how they were seduced, and how much money each of them lost. The schemes themselves are very simple. Everything seems so obvious, embarrassingly so, after the scammer's ruse is exposed. Yet often it can take years, sometimes many years, before these charades are uncovered.

There are two reasons for this. The first is self-evident: no investor will ever complain if he is getting what he was promised or, perhaps equally important, if he thinks he is getting what he was promised. I asked a friend of mine, one of Bernie Madoff's many victims, how much money he lost. He said, "$11 million." Then he paused and said, "Actually, I don't know. The last statement said I had $11 million. But to be honest, I don't know." It is still not entirely clear how much money was really "lost" in the larger Madoff scam. A figure of $50 billion has been tossed about with regularity, but that number represents actual investor capital plus fictitious profits. In other words, Madoff's victims thought they lost $50 billion, but in all likelihood, their actual out-of-pocket losses were much less, perhaps $19 billion or less. As of June 2017, $10 billion had been recovered.

Clearly, if Madoff's victims believed that all was well, there would be no reason for them to sound an alarm. And on the surface, all was well. If Madoff could have honored redemptions, i.e., cash out investors who needed some liquidity, he would have been able to perpetuate his hoax indefinitely. It was the financial crisis of 2008 and the horrendous stock market decline that followed that did Madoff in. His investors, like investors everywhere, panicked, and too many of them wanted to get out of the market at the same time. He couldn't keep up with their requests for cash.

Second, a scammer needs to develop and maintain a deep level of trust with his victims. Madoff certainly did. He founded Bernard L. Madoff

Investment Securities Inc. in 1960; it grew to become one of the top market making firms on Wall Street. He was Chairman of NASDAQ, a very visible member of the social scene in New York City, and well known as a philanthropist within the greater Jewish community. His reputation and standing enabled him to steal with impunity. After a few years, his entire operation grew by word of mouth. Madoff, ever the con man, told his victims even though his practice was closed to new business, he would do them a favor and make an exception by letting them in.

Another scammer, Allen Stanford, the architect of a $7 billion Ponzi scheme, did much the same thing. After a series of highly successful real estate investments in his native Texas, he devoted his time to running Stanford Financial and opened a bank in Antigua as its chief subsidiary. He was the toast of the town, praised by the Governor of Antigua for his generosity and good works. Ultimately, Stanford was knighted by the Antiguan government and was often referred to as Sir Allen. Stanford's operation, like Madoff's, was a complete fake. He simply pocketed the funds his clients had entrusted to him; after his fraud was exposed, he was sentenced to 110 years in prison. Madoff received a sentence of 150 years.

Fraudsters like Stanford and Madoff have been around forever. There are more of them now, and some of the hustles today, like theirs, reach into the billions of dollars, but in all other respects, the methods used by perpetrators of investment scams haven't changed a great deal over time. This was certainly the case with Walter Curran, a broker who worked for Dean Witter (now Morgan Stanley) in Boston in the 1980s. Anyone who knew him would never forget him; he had an unbelievably outgoing, affable personality, and he also possessed an unnatural amount of energy; he was one of those people that could seemingly get along on two hours' sleep. He was known to take friends and coworkers on impromptu pub crawls, picking up their tabs and sometimes those of anyone else within shouting distance. His career got off to a fast start; he could attract clients with ease, almost magnetically. After a few years, he was driving a Jaguar and wearing a gold Rolex. He joined the Oakley Country Club in Belmont, MA, where he played golf frequently and became close to a number of its members.

In time, he persuaded them to set up segregated accounts, created (so he said) only for his best clients so that they could take advantage of special investment opportunities. Of course, he promised high returns. Why not? He had begun to run a Ponzi scheme.

After the market crash of 1987, it all fell apart. Several of Curran's customers called him at his Dean Witter office, but he wasn't available. No one seemed to know where he was. When some of these clients said they hadn't received the funds they had requested from their "special accounts," management was alerted, and then they notified the NYSE, the SEC, and the FBI. Curran became a fugitive from justice. Shortly thereafter he was arrested at a Canadian border crossing trying to get *back* to the United States; customs officials had become suspicious since he was driving a rented Canadian car while carrying a Massachusetts driver's license. A search of his luggage turned up over $100,000 in currency that he had never declared; police in the United States were immediately contacted, and after they confirmed that a warrant was out for his arrest, he was quickly taken into custody.

Those who knew him fairly well whispered that before his odyssey through Canada, he had been golfing; others said he had taken his family to Europe to travel on the Orient Express. There were rumors that he had been in Las Vegas, or even if he had not, he had run up enormous gambling debts. I have no idea if all of these stories, or none of them, was true. Whatever the case, his life had become quite a spectacle, a constant topic of conversation and gossip for the financial community in Boston. In times like this, we often forget about shame and betrayal, family and victims. We become voyeurs. We can't help it. This story was just too juicy, and soon it got juicier. Curran had run up a small mountain of debt at the Bank of Boston, and after his arrest was made public, the bank filed suit against him and froze whatever remaining assets he had, including his house and car.

He was sentenced to over ten years in prison, but in time, a federal appeals court overturned Curran's sentence; it turned out that his wife, family members and some victims (yes, victims!) had written letters of support to the district judge, none of which were present in the presentencing report to the court or even made available to Curran's attorneys. (These letters were sent to the probation office, but Curran and his lawyers had no knowledge of this and never saw them.) The district judge had sentenced Curran to a longer term than had been recommended by prosecutors; he referred to only one letter he had received from another victim, who wrote, "We beg that the court to impose the strongest, severest of penalties that the law provides..." In the end, it was determined that all of the issues concerning presentencing, sentencing, and victim impact statements raised concerns regarding due process, and as a result, Curran's sentence was vacated in February 1991. This happened only two years after his arrest. Walter Curran may have been free, but his life was in shambles, and his victims deeply scarred.

We never seem to run out of Currans and Madoffs and Stanfords. You may remember Frank Gruttadauria, a successful broker in the 80s and 90s whose career went up in flames when a Ponzi scheme he had been running for perhaps fifteen years became public knowledge. In January 2002, he shocked his associates by disappearing from his office after leaving a letter behind that described his illicit activities. At the time of his disappearance, Gruttadauria was the branch manager for Lehman Brothers in Cleveland, having come to that firm in 2000 from S.G. Cowen, where he had worked since 1990. The timing of his exodus was no accident. The stock market was in the midst of a terrible decline, and Gruttadauria's clients, his unknowing victims, were understandably anxious. However, Gruttadauria was in no position to continue his shell game. When he finally turned himself in after being on the run for approximately one month, he had the princely sum of $6.55 in his Lehman Brothers personal account, not the $12 million he claimed when he had applied for a loan from National City Bank.

Gruttadauria was able to run his Ponzi scheme the old-fashioned way—by taking advantage of a small group of wealthy clients who trusted him. His task was made easier because he was able to generate false statements from a secret personal computer. He was also poorly supervised, in some cases actually monitored by subordinates in his own office. At the time of his arraignment, no one, not even the SEC, could pin down how much money was lost. Initial newspaper accounts tossed around a number as high as $300 million. The SEC's original complaint spoke of $40 million. Later, that was amended to $115 million. The statements Gruttadauria generated indicated his clients' accounts were worth $289 million in aggregate, when in fact they contained $12 million. Settlement with all of the victims proved to be difficult. Some insisted on being paid what they lost, plus the "fictitious profits" that Gruttadauria claimed they had earned. In other words, they wanted their money back along with what they would have, could have, or should have earned. The *Wall Street Journal* reported that by the end of 2002, Lehman and Cowen were in the process of repaying the victims as much as $100 million. Gruttadauria, meanwhile, went to prison for seven years and after his release wrote a book titled *Under the Banner of Justice*. It is a critique of the American legal system.

Countless scams have been run in recent years. They have occurred everywhere and do not discriminate by reason of geography, although they are likelier the closer one gets to the Money River. I've witnessed a few where I now live in Sarasota, FL, where, in the years immediately following the financial crisis, real estate values throughout the state plummeted as much as 50 percent. Just like stock-market-based scams that became public knowledge following steep market declines, real estate fraud was revealed only after that bubble burst, and property owners found themselves upside down on their homes and investment properties. It was then that prior fraudulent activity was exposed in the form of forged signatures, falsified applications, fake identities, and bogus appraisals.

Sarasota has not been immune from stock-market-related investment scams either. Arthur Nadel, known locally as a mini-Madoff, bilked investors out of more than $300 million. At the time of his disappearance in 2009, Nadel's hedge funds had assets totaling less than $1 million. Like Gruttadauria, Curran, Madoff and many other Ponzi scheme operators, Nadel kept his operation going until he was out of money, and then he went on the lam. His flight occurred, not surprisingly, during the bear market of 2009. He left his wife (his fifth) a note that told her how to access funds he had somehow managed to set aside during the last chaotic months he was able to keep operating. In this note he also suggested that she, "sell the Subaru if you have to," but no such thoughtful instructions were left for his victims. Sentenced to a fourteen-year term, he died in prison in 2012 at age seventy-nine.

General Douglas MacArthur said, "Old soldiers never die, they just fade away." The same can't be said for old scammers, who never seem to fade away but rather keep coming back for more. Two other senior citizens in Sarasota, Sheldon Rose and Alvin Mirman, were both near eighty when they pleaded guilty to a $6 million securities fraud scam in March 2017. Their scheme involved selling "blank check" or shell companies to investors who believed they were acquiring stock in legitimate corporations with genuine operations. Rose and Mirman were then able to manipulate trading in these stocks in a classic pump and dump scheme. During sentencing, the court cut both some slack because they were first-time offenders and promised to make restitution to their victims. Rose got forty months, and Mirman received twelve. Mirman's lawyer duly noted that he was President and Trustee of his synagogue, Temple Emanu-El, but apparently did not mention that he had been permanently banned from the securities industry in 2007. A minor oversight, to be sure.

CNBC's *American Greed* series about financial fraud and white-collar crime debuted in 2007 and was renewed for its 11th consecutive season in 2017. It is unlikely it will ever run out of material, or that viewers will lose interest in watching the program. Approximately 150 episodes have been aired since its inception, and of course, they feature only the most lurid, jaw-dropping stories. After all, this is entertainment, is it not? Some of the titles, like *Michael Lock: Pimp, Preacher, Profiteer* or *Allen Stanford: The Dark Night*, are obviously designed to get viewers (or perhaps voyeurs?) amped up.

Financial advisors running Ponzi schemes are in no way the only practitioners of fraud on Wall Street. Insider trading is the moral equivalent of robbing a bank, as is accounting fraud and money laundering. We've seen that the incidents of financial fraud have grown alarmingly in recent years, and if it appears that as a society we are being overwhelmed by this, it's probably because we are. Regulators complain that they do not have the resources or manpower to keep up with their workload. That's disconcerting enough. Keep in mind that regulators enforce, they do not prevent. That makes their task—let's call it the War on Fraud—even more difficult than the country's War on Drugs in the 1980s.

This issue of prevention versus enforcement brings us back to the notorious Bernie Madoff and his so-called scam of the century. Madoff's surrender to authorities may have marked the conclusion of his massive swindle, but it provoked a great number of unanswered questions as well. When did it start? How much money was really lost? How could so many wealthy investors have been duped? What due diligence did Madoff's institutional investors perform? How could this ruse have been kept secret for so long, even from his sons who worked with him? What about FINRA and the SEC? How could his charade have gone undetected?

First, Madoff was a master at building trust. Another friend of mine (and yet another Madoff victim) is a retired pathologist who was introduced to Madoff's make-believe money management operation in the 1990s by his father-in-law, who himself was referred by other Madoff clients. These future victims were sophisticated and savvy investors, very much connected to the New York-Palm Beach extended community where Madoff was able to do most of his damage. Their collective confidence in Madoff imbued him with an additional aura of credibility—one that he really didn't need. As Chairman of NASDAQ and an established philanthropist, Madoff was universally respected and admired. He did not seek out clients; they were drawn to him as if he possessed the irresistible attraction of a vampire.

My friend recalls feeling grateful that Madoff consented to take him on as a client. Soon other family members, siblings and cousins, were brought into the fold, and several of them ended up staying on with Madoff until the very end, and in the process, of course, losing everything. I asked him how he felt and what he was thinking the morning that he learned

of the scam, and he just laughed nervously. He admits he did no due diligence, and in fact never met Madoff personally. He was told that if he had
any questions to call "Frank." (This would have been Frank DiPiscali,
Madoff's lieutenant and operational mastermind whose official title was
Chief Financial Officer.) He is strangely accepting of his experience, of
Madoff's behavior, and of his own blind faith in the recommendations of
relatives and close friends. He mentioned an oft- repeated aphorism, "If
it's too good to be true, it probably is," and noted that it's easy to let your
guard down when a herd of people jump on the bandwagon.

Madoff's herd included ultra-high-net-worth investors, foundations,
non-profit social service organizations, pension plans, educational institutions and hedge funds. None of them questioned Madoff's legitimacy or
his purported investment results. This is particularly remarkable since his
alleged investment track record would have qualified for the Guinness
Book of World Records if it were real. He claimed he never suffered a
down month, and his clients' statements reflected this fantasy: 1 percent
a month, 12 percent a year, with monotonous regularity. No other money
manager has every achieved this type of consistency—it was perfection,
really—when investing in the stock market. It would have been easier for
him to contend he could climb Mt. Everest in flip-flops. His level of arrogance was beyond belief.

When asked about his trading strategies, Madoff was both coy and
evasive. He spoke vaguely of proprietary methodologies and secret algorithms, but when pressed, he revealed he was using a technique well
known to established option traders: the split-strike conversion strategy.
For those unfamiliar with options trading, it is best to think of this as a
hedging technique; it represents a more conservative way of investing in
the stock market by limiting downside exposure. However, it does not
eliminate risk, and any experienced options trader can attest to that.

One of them was Frank Casey. I worked with Frank forty years ago
and couldn't imagine a better source of information concerning Madoff.
Casey, along with Harry Markopolos and Neil Chelo, managed money for
Rampart Investment Management in Boston, and the three of them were

soon to become central figures in the Madoff saga. Rampart was (and is) a well-respected boutique that managed about $9 billion in options over-lay programs for institutional clients and hedge funds, the same kinds of clients that comprised represented the core of Madoff's business. Bernie Madoff and Rampart were competitors, if it is possible to call them that, because one business was phony and the other legitimate.

Casey first discovered Madoff in early 1999 when he was having a hard time persuading a potential client to sign with Rampart, even on a trial basis. This prospect was a "feeder fund," a type of hedge fund that doled money out to individual money managers and functioned as a manager of managers. Casey was told that the fund, Access International, had already invested $300 million of its own clients' money with another money man-agement firm specializing in options and was achieving remarkable success. Access International's CEO, Thierry de la Villehuchet, had inadvertently raised a red flag, the first of many, by telling Casey that he was pledged to secrecy and could not reveal the name of the firm that was achieving such astonishing results. Frank was immediately suspicious, since the trading history of this client, like every other Madoff client, showed a positive return every month, regardless of market conditions. Rampart, like other money management firms, used the split-strike conversion strategy often, and it did for them what it was supposed to do—it smoothed out the road bumps by reducing volatility. It did not eliminate risk. It couldn't. Nothing could, except Bernie Madoff's magic wand.

Casey was committed to earning a piece of Access International's busi-ness. By the end of 1999, he had learned where Access had invested the $300 million—with Madoff. That was Red Flag #2. Madoff wasn't even registered as an investment advisor. It turned out that Bernie Madoff, Chairman of NASDAQ, was illegally running an unregistered hedge fund. This revelation was just the beginning; dozens of red flags would surface in the months and years ahead, yet Madoff was able to continue his scam with impunity. De la Villehuchet, by all accounts a decent and sincere man, remained oblivious to Madoff's chicanery until the very end, when he took his own life in his Manhattan office.

Knowing that Rampart couldn't come close to matching Madoff's numbers (who could?), Casey turned the information he had gathered over to one of his associates, Harry Markopolos. Harry had an intuitive knack for forensic accounting and within a matter of hours determined that Madoff's performance claims were entirely bogus. Markopolos recalled his feelings at the time when he was interviewed on NPR's *Morning Edition* after Madoff's arrest and guilty plea:

> It's hard to compete with a Ponzi scammer because all he has to do is type his performance returns into the computer. He doesn't have to manage his returns according to the market, whereas I had to. I read his strategy statement, and it was so poorly put together. His strategy as depicted would have trouble beating a zero return, and his performance chart went up at a 45-degree line: that line doesn't exist in finance, it only exists in geometry classes. They [legitimate hedge fund managers] bought into his patina of respectability that he was a market maker — one of the largest on the street. They thought he was a Wall Street titan, and they had no reason to doubt him. But they didn't know that math like I did.

Madoff continued to turn clients into victims for another ten years. The timeline of what the whistleblowers at Rampart tried to do, and what the regulators, especially the SEC, failed to do, is nothing short of amazing. In May of 2000, Markopolos submitted an eight-page report to the SEC, the first of six that he would end up filing during the next half-dozen years. The report clearly and methodically documented Madoff's fraud. No response was received. More than a year later, an amended and expanded filing was made. The SEC opened an investigation of sorts, but its behavior was strangely passive. No one at the agency ever asked Casey or Markopolos to come in for a face-to-face meeting.

During this time, Casey contacted Michael Ocrant, a writer for a hedge fund trade journal, *MAR Hedge*. Frank made no secret about his motivation—he wanted to out Madoff. Ocrant, a respected journalist, took a close look Madoff's operation; what he saw raised the same doubts in his mind that it had in Casey's. Ocrant penned an exposé of Madoff's operation in May 2001 entitled "Madoff Tops Charts; Skeptics Ask How." A similarly damning report, Erin Arvedlund's "Madoff Scheme: Too Good to be True," appeared in *Barron's* just a week later. When she asked Madoff how he was able to achieve such amazing returns, he said, "I can't go into it a great deal. It's a proprietary trading strategy." Why couldn't anyone else reverse engineer what he was doing and achieve similar results? Simple. Madoff suggested they "didn't do a good job." The world shrugged its shoulders.

Casey's conviction that Madoff was running a Ponzi scheme mounted quickly. When he first ran into Madoff, Casey had been in the business for twenty-five years, almost entirely focused on options and derivatives. He knew all of the players—floor traders as well as his counterparts at other firms. None of them had ever seen any traffic from Madoff. Even these people were suspicious that Madoff was a fake, and they had nowhere near the first-hand knowledge that Casey possessed.

Madoff had an explanation for everything. He told his victims that he would not charge them a management fee, only commissions. That's why he didn't register as an investment advisor. He wanted to be thought of as a broker-dealer and nothing else. He told his clients he could make enough money on the commissions associated with trading in their accounts. To Casey and Markopolos, these terms ended up being red flags because the fees that hedge fund managers typically charge their clients—1 to 2 percent of assets plus 20 percent of profits—would dwarf the commissions paid out to brokerage firms. By disclaiming management fees, Madoff was walking away from a huge amount of money. Why would he do that? Simple—to avoid being examined as an investment advisor.

He set up arrangements with several hedge funds that ran trades through Madoff's broker-dealer subsidiary. One of the largest was the Greenwich Sentry Fund; it falsely claimed to oversee the implementation of Madoff's strategy, when in fact it did nothing of the sort. Madoff ran the money (more accurately, he ran away with the money) and had total control of every decision. Fairfield Sentry, a feeder fund, invested a small amount its clients' money with several other independent money managers, but they had the lion's share of their assets under Madoff's purview. They were hypnotized by his success.

Madoff insisted he was not managing money, simply executing trades, and his BD subsidiary was a perfectly legitimate firm that had no problem making it through regulatory audits and examinations. As mentioned before, clients were sworn to secrecy, so much so that when whenever rankings of hedge fund results were published, Madoff's operation was never mentioned, even though it was, at least in the minds of its clients, one of the largest in the country. Fairfield didn't complain. One of its principals earned as much as $300 million in a single year from his firm's management fees. Their "management" strategy could be explained in one short sentence: "Give the money to Bernie." Did Fairfield suspect that Madoff was a sham? No more than did any individual client. Did they turn a blind eye to what was going on? Could they have known? Should they have? Perhaps, but in the end, Madoff took them down, just like everyone else.

After Markopolos first contacted the SEC, and especially after the Ocrant and Arvedlund articles were published, the SEC did open its eyes to possible wrongdoing, but in a way that was both apathetic and incompetent. Even before Madoff's cover was blown, Markopolos and Casey had specified dozens of red flags that the SEC subsequently passed over. Some of them were quite egregious. First among them was Madoff's Svengali-like performance record—too good to be true, preposterous, really—but his clients and to a degree the SEC quietly ignored it because of his standing and credibility within the industry. Second, Madoff did not allow outside performance audits; his own auditing firm, Friehling and Horowtz, was a tiny storefront operation. (It was later revealed that they rubber-stamped everything Madoff gave them, and never performed a legitimate audit.) Third was the issue of secrecy and the charade of pretending he wasn't an investment advisor. Fourth, there was Madoff's failure to register as an investment advisor, mentioned above. Lastly, and most damning of all, was the simple fact that there weren't enough option contracts available to accommodate the trades that Madoff claimed to have processed. Yet no one bothered to take notice that this mismatch was clear proof that the books were being cooked.

The SEC investigated Madoff's Ponzi scheme after Madoff's fraud was exposed. In an embarrassing 477-page report, the agency had no alternative but to point the finger at itself. There were countless missed opportunities and incidents of lax follow-up. After Markopolos sent written submissions to the SEC in 2002 and 2005, he placed several calls to Meaghan Chung, Head of Investigations at the SEC's New York office, but she would neither confirm or deny that Madoff was being investigated. It turned out that Chung was indeed looking at Madoff, but in the end, took no action against him. Perhaps she as well as others at the SEC were influenced by Madoff's standing in the investment community and assumed that the whistleblowers at Rampart were simply disgruntled competitors. The atmosphere changed abruptly after Madoff was exposed. The SEC, which, as we know, never even bothered to meet with Markopolos or Casey, was suddenly all ears. Casey and Markopolos were both asked to testify before Congress. Casey's testimony alone, taken under oath, ran seventy-two pages. Markopolos was especially pointed in his criticism of Chung; he believed that her failure to act allowed Madoff to perpetuate his scam. In an interview with the *New York Post*, an emotional Chung asked rhetorically, "Why are you taking a mid-level staff person and making me responsible for the failure of the American economy?" She has a point, even though she clearly bears some responsibility for the Madoff debacle. But others do as well. There were many people, all bright, financially sophisticated, Wall Street professionals who could have known and should have done something—but didn't lift a finger. They remained inert throughout the entire fiasco.

The SEC did pay Madoff a few visits before he surrendered, but apart from motivating Madoff to register as an investment advisor in 2006, all it did was kick the can down the road. A number of the SEC staffers who talked with Madoff over the years were young, inexperienced attorneys who had very little knowledge of the securities industry or options trading.

It seemed as if every time they started to look at Madoff, they closed the book on him. Why else would Markopolos have made six submissions to the SEC over an eight-year period?

All of us knows what an audit involves—the verification that financial statements are accurate representations of the truth. Auditors do not verify every transaction, account, invoice, and receipt, or item of inventory, but they do spot check rigorously to get a meaningful sample. We've already seen that Madoff's chosen auditing firm never examined Madoff's books and simply signed off on all the statements that Madoff produced. Did the SEC not become curious how such a tiny CPA operation could audit the books of one of the largest and most successful broker-dealers on Wall Street? Apparently not.

The bungling didn't stop there. During one SEC visit in 2006, examiners asked Madoff what his DTC number was. The Depository Trust Company is, for want of a better word, an electronic clearing house where all of Wall Street's trading activity is processed and recorded. The DTC holds book-entry security positions for all of its members, such as Merrill, Morgan Stanley, and the rest. Madoff's broker-dealer firm was of course represented at the DTC. It would have been child's play to verify Madoff's trading history. If, for example, he reported to clients that he had purchased two hundred thousand shares of Bristol Myers on a given day, that transaction would be reflected on the books at the DTC. To Madoff's amazement, the SEC never bothered to verify anything. He later revealed in a prison interview that as soon as he was asked for his DTC number, he felt the game was over. He also opined that if he had been forced to register as an investment advisor before 2006, he would have been caught earlier.

While the SEC's particular record in the Madoff scandal was embarrassingly poor, it would be unfair to dismiss the agency out of hand as a total train wreck. I spoke with Frank about the SEC's mission as well as its limitations. One of their major roles is to enforce compliance with securities laws and regulations. The SEC has the power to impose sanctions and penalties, and it can refer criminal cases to the Justice Department for prosecution, but the agency really has no ability to prevent fraud from happening in the first place. It cannot ask for wiretaps or create a network of informants or set up a sting operation. For all of its powers, in this one important respect, it is powerless. Our right to privacy, guaranteed by the Constitution, will probably ensure that the status quo will not be disturbed.

There has been a fair amount of debate regarding the SEC's inability to be more proactive in rooting out fraudsters. One of the methods might be through greater regulatory oversight of transfer agents. Sometimes fraudsters can rip off transfer agents in the same way money launderers can scam banks. For example, assume a fraudster acquired restricted shares, i.e., those acquired in a non-public transaction. He would need a legal opinion to authorize a transfer agent to remove the so-called restrictive legend from the face of the certificate; this would enable him to sell the shares in the open market. If he were able to identify a thinly traded stock and come up with a bogus legal opinion, he could then "pump and dump" the stock by publicly issuing a stream of highly optimistic (and totally false) comments and opinions. This would entice unwitting buyers, and when the shares popped up in price, our fraudster would sell.

Given this, creating an enhanced level of communication between the SEC and transfer agents on some level would seem like a good idea; but agents have their hands full, currently managing over 250 million shareholder accounts. They are likely to resist the costly and perhaps overwhelming task of becoming fiduciaries and gatekeepers for the SEC. Furthermore, individual states can, and do, have different requirements governing the removal of restrictive legends. Any movement toward greater SEC powers will likely come at the expense of the states. The workout here faces a long, almost tortuous future. Besides, this particular type of fraud is just one of innumerable get-rich-quick schemes.

A federal whistleblower program was established for the first time in 2010 when Dodd–Frank legislation was passed by Congress and signed into law by President Obama. It fell to the SEC to establish an "Office of the Whistleblower" and make payments to claimants that provided the agency with what it considered to be "high quality, original information" leading to a successful "enforcement action in which over $1,000,000 in sanctions" was ordered. Whistleblowers need to apply for these awards after the SEC has acted, and this process takes time. Over two years elapsed before the SEC paid out dollar one. Many claims were denied, no doubt because all of the tips the SEC received were neither original nor high quality.

The whistleblower program has been a qualified success. Keep in mind that since 2010, approximately $1 billion in sanctions—in total— were ordered as a direct result of whistleblower tips, and only a bit more than $150 million was earmarked for whistleblower rewards. Just thirteen such payments were made in 2016. Obviously, the program has gotten off to a very slow start, and part of the reason may be that the SEC has done a rather poor job in publicizing it. The agency's home page on the internet, www.sec.gov, doesn't mention it. A drop-down menu of over twenty SEC offices, one that includes the under-the-radar Offices of FOIA Services and Administrative Law Judges, doesn't even list it. The whistleblower program may not be totally invisible, but so far one would have to categorize it as an underachiever.

The responsibility of enforcement does not lie exclusively with the SEC. Every state has its own set of rules and regulations; some of these may parallel federal requirements, but others do not. There is very little if any coordination between state regulators and the SEC. Yes, they do cooperate with each other, but they are not on the same team. Perhaps there are not outright turf battles, but sometimes there are overlaps, and on other occasions, there are gaps. Each state has its own licensing requirements for registered representatives and investment advisors and is free to establish its own disciplinary procedures as well. States can and do set their own rules regarding securities offerings, and these can be more stringent than the SEC's, or in the case of offerings that do not require federal registration, less so.

The NASAA is the North American Securities Administrators Association. It claims to be the "preeminent organization of securities regulators," but in practice, it functions much like a trade association. It is an advocate for investor protection in much the same way AARP is a resource for older Americans. Like other advocacy groups, it has a very public face, and in the past, has been quite active in lobbying for legislation that can advance its agenda. On one level, it is relatively powerless, but the NASAA nevertheless has played a valuable role in advancing the cause of regulatory reform. The organization is not shy. A few years ago, shortly after the credit crisis and the collapse of Bernie Madoff's Ponzi scheme, it announced:

> NASAA has long called upon Congress to extend the fiduciary duty standard to all financial professionals who give investment advice regarding securities. Currently, investment advisers have this duty, but broker-dealers do not. What is fiduciary duty? It is simply the duty to put the client's interest first. Differing standards of care create confusion and distrust and do not serve the best interests of investors.
>
> State securities regulators should also urge Congress to increase the number of investment advisory firms under our jurisdiction. States have an efficient and effective system in place for the regulation of investment advisers, and we are developing systems to better deploy our resources should we take on greater regulatory responsibilities.
>
> Another area of concern is mandatory, industry-run arbitration for investors. Investors should have the right to choose litigation or independent arbitration as the forum for resolving disputes with their financial services firms. As the debate over regulatory reform gathers steam in Congress, so too have efforts by powerful interests in the financial services industry to delay, derail and distort the regulatory changes to the status quo that are necessary to strengthen investor protection. But business as usual doesn't work anymore. Nor does regulation as usual.

There is a bit of bravado in the NASAA's exhortations. As a former industry insider, I cannot help but feel offended when I read about "powerful interests in the financial services industry (that) delay, derail, and distort regulatory changes." That is a naive oversimplification if not total nonsense. The NASAA is not the sole occupant of moral high ground, nor does it have all the answers to the challenges we face. The issues it addresses are important, but, as we shall see later, they are complex and nuanced. A good example of this is the ongoing conversation about the fiduciary duty of broker-dealers, a subject with many shades of gray.

In the end, though, such discussion is imperative. Healthy debate over regulatory issues is needed more than ever. Over time a free and open exchange of ideas should enable all of the players at the table to identify common ground. After all, investors, regulators, and the financial services industry all share the same long-term goals. Perhaps the most significant of these is our desire for fair and open markets that are so well-structured and policed that bad guys like Bernie Madoff are rendered powerless, incapable of defrauding innocent victims. Unless all of the stakeholders here—regulators, investors, brokerage firms, investment management companies and more—are successful in overcoming financial fraud, the financial services industry will find it next to impossible to rebuild the confidence and trust that have been forfeited in recent years.

Not Your Grandmother's Stock Market

● ● ●

IT WOULD BE IMPOSSIBLE TO understand where the industry stands today without looking at the people who shaped it. We've seen how Chuck Schwab parlayed his vision, single-mindedness, and the use of technology to broaden the appeal of investing through lower costs and greater ease of access. His work followed that of Charles Merrill, whose influence at an earlier time was no less impactful than Schwab's.

Before we get to the present, let alone the future, a little history is in order. Charlie Merrill died when I was nine years old, fifteen years before I joined the company. Many of my colleagues and clients, of course, knew him well, and they all spoke about him with a combination of fondness and awe. Surprisingly, there was nothing about his earlier years that would have indicated he was destined for greatness. He was a two-time dropout, failing to graduate either from Amherst College or the law school at the University of Michigan. He spent more time playing semi-pro baseball than he did attending classes. At the end of the baseball season in 1907, Merrill moved to New York to take an entry-level job on Wall Street that paid him $15 a week, and he rented a room at the YMCA (where coincidentally he met his future partner, Ed Lynch). Six years later, when he was twenty-eight, he started the firm that was to become Merrill Lynch. It consisted of two employees, himself and his assistant, Lilian Burton, who was to remain with him for forty years.

Scarcely a decade later, he had achieved phenomenal wealth. The company established offices throughout the country and had become the nation's dominant underwriter for chain store financings. Now known as Merrill Lynch, the firm's clients included Safeway, Kresge, J.C. Penney and many others, and Charlie Merrill had achieved celebrity status on a national level. Yet, despite his firm's spectacular success, the general prosperity that typified the Roaring 20s, and a record-setting bull market, he became deeply concerned about the future direction of the stock market. He had witnessed years of unbridled optimism and a parabolic rise in stock prices, and so, over a year before the 1929 crash, Charlie sent an ominous letter to all Merrill Lynch customers. He warned them of the dangers of leverage (margin debt) and speculation: "We advise you in no uncertain terms that you take advantage of the current high prices and put your financial house in order. We recommend that you sell enough securities to lighten your obligations." Imagine a Wall Street CEO saying that today.

Merrill gave the same message to his partner, Ed Lynch, and after meeting with initial resistance was finally able to persuade him to sell and in so doing vastly increasing the company's odds of riding out a future downturn. (Merrill Lynch was a partnership, and the securities that Merrill and Lynch owned made up a large chunk of the firm's net capital.) The decision was also consistent with Merrill's oft-repeated desire to get out of the retail brokerage business altogether. A few months after the Great Crash, Merrill Lynch and E.A. Pierce and Co. merged, with Pierce acquiring Merrill Lynch's retail operations. While Charlie Merrill had significant equity in the new company, his role had changed dramatically. No longer the face of the firm, he was now not much more than a passive investor—a large one, to be sure—but passive nonetheless.

During the Depression, Ed Lynch lived the good life—extended trips abroad (especially to Paris), a luxurious sailboat, and homes in the Caribbean, Palm Beach, and Southampton, NY. Like Lynch, Merrill was a bon vivant and enjoyed an opulent lifestyle as well, but in contrast to his partner, he spent most of the 1930s working as diligently as he had as a young entrepreneur on Wall Street. Much of this time was devoted to the grocery business, specifically Oakland-based Safeway Stores. He was Safeway's largest shareholder and exerted a powerful influence on the company, playing a critical part in its continued growth.

Another one of life's decision points presented itself to Merrill in the late 1930s. E.A. Pierce had continued to struggle, and there were serious doubts that it would be able to continue as a going concern much longer. Merrill was approached by Winthrop Smith (a former ML partner, now an E.A. Pierce partner) to come back to the retail brokerage business in the only way he knew how—active and fully engaged. Merrill saw opportunity where others saw obstacles. He said yes. And so, in 1940, the latest iteration of Merrill Lynch came into being. It was to flourish for another sixty-plus years, redefining the role of retail investment firms and the way in which they connected with customers. My grandmother at the time was in her late thirties, the mother of two pre-teen children. This was my grandmother's stock market.

Charlie Merrill's presence was immediately felt. Early on, he took a firm stand on behalf of the small investor. He stressed that no account was too small for Merrill Lynch (initially known as Merrill Lynch, E. A. Pierce and Cassatt), and all clients, regardless of size, would be treated as equals. He believed in full disclosure and authorized that the firm, which was privately held, release its financial statements to the public. He decried the practice of churning accounts for commissions, and he did something about it—retail brokers were to be paid a salary plus a bonus. This practice continued until the late 1970s. In time, formal training programs for brokers and then branch managers were established, the first of their kind on Wall Street.

Leaning on his experience at Safeway, Merrill applied his knowledge of advertising and marketing to the brokerage industry and did so with great success. He brought Wall Street to Main Street, offering educational books and pamphlets along with public seminars designed to inform and enlighten. He instructed his brokers to provide information so that their customers could make informed decisions and to never give out advice unless it was requested. This represented a remarkable break from the established norm. He built a culture of doing one's job only one way—the right way. Any deviation from the expected standards of ethics and integrity would not be tolerated, something that was drilled into every new employee on Day 1. In 1948, the *Saturday Evening Post* ran a series of articles about Merrill Lynch that were so favorable one might have guessed it was paid advertising.

The 50s and early 60s represented the golden years of the retail brokerage industry. This era is now looked upon with fondness and nostalgia by baby boomers, but it also benefited from its own advances in technology that had occurred since the turn of the century. Commercially produced computers made their first appearance. Radio and television began to crowd out print media; automobiles and airplanes revolutionized transportation. Electronic quote machines similarly displaced the teletypewriter, just as teletype had done to chalkboards. However, while technology may have been a force for change on one level, the underlying culture of Wall Street was largely unaffected. In a sense, many of the changes the Street experienced during this era were little more than surface, because the strategy and tactics of doing business in 1965 were not terribly different than they had been ten or fifteen years earlier. In retrospect, it all made perfect sense. Commissions were fixed and high, and the American economy was booming. Why rock the boat?

Soon, Merrill's major competitors followed suit. E.F. Hutton, Shearson, Paine Webber, Kidder Peabody, Dean Witter, Smith Barney and others each built a successful national network of retail offices; these firms in many ways bought into the business model and the principles that Charlie Merrill had established years before. It looked like the white-shoe firms of Wall Street were about to enter the promised land. Business was good and kept getting better—until it didn't.

You may have noticed that none of these firms, not even Merrill Lynch, exist today as independent companies. One of the reasons was that all of them were slow to anticipate shifts in consumer tastes and preferences, almost always reacting, often grudgingly, to changes after the fact. The clients of Wall Street wire houses kept getting older. All of the major old-line brokerage firms were slow in bringing new technology into their branch offices. When online trading was first offered by Fidelity and Schwab, and then other discounters, the competitive threat this posed wasn't taken seriously. Instead, it was rationalized away the same way that the American steel industry reacted when business started going sour in the 1970s. (With Big Steel, it was always someone else's fault—the unions, the economy, foreign competition, trade policy, high interest rates, etc.) Even after the long bear market of 1968-1983 finally ended, traditional brokerage firms struggled; profit margins and return on equity were anemic, and stock prices of most public investment firms flatlined. Worst of all, client satisfaction remained distressingly low. Revealingly, Merrill Lynch's closing 1990 price was unchanged from the IPO that had taken place almost twenty years before.

The 1970s and 80s were transitional years on Wall Street. The old world did not disappear in a flash. Discount brokers maintained a relatively small market share, and they suffered growing pains common to many startup companies. While the advent of negotiated commissions in 1975 did have an immediate and dramatic impact on institutional business, the effect on full- service retail brokerages was somewhat limited and slow to take hold. Internet trading didn't even exist before the mid-90s; until then, all trades at established discounters were processed manually by registered customer service representatives. Compared to today's bare bones rates, commissions remained relatively high.

In the 1990s, the business continued to evolve. Some change was substantive, some cosmetic. Branch offices got spiffier, back-office operations streamlined, and desktop computers were introduced system-wide. All the major firms expanded their footprints nationally by opening satellite offices in small cities. Additionally, large amounts of money were spent on recruiting deals for the established big producer, the Tyrannosaurus Rex of the financial world. Through it all, one thing remained constant: research, sales, and trading were all done in the time-worn, traditional way—face to face, eyeball to eyeball, mano a mano. Machines were indispensable, but only to the extent that they helped people make decisions. And then, without much warning, the playbook changed. May Day was the shot across the bow. Computer-based trading sealed the deal, and Charlie Merrill's world ceased to exist. In 1950, he was a visionary, a game-changer, a maverick. Fifty years later his firm in some ways had become an anachronism. Although many of the principles he had espoused years earlier continued to live on, and every brokerage office still had its share of dinosaurs, change accelerated with every passing year. Merrill Lynch and its traditional competitors started to lose market share, and those losses are continuing today.

When I first arrived at Merrill Lynch in 1972, computers were primitive by today's standards. Desktop computing was years away, and many office functions were still performed manually. Most customers preferred to take physical possession of their stock certificates; delivery normally took two to four weeks and was provided at no cost. Some brokerage firms now charge as much as $500 as a processing fee just to mail a stock certificate to one of their clients. Also, since there were no sweep accounts or money market funds, all customers wanted to receive checks for their cash balances for an obvious reason—brokerage firms didn't pay any interest. I remember that it was Rita Rogers' job to issue these checks, and it kept her busy all day.

Technological innovation soon turned the business upside down. I am sure I heard about program trading before the 1987 market crash, but it was not until after that debacle, a 20 percent one-day decline, that it became a common topic of conversation. The '87 crash was the largest one-day meltdown in the history of Wall Street, even exceeding the losses that took place in 1929. Putting the magnitude of the decline aside, in many other respects nothing quite like this had ever occurred before. There was no catastrophic event that triggered it—no war, assassination, or natural disaster. Nor was it a harbinger of future economic distress. A mild economic recession didn't begin until late 1990, about three years later. How, then, could the crash have taken place when it did? Causes and effects were debated endlessly. They still are.

One thing is quite clear: the conditions that existed in the spring and summer of 1987 (leading up to the crash) were virtually identical with those that have existed before other major market declines. Stocks had been on a run for several years. Valuations were high. So was public optimism. Margin buying had increased dramatically—a clear sign of increasingly speculative sentiment on the part of investors. There was a widespread consensus among market participants that continued economic growth would serve as a catalyst for prices to rise in the future. Few were concerned that U.S. Treasury bonds yielded 10 percent, and stocks on average yielded just 2 percent. The momentum behind the mid-80s bull market was powerful enough to overcome many of the most cynical among us.

Program trading made its initial appearance in the 1980s. It represented the first time that computers were used to do more than administrative tasks like accounting, payroll, trade settlement, and the like. Program trading put the computer in the front lines; here, a machine (the computer) was programmed by engineers to enter trades for large baskets of securities, but only when certain predetermined conditions were met. The rules upon which trading decisions were made are called algorithms. Rules-based trading was not especially new; trading (and decision making) initiated by high-speed computers was. Program trading was embraced only because human beings couldn't get the job done fast enough. The concept grew in popularity among large financial institutions and hedge funds because it offered them, or so they believed, a means of nimbly trading substantial holdings of securities at a reduced level of risk.

Program trading involved portfolio insurance and index arbitrage, two strategies that are like cousins. Of the two, the use of portfolio insurance was far more widespread and is looked upon by many as being a root cause of the '87 crash. It is easy to get lost in the weeds when talking about this, so, for the sake of simplicity, think of portfolio insurance as a hedging technique. Ideally, stock index futures would be used to offset portfolio losses in a declining market. The weaker the market, the more one would hedge. In theory, it made perfect sense—so perfect, in fact, it sounded too good to be true.

For a strategy like this to be successful, speed and reliability were essential. Large multi-million-dollar baskets of stocks would need to be purchased (or sold) in the blink of an eye. (Exchange- traded funds would have made this task easier, but they did not exist at the time.) These stock purchase transactions would need to be quickly offset by corresponding trades in the options and/or futures markets, where contracts on popular stock indexes like the S&P 500 were traded. Any programming error, mechanical malfunction, or trading disruption on the exchanges themselves could have catastrophic consequences.

And on October 19, 1987, there were malfunctions and disruptions galore, and these were made worse by the fact that the NYSE and the CBOE were in different cities some 791 miles apart; New York and Chicago had different trading hours, computer systems, rules, regulations, and supervisory personnel. During the day of the crash, trading became chaotic. There were delayed openings in New York, and once trading was underway, selling accelerated, with wide gaps appearing between trades. Futures and options followed suit until there was a near meltdown in Chicago, and trading on that exchange was halted altogether. Having now lost the ability to hedge, institutional investors panicked and precipitated a selling stampede in New York. When the CBOE reopened, its prices were totally out of whack with New York.

Volume was so heavy that some orders never found their way to the exchange floor; many of those that did and got executed were not reported back for hours, sometimes days. Questionable executions were common. An order for XYZ paced at 1:00 could have been filled at that time, or two hours later, or never. I remember trying to buy Gillette when it was trading around $23, and it came back to me at $31. Since this was a trade for my own account, and I never put a price limit on the trade, all I got was a pat on the back and a lot of teasing.

On the twenty-fifth anniversary of the 1987 crash, veteran financial journalist Floyd Norris wrote in the *New York Times*:

On one day, the Dow Jones industrial average lost 23 percent of its value. People wondered if that heralded a new Depression. A front-page headline in The New York Times asked, "Does 1987

Equal 1929?" It did not. The next recession, a mild one, was more than two years away. What it did signify was the beginning of the destruction of markets by dumb computers. Or, to be fair to the computers, by computers programmed by fallible people and trusted by people who did not understand the computer programs' limitations. As computers came in, human judgment went out. That process, then in its infancy, gained speed over the next two decades. By 2008, it really did threaten a new Depression.

Norris quite correctly points out that program trading was not the singular cause of the crash of 1987. Nor has the ever-increasing reliance on computer-driven strategies been the primary cause of every major market decline since then. Yet it would be ridiculous to contend that the practice of allowing machines to run on autopilot while trading billions of dollars' worth of securities is a welcome, entirely beneficial development. One computer-aided market crash is one too many.

Portfolio insurance as it was practiced in the 80s quickly disappeared. Don't think for a minute this was a result of some epiphany or spiritual awakening on the part of hedge fund managers. In truth, the portfolio insurance method of program trading was effective only part of the time, and "partly effective" is not something one looks for in insurance. Besides, the introduction of exchange-traded funds a couple of years later made the job of acquiring "baskets" of securities an effortless task, something available even to the smallest of individual investors. More important, though, was that the speed and capabilities of computing were growing exponentially in the 1990s, and traders on Wall Street were, as always, on the lookout for novel and more creative ways of making money.

When I say that this is not my grandmother's stock market, I couldn't be more serious. First, the New York Stock Exchange, once the only game in town, is today one of many exchanges where stocks are traded in the United States. Less than 25 percent of total daily volume takes place on the NYSE. While estimates vary greatly, at least 50 percent, and perhaps as much as 75 percent, of all trading is done through computer-generated high-frequency trading. Most people have no idea what HFT is and where much of the trading takes place. One thing we do know is that HFT trading is processed by computers on fully electronic, highly automated exchanges, where many orders are entered and filled by high-speed computers—without the assistance of a human being. Nowadays, the NYSE is just one of these exchanges. So is NASDAQ. In the space of a generation, both became unrecognizable.

Have you heard of Bats Global Markets? Probably not. Bats Trading, Inc. was founded in 2005; in November of 2006, it recorded a one-day record volume of 100 million shares. Today it processes around seven hundred million shares of trading daily. The IEX, established in 2012, handles about two hundred million shares each day. There are other electronic exchanges like these, and there are also dark pools, an ominous-sounding term describing a private exchange that serves large institutional investors.

High-speed computer-powered algorithmic trading is not necessarily a bad thing, and it has many defenders. Both large and small investors have benefited from greater liquidity and smaller spreads. All things being equal, buyers now pay less and sellers receive more than would have been the case twenty years ago. In the 70s and 80s, stocks were typically quoted in fractions (⅛, ¼, etc.); today, they are quoted in decimals, with the difference between best bid and best offer often only one cent. Not too long ago even the most liquid NASDAQ-traded companies like American Express and Microsoft traded with spreads of nearly a dollar a share. Retail customers were then charged a fat commission in addition to the market maker's spread; clearly, this was a highly lucrative operation for brokerage firms.

High-frequency trading nonetheless has many critics. Like many other innovations, HFT has been the cause of unintended consequences. As an example, modern air and auto transportation have transformed the way we live, but they also pollute the air we breathe. Modern computers have provided society with countless benefits, but they have also opened up a window to criminal acts such as hacking and identity theft. As one of my mentors liked to say, everywhere in life "there are gives and there are gets." This applies to HFT as well. HFT has many benefits, but it must also be said that without high-frequency trading, it is highly unlikely we would ever have experienced a flash crash. To some, and I am one of those folks, an instantaneous massive drop in stock prices caused by a mechanical or design error is too great a price to pay for enhanced liquidity. Apart from the staggering potential for financial loss, flash crashes erode public trust in Wall Street.

After the '87 crash, regulators and the exchanges collaborated to create a system of trading suspensions called circuit-breakers. These rules-based trading halts would, it was believed, allow time to elapse so that panic would dissipate, and the markets would be able to function normally. But regulators and the principal stock exchanges were reluctant to overreact. Sometimes it seemed as if they were reluctant to act at all. The establishment of temporary trading "time-outs" proved to be only partially effective. This means they are partially ineffective as well. Think about a homeowner who has a surge protector installed. The surge protector no doubt will serve a useful purpose, but it cannot guard against a direct lightning strike, or prevent the home from burning to the ground.

The circuit-breaker concept was put to the test in 1997 when the Dow Jones Industrial Average suffered a horrendous one-day meltdown of nearly 7 percent. The SEC noted that the 350-point circuit breaker in force at that time was too *small* because the decline "was not of a magnitude to offer a true test of how circuit breakers might operate during more severe declines." How much more severe would one look for? At the time, the October 1997 mini-crash represented the largest one-day point decline in DJIA history and currently stands as the fifteenth worst percentage loss in the past one hundred years. Circuit breakers can work, but only if they are aggressively utilized. Protecting the public needs to be the focus, not keeping the markets open at virtually all costs.

In any event, even HFT's most vocal supporters would agree that it is not without risk. One of the most troublesome byproducts of high-frequency trading was the so-called flash crash, a term that did not come into popular usage until May 6, 2010. In a matter of minutes, the Dow Jones

Industrial Average inexplicably plunged seven hundred points and almost immediately recovered most of the ground it had lost. At its low, the Dow was down a thousand points on the day. Investors suffered nearly a trillion dollars' worth of losses. Some trades for a given stock took place at a penny a share; others at $100,000. The market became completely dysfunctional. To this day, no one knows why and how it happened. Initially, a Kansas-based mutual fund company, Waddell and Reid, was singled out as a bogeyman. It turned out the firm was engaged in perfectly legitimate hedging activities. There were rumors of a cyber-attack engineered by Al Qaeda.

John Carney of CNBC pointed the finger at high-frequency trading, and his assessment was both colorful and reasonably accurate. He opined that before May 6, "smart traders were devastating the High Freaks." To Carney, smart traders are hedge fund managers, and High Freaks are high-frequency traders. (This is a bit misleading since many hedge funds also partake in HFT.) In any event, Carney continued, "And so the High Freaks did the smart thing: they stopped trading." He reckoned that by temporarily pulling out of the market, high-frequency traders precipitated a market collapse because they weren't there to provide support as stocks tumbled. His statement is a bit simplistic, but overall it is spot-on. The only folks who are obligated to provide support for the market during volatile times are the NYSE "specialists." Today, they have a greatly reduced role and a fraction of their former influence. They had nowhere near the capital to absorb the avalanche of selling on May 6.

It later was learned that a young, unknown day trader in London, Navinder Singh Sarao, may have had a meaningful role in the events of May 6. Sarao lived with his parents and traded from his bedroom. He purportedly made $40 million during a five-year period by engaging in a practice called spoofing. Electronic spoofing occurs when you enter a trade and withdraw it before it can get executed, much like a fighter who feints a punch in order to make his opponent react. All you need is a criminal mind, modified software, and a very fast computer. Spoofers like Sarao, for example, could establish a long position and enter a blizzard of buy orders in a micro-second—enough to excite high-frequency traders who may take the bait and buy for their own accounts. Their buying would push prices up a little more, creating a window of opportunity for the spoofer to sell.

Sarao was exposed several years later by a whistleblower named Eric Hunsader. Hunsader, himself a vocal critic of high-frequency trading, runs a small software firm in Winnetka, IL. Like Madoff whistleblowers Frank Casey and Harry Markopolos, Hunsader found it hard to get the prompt attention of the SEC. He said that he was onto Sarao's manipulation as early as 2010, but no action was taken against Sarao until 2015, when he was arrested. Hunsader was paid a $750,000 award by the SEC. While not chopped liver, his award represented only 15 percent of the fine that the SEC levied against the NYSE—at the low end of a 10-30 percent that is authorized. The NYSE paid a fine of $5 million. To the Exchange, this must have felt like a parking ticket.

Notwithstanding the above, no one, not even Hunsader, believes Sarao was solely responsible for the flash crash. Hunsader opined that Sarao brought the kindling wood to a forest fire, not the gasoline or the matches. A master of metaphors, he later concluded that "if this was a cake recipe, then Sarao was a pinch of salt." Others have taken it a step further, claiming that Sarao was falsely accused and in no way responsible for the carnage that took place on May 6. This was the principal finding of a study co-authored by a former SEC Commissioner and two University of California professors. They wrote, "it is highly unlikely that, as alleged by the United States Government, Navinder Sarao's spoofing orders, even if illegal, could have caused the flash crash, or that the crash was a foreseeable consequence of his spoofing activity." They went on to say, "at most, we can conclude that Sarao was operating in an extremely complex environment, in which any of the millions of financial market actions on May 6, 2010 (including his own) could have unforeseeably precipitated a critical event and a downward cascade of prices." Interestingly, there have been other flash crashes and mini-crashes since May 6, 2010, and Navinder Sarao was off-line for all of them.

One of them occurred during the summer of 2012. Technology difficulties experienced by trading firm Knight Capital were responsible for extremely volatile trading on approximately 150 companies listed on the NYSE. Knight confirmed that it then advised customers to route orders for these securities through other trading firms. The NYSE announced (as did Knight) that it would review trading in these stocks. Forbes reported that the mini-crash would "unquestionably renew the debate over electronic trading and whether market participants have sacrificed safety or soundness for speed." If it did, the debate ended in a draw.

The markets experienced another horrific meltdown on August 24, 2015. On that day, the DJIA dropped an astonishing thousand points minutes after the market opened, and recovered more than half the ground that it lost almost as quickly. During the course of the day, trading in a multitude of issues was temporarily halted an amazing twelve hundred times as the exchange's circuit breakers were activated to offset the extreme volatility. Surprisingly, some of the most bizarre trading occurred in ETFs (exchange-traded funds), whose prices often became seriously decoupled from the underlying indices they were designed to replicate. Neena Mishra of *Zacks* described the trading as "crazy" after observing that approximately 80 percent of the trading halts occurred in ETFs. She was spot on. In some cases, ETFs opened for trading before many individual stocks that they held could do so.

Analysts felt that the cause of that particular crash was investor concern over growth prospects in the Chinese economy. Seriously? Perhaps it was a catalyst, but it cannot explain the magnitude of what transpired during the day. (I certainly don't remember waking up that morning racked with worry about the growth rate of the Chinese economy.) Afterwards, there were more reviews, more committees, more studies—and more flash crashes.

Fast forward to 2017. On July 7, a CNBC headline shouted, "Silver Plunges in yet Another Mysterious Market Flash Crash." The network went on to say, "Traders could not name a fundamental reason for the drop, but considered it another case of computer-driven trading that disrupted markets during a period when few were actively trading." This particular flash crash followed another that had occurred just a month earlier when "bitcoin rival ethereum crashed in New York afternoon trade on June 21 from near $317 to ten cents on a major U.S.-based digital currency exchange called GDAX." Yes, that is $317 to ten cents—in a matter of seconds.

In *Transforming Wall Street*, Kim Curtin spoke with dozens of investment professionals and executives and posed the following question to each: "if you had a magic wand to wave over Wall Street, what would you do?" Some of the answers were surprisingly unrealistic, e.g., "End retail brokerage tomorrow," or "Do away with the Federal Reserve Bank." Several dyed-in-the wool, old-school, *laissez-faire* capitalists predictably responded, "Do nothing." Not one mentioned high-frequency trading.

All the large, memorable flash crashes we have experienced represent unintended consequences of HFT. Five hundred and thousand-point flash crashes, of course, are spectacular news events that capture the public's attention. It is probable that without them, the average investor would have never heard of high-frequency trading in the first place, how it came into being, and what its participants are trying to accomplish. HFT has already transformed the way stock markets function, at times for the better, at times not. Rod Serling might have said that HFT lies in the Twilight Zone, the "the middle ground between light and shadow, between science and superstition, and between the pit of man's fears and the summit of his knowledge."

A sudden market decline doesn't have to be big and noisy to qualify as a flash crash. Smaller, inexplicable violent drops in stock prices constantly occur today, but they don't seem to attract much attention—perhaps their frequency has led us to believe that this type of market action is normal. To me, it is anything but normal. It is disturbing to me and others to see stock prices collapse, and then immediately recover, without a rational reason. Is this investing or casino gambling? Inexplicable short-term market volatility is a key reason why investors don't trust Wall Street and feel the system is rigged.

It wasn't until the 1990s that fully electronic securities trading became broadly available to institutional investors. Until then, NYSE market makers called "specialists" conducted business as usual, and virtually all trading in listed stocks went through them directly. They were charged with providing liquidity by making stock available for sale when there were no sellers, or offering shares to buy when there were no buyers. Their role as an exchange specialist obligated them to maintain an orderly and fair market. For decades, the system worked reasonably well, until technology intervened.

For many years, the NYSE enjoyed a monopoly on securities trading in the United States but lost its position of dominance in a virtual instant. The old specialist system still exists to a degree, but specialists are now called DMMs (direct market makers), and much of the trading now taking place on the exchange goes directly from computer to computer, untouched by human hands. It appears that NYSE specialists are dinosaurs in waiting. The NYSE was once, for want of a better description, a not-for-profit club; it went public in 2006 and became a for-profit corporation. For the first time, it was forced to compete with any number of other stock exchanges that were also organized as for-profit entities. Throughout the 1990s and early 2000s, competition provided immense benefits to investors. Bid-ask spreads narrowed, and commissions came down.

All the while computers kept getting faster and faster, by 2008 capable of taking on tasks and running at speeds that were unimaginable back in the old days, like 2005. Some folks got the idea that if one could create a direct, high-speed connection between the data centers of NASDAQ and the Chicago Mercantile Exchange, and if this connection could provide certain traders a time advantage like a head start in a footrace, then the data link could become a very valuable commodity indeed. It could be leased, so to speak, to the highest bidder, to hedge funds and brokerage firms that valued speed above all else. And so, in 2008, construction crews completed an 800-mile trench between Chicago and New Jersey, and high-frequency trading was born.

Michael Sanderson was CEO of Instinet in the 1990s and later served as CEO of Bonds.com and Interdealer Information Technologies. He has vast experience in electronic trading of both equities and fixed-income securities, and he also has strong opinions about the state of the markets today. He is not a fan of HFT as it is currently practiced. I asked him what he would do if he had the power to fix the system where he feels it has failed us and where the collateral damage has far outweighed the benefits. He laughed and said, "That's like asking a London black cab driver, 'what are you going to do about Uber?'"

Sanderson rightly points out that the problem with HFT is neither that it is fast or that it is frequent. He knows that technology is not going to go away, and it is naïve to expect that it will. In his lifetime, he has seen innumerable advances that have served to benefit all investors, whether large or small. The cost of doing business has come down because of lower spreads, commissions, and fees. A broad array of information is available on the internet. Investors may take comfort that regulatory authorities have their best interests at heart. And to a degree so does the NYSE, although the Exchange has a habit of laying it on a little thick. The following appears on the NYSE website:

> Though all of our markets operate electronically using cutting edge, ultrafast technology, we believe nothing can take the place of human judgment and accountability. It's this human connection that helps ensure our strength, creating orderly opens and closes, lower volatility, deeper liquidity and improved prices. For over 200 years, we've maintained a steadfast commitment to stronger, more orderly financial markets. And we intend to keep that tradition going for the next 200.

It all sounds wonderful, but here are the facts. The high-speed data link between Chicago and New York was built to provide traders willing to pay a fat subscription fee with the ability to have their trades executed faster than anyone else. What we are talking about here is a head start of three milliseconds, or three one-thousandths of a second. A high- frequency trader can program computers to see a buy order, for example, as it is about to become visible electronically, and then, with blinding speed, after purchasing the same securities for a penny or a fraction of a penny less, immediately sell those securities to the "slowpoke" buyer. The profit margin on each trade may be a small fraction of a penny, but with a daily trading volume of hundreds of millions of shares, the profits can add up awfully quickly. Does this sound like investing? The whole process seems more akin to cutting in line, counting cards in a casino, or receiving incorrect change and keeping it. HFT is not illegal, but it just doesn't pass the smell test. Not for me. Not for Sanderson. He says, "Just because you can do something doesn't mean you should."

High-frequency traders trade on multiple exchanges and can often arbitrage one exchange against another. This is because a given exchange may be one or two milliseconds faster or slower than another. HFTs look to take advantage of this disparity. If their computers are powerful enough, if their data links are fast enough, and if their algorithms are nearly bullet-proof, they can game the system. All they need is some stock to trade. Keep in mind, HFTs are not trading their own securities for their own accounts. They use "other people's money." At the end of each day, high-frequency traders will normally end up with a net zero position, and in order to maintain a viable business, they need access to a supply of shares held by financial institutions and hedge funds. They often *pay these customers* to trade with them. That in itself doesn't pass a smell test either, but to make matters worse, their arbitrage activities—picking off a better price on one exchange as opposed to another—allows them to profit at the expense of their customers.

High-frequency traders, however, have never been accused of occupying an especially high moral ground. The odd thing is that major problems usually do not occur when these folks are actively trading, but rather when they *stop*. When things are going well, high- frequency traders will become more active, and in relatively stable markets it is quite true that HFT provides investors with greater liquidity; but when the situation gets dicey, these electronic cowboys quickly lose their nerve, turn off their computers, and walk away. As we've seen, that's one thing that people didn't pick up on when examining Navinder Sarao's role in the '97 crash. In the middle of the firestorm, he stopped trading.

NYSE floor specialists do not possess the capital to maintain any semblance of an orderly market given the order flows of large financial institutions. Not only do the five hundred and thousand-point crashes bear witness to that, but so do the smaller, but far more frequent sudden stops and starts that now occur in the stock market on a regular, almost daily basis. Often they occur with individual stocks. Such inexplicable 180 degree turns followed by an immediate recovery have become an everyday occurrence.

I asked Sanderson if this short-term volatility, too small to be called a crash, too large for any rational investor to be comfortable with, is a serious problem. He said, "Huge!" and then repeated the word two more times. It's easy to see why. Collectively, high-frequency traders have great power and influence, but they have no real responsibilities when it comes to the maintenance of orderly, efficient trading. They are in the market for one reason only—to make money for themselves. Ideally, they would like to be in the market every day, every hour, every millisecond. But if for some reason they stop trading in a broadly held stock for any period of time, all hell may break loose. It often does. While high-frequency traders go on siesta, other investors can end up getting screwed.

Actively managed mutual funds have been underperforming broad-based indexes like the S&P 500 for years. Is this any surprise, especially given the built-in advantage that high- frequency traders enjoy—and the obvious handicap endured by traditional investors? No, it should not, nor should a recent announcement from BlackRock, the largest asset manager in the world, surprise us either. Recently this company announced that it would be using computers to manage some of its mutual funds. The *New York Times* reported in March 2017 that BlackRock "laid out an ambitious plan to consolidate a large number of actively managed mutual funds with peers that rely more on algorithms and models to pick stocks." We are not speaking of index funds or ETFs here, but conventional, plain-vanilla mutual funds that will be managed by programmed machines instead of people. BlackRock will probably be very successful at promoting this since many investors (and a number of their advisors) are convinced that they cannot compete with HFT. If that happens, Sanderson mused, we may soon witness a race to the edge of a cliff.

Charlie Merrill would have a difficult time understanding Wall Street today. Robo advisors, dark pools, algo funds, high-frequency traders, and leveraged exchange-traded funds don't have much in common except they all have a significant influence on the market, exponentially greater than that of retail investors who may occasionally trade a few hundred shares of stock at a time. The features of today's market are also opaque and poorly understood by the public. A good example of this can be found in structured notes, a relatively recent creation of Wall Street math whizzes. These oddball securities are typically packaged and sold to retail customers who have very little if any idea of what they are buying, perhaps because their advisors don't either. Here's an example of one put together by Goldman Sachs:

5y NC1y Issuer Callable Contingent Coupon Notes linked to the S&P 500® Index and the Russell 2000® Index, [6.00-7.00] % p.a. Contingent Coupon paid quarterly 50% Coupon Barrier, 50% Euro Barrier

Do you understand this? I don't either. It is no secret that technology has reshaped the world we live in. And it is also no secret that immense changes have taken place on Wall Street as a result. High-frequency trading particularly has received a good deal of publicity from two best-selling exposés, Michael Lewis' *Flash Boys* and Scott Patterson's *Dark Pools*. Both are clear about the potential hazards we all face in a high-tech, high-speed world. Computers are engineered for speed and accuracy. They have no conscience or sense of morality, no mission, no vision, no goals. It's up to all of us—investors, traders, brokerage firms, banks, mutual funds, pension funds, hedge funds and yes, even high-frequency traders—to decide what kind of society we want to live in and to muster up the courage to do something about it.

We must remember that as part of this process, it will be essential to define the role that technology needs to play as well as what it must not. This discussion cannot be limited to the area of financial services since these very issues apply to many elements of our civilization. On July 18, 2017, CNN reported that America's second-highest ranking military officer, Gen. Paul Selva, advocated for "keeping the ethical rules of war in place lest we unleash on humanity a set of robots that we don't know how to control."

Cleaning House

• • •

ADVANCES MADE BY SOCIETY DURING the past hundred years have been truly remarkable. Medicine, transportation, communication, and science have been transformed; life expectancy and levels of literacy have increased dramatically. Space exploration and genetic research have opened pathways of knowledge to subjects previously uncharted and remote. With this in mind, it is hard to believe that Wall Street is incapable of improving its public image and restoring trust with investors. The Street does not need faith healers or Aladdin's magic lamp—just some common sense and a willingness to cooperate in meeting a challenge that affects every participant in the business in a meaningful way. The government can police, protect, and regulate, but it cannot help the industry help itself.

Let's start with an event that touched virtually every American, even those without investment holdings. The credit crisis of 2008-2009 and the Great Recession that followed it resulted in financial loss, human suffering, unemployment, and homelessness on a scale not seen in our nation since the 1930s. It also brought tremendous reputational damage to Wall Street. This is something that the investment business is still dealing with today, long after the recession came to an end, and unless major changes are made, this collateral damage is likely to continue to taint the industry for years to come. It is hard to imagine our economy ever reaching its full potential if there is little trust in the Street's bankers, brokers, traders, analysts, and money managers.

Monday morning quarterbacks have blamed the credit crisis on any or all of the following: Barney Frank, Fannie Mae, greedy developers, mortgage lenders in general, mortgage lenders not in general, irresponsible speculators, the Federal Reserve Bank, interest-only loans, no-money-down loans, crooked realtors, crooked attorneys, crooked appraisers, and, lest we forget, Wall Street. If all else fails, blame Wall Street. It's easy—but only partially accurate.

We've seen that the credit crisis was caused by too much credit. How's that for a simple answer to a difficult question? Yes, credit is an absolute necessary for a healthy and vibrant economy, but when the amount of credit extended exceeds prudent limits, when any small hiccup restricts a borrower's ability to make payments to his creditors, significant problems will surface very quickly. Lenders are not our friends, and they never were. If you don't believe me, let a loan go delinquent and see what happens.

In the early 2000s, credit was readily available to virtually anyone. Mortgage loans, some of them quite exotic, made it possible for marginal borrowers to believe they could join in on the real estate boom and get rich. Buyers could choose from no-doc, option ARM, interest only, or zero-down mortgage products. It was too good to be true. All you needed was a pulse, a decent credit rating, a willingness to live dangerously and voilà—you had suddenly become a player in a game where you couldn't possibly lose. Or so it seemed. The real estate bubble, however, was no different than the stock market in 1928, junk bonds in the 1980s, or internet stocks in the 1990s. Ultimately, the law of gravity would prevail.

The government took swift action in 2008 and 2009 to save the economy from cratering completely. It would be foolish to say that many of the emergency measures like bank bailouts and Federal Reserve interest rate manipulation didn't work. They did. But we need to recognize that whatever the government did was either a short-term fix or a Band-Aid. The conditions that existed before the credit crisis became a crisis still exist today.

Fortunately, there are a few simple steps that Wall Street could take that would make it far more difficult for a housing-based credit crunch to reoccur. First, could we not require that lenders hold on to their mortgages for at least a year after they are originated? Is that too much to ask? Is it unreasonable to expect that the original issuer of a mortgage be willing to take such risk rather than immediately pass it on to a third party? The history of the credit crisis is clear on this: lenders who had no intention of holding mortgages long term had no real incentive to exercise caution when a loan application was made or being reviewed. Their goal was to close a loan as quickly as possible, sell it to someone else, and then move on to the next.

Second, let's think about creating an environment where borrowers must make a meaningful down payment to qualify for a mortgage loan. There is no reason Fannie Mae and Freddie Mac cannot require minimum down payments of at least 10 percent on all conventional loans. This would be a short-term negative for the housing industry, but the long-term benefits would be powerful and enduring.

On this subject, Silicon Valley Bank's Oscar Jazdowski makes an interesting point. Jazdowski spent the last several years living in Shanghai as Head of Corporate Banking for SVB. I was surprised to learn that a typical down payment for an owner-occupied residence in China is 40-50 percent; for a second home, 60-70 percent. Home equity lines of credit do not exist. There has certainly been a real estate bubble in China, but it has not been made more extreme by excessive lending. When the inevitable contraction takes place, it will not have anywhere near the devastating effect that it did in the US and Europe, where many homeowners were overextended.

With 0-5 percent equity, it doesn't take much to go underwater. Even today, almost ten years after the credit crisis, if you have good credit you can obtain a minimal down-payment loan. FHA loans require only 3 percent down, as do many mortgage programs available through state housing agencies. Some VA loans require nothing.

Another way of tamping down speculation would be to further restrict the deductibility of mortgage interest, currently topped at interest on a $1 million home. This sacred cow has been defended mightily by the real estate lobby for obvious reasons, but let's remember that the world did not end when the $1 million cap was introduced. Our current tax system, at least in this regard, encourages borrowing—not saving and investing. It's not just that lenders need to have skin in the game—so do borrowers. Reforms like these would help to protect people from their own poor judgment, just like mandatory seatbelt laws. Our current system makes it easy for both lenders and borrowers to run away from their responsibilities. Often the American Dream of home ownership becomes an American nightmare—if it involves taking on a mountain of unaffordable debt. Lax and imprudent lending policies will inevitably bring about a short-term boom and a long-term bust.

Next, high-frequency trading. It's clear that technology is not going away, nor are computers, and neither is HFT. Even Michael Lewis, who delivered a blistering critique of HFT in *Flash Boys*, recognizes that reality, but more interestingly, he makes the point that the problem is not with the existence of HFT but rather its social consequences. Lewis writes that he "didn't feel that strongly about high frequency trading (per se)." He goes on to say that the "big banks and exchanges have a clear responsibility to protect investors."

This, of course, would necessitate a sea change in behavior. And on at least one occasion, it actually happened with the opening of the Investors Exchange, IEX. Brad Katsuyama became a pioneer in the HFT world when he followed his moral conscience in 2011. He quit his job, was joined by a few associates who did the same, and went out on his own to establish a new stock exchange whose guiding principles would be rooted in investor protection. IEX does not pay for order flow and does not use exchange arbitrage to profit at the expense of its customers. It has enjoyed a reasonable amount of success, and Katsuyama and his co-founders should be justifiably proud of their achievements. Yet one must recognize that the IEX is still something of an oddity, almost an outlier, in a world of electronic cowboys. In time, perhaps it will become a power of example, and its way of doing business will become the norm.

The SEC has been taking a closer look at HFT practices and pulling in the reins on some of the more controversial practices like payment for order flow. This practice, known within the business as maker-taker, is in plain English known called a rebate. It is what it sounds like: paying a customer to do business with you. In the world of retail brokers, rebating is expressly forbidden and considered unethical. As a twenty-four-year-old dinosaur in training, if I'd tried something like this, I'd have been fired.

For institutional investors, a different set of rules applies. As an example, so-called "soft dollar" payments have been earned by brokerage firms for years. Here a broker may provide an investment advisor with research, electronic terminals, and more in return for a certain amount of directed commissions. This arrangement is a formal *quid pro quo*. The maker-taker way of doing business operates similarly, only here it is stock exchanges paying brokerage firms and market makers for order flow. The greater the order flow, the greater the opportunity to attract high-frequency traders, and of course, this increased activity will enable the exchanges to make more money.

Joe Saluzzi is one Wall Street executive who has spoken out forcefully on this issue as well as others. Saluzzi, co-founder of Themis Trading LLC, has been a candid critic of certain elements of high-frequency trading that he classifies as predatory. Maker-taker is one of them since orders often end up being routed where they shouldn't. This happens because the brokers sending them orders for their *own* customers are conflicted. For example, an order may be sent to "Exchange A" not because it offers the best price, but primarily because it is paying for the business. As we have seen, the reason an exchange will pay for the business is to attract high-frequency traders. In this scenario, unknowing customers can and do become victims of a system where investors take a back seat to the exchanges. You don't have to be a big-time trader to be a victim. Conservative mutual funds and pension plans can get scalped just like your next-door neighbor.

Saluzzi's efforts in this area—testimony before Congress, frequent media appearances, a 2012 book (*Broken Markets-How High Frequency Trading and Predatory Practices on Wall Street are Destroying Investor Confidence*)—have all helped broaden public awareness and increase the chances for badly needed reform. He is passionate about cleaning up HFT's abuses and has put the principles he espouses into action. His firm's mission is clear; its website proclaims, "Themis Trading is an independent, no-conflict, institutional agency brokerage firm specializing in equities." Who knows? Saluzzi's sincerity and commonsense approach, much like Brad Katsuyama's at IEX, may shame the Street into action before the SEC can finish the job itself. In any event, the maker-taker practice must be effectively restricted, regulated, and supervised. A continuation of the status quo is simply unacceptable.

The SEC has, in fact, become increasingly aware HFT abuses. Some of these have taken place in "dark pools." When I first heard the term, I thought it represented some sort of a secret slush fund. In a sense, it does. A dark pool is an alternative stock exchange that serves institutional investors. They NYSE has one; so do Goldman, Morgan Stanley, and most other major Wall Street firms. Dark pools must publicly report trades after they take place but are not required to reveal any information, such as bids, offers, size, etc. beforehand. This gives an investor the ability to place an order without telegraphing his intentions to the rest of the world. In a number of dark pools, however, regulatory compliance has been anemic and supervision lax. The SEC now has Wall Street's dark pools in its crosshairs. Credit Suisse, UBS, Citigroup, and Barclays have been singled out and fined by the SEC, with Barclay's fine coming in at $70 million.

Saluzzi spoke of another problem that has cropped up since the appearance of alternative exchanges and high-frequency trading: the demise of the specialist system. This is probably the inevitable result of technology, and not necessarily something to be mourned. However, if the specialist in time fades away and becomes an anachronism, the SEC's goals of market fairness and transparency will not disappear—but the ability to achieve those goals will have been severely compromised. In some form, action must be taken. It is absurd to think we can have smooth, equitable, and efficient trading unless all participants—and this includes dark pools and alternative markets—are charged with the kinds of responsibilities that specialists have willingly taken on for decades.

There is one last issue with HFT that is worth mentioning. The idea of a transaction tax has been brought up often in recent years, and it has always gone nowhere because it was looked upon as a way to punish high-frequency traders (probably correct), something that agitated Wall Street and its lobbyists to no end. Apart from that, many people have a visceral, negative reaction to the word "tax." Still, there may be a slightly warmer response if one were to call this a usage fee, where traders would be subject to a small fee based upon the number of transactions they complete in a given period. Proceeds could be used for enhanced surveillance systems designed to police high-frequency activity.

High-frequency trading and the credit crisis are just two of the factors that have damaged Wall Street's public image. The industry has had more than its share of bad actors—from bit players to Bernie Madoffs—who have preyed on the public for years. Even if we admit that bad people who do bad things will always do bad things, the industry must take a much harder line toward its vultures. Failure to do so invites continued misfortune and reputational pollution.

The industry likes to think of itself as exclusive, but in many ways, it isn't. It is relatively easy to get a securities license. One needs only a background check, a set of fingerprints, and enough intelligence to pass several mandatory examinations. Once in the business, it is almost unheard of to be booted out. It is extremely rare for someone's license to be suspended or revoked by the SEC or a state securities administrator. Anything short of fraud is ordinarily tolerated. Major investment firms with large compliance departments will from time to time dismiss "problem advisors," but often these individuals will be quickly picked up by another firm. I know of one advisor who was fired after innumerable sales practice complaints; all of the formal ones (nine in six years) were, of course, disclosed to regulators, fully documented, and appear on FINRA's Broker Check website. After his dismissal, he was able to land another job and remains active in the business today.

To make matters worse, big producers often get a free pass. I know of another advisor who was fired because he forwarded a graphic, pornographic email to one of his friends. Since the email was received by and sent from a company email account, he had crossed the line by clearly violating his employer's "zero tolerance" policy toward such activities. The advisor was highly talented and successful, so, as one would expect, after he was terminated, he was snapped up by another firm. It should not surprise anyone that his new employer had its own zero-tolerance policy regarding pornography. This is beyond ironic. It is shameful, and a reckless way to conduct business.

Small firms present a special challenge of their own, and in one sense the smaller the firm the larger the problem. Would the owner of a boutique investment advisory firm fire himself if he was guilty of fraud or creating a hostile work environment? The answer is obvious. Would he terminate a key employee, one whom he had hired, trained, groomed, and worked shoulder to shoulder with for ten or more years? What if that person was a family member? Of course, he would be prone to cut the employee some slack and let the situation slide. Decisions like this become more challenging in small firms where there are no large compliance departments, in-house attorneys, and reams of policy manuals that can make the decision-making process more formulaic.

What I am trying to say is that there are a lot of sketchy folks who hold a securities license, and they have abused that privilege. Large firms with hundreds of compliance professionals may have the wherewithal to police themselves but often fail to do so. Tiny owner-operated advisory firms are a special case; they'll never point the finger at themselves. The responsibility of supervision here rests with our regulators and the exchanges. They need to play hardball. No one will complain, and the world will be better off.

Just as there are conflicts of interest embedded in high-frequency trading, there are also similar conflicts in retail brokerage. I suppose they can be present in any business. Traders, analysts, administrators, executives, and advisors confront temptation frequently, but it is the advisors, particularly commission-based advisors, who come up against it on virtually every transaction. The conundrum has been made more difficult by the industry's distinction between what is "suitable" and what is in the customer's "best interest." Until now, commission-based brokers only needed to concern themselves with suitability and were not subject to fiduciary standards of behavior. New regulations imposing adherence to fiduciary standards in retirement accounts were set to take effect in 2017, but President Trump has made it clear he is in favor of a rollback. Currently, it is not clear which way this will play out, but it is an important issue, one that needs ongoing attention. The vast majority of financial advisors are not sociopaths like Bernie Madoff, but some do work just inside the line or on the edge. They need to be reined in so investors can get (and feel they are getting) a fair shake.

An old friend of mine, a senior sales executive with a leading global asset management company, sincerely believes the business can be a "noble profession" for those who practice it properly, but he recognizes that the industry has done a poor job of managing expectations. Advisors and money managers tout their performance excessively, often failing to explain what they do and how they do it.

He is also concerned about the industry's bad apples, those folks that occupy financial purgatory—a zone where sleazy operators who are not quite criminally disposed operate with regularity. Even when their actions become intolerable to their employers, they are frequently given the option to resign when they should be dismissed for cause. As a result, their U-4s, a kind of official dossier maintained by FINRA, is sanitized, and it presents a false picture of the individual's true compliance record. In this way, people who shouldn't remain in the business get to do so. Such arrangements are commonplace. They are no different than standard legal settlements where both parties neither admit nor deny guilt. However expedient, such settlements can have long-standing, harmful effects by allowing shady characters to remain active in the securities industry.

Ridding the business of rogue brokers and advisors may be a pipedream, but one way to start would be to look at the concept of sentencing guidelines, something that is well established within our legal system. In this scenario, potential violations and infractions could be identified, along with appropriate penalties. This is an area where the industry should take a leadership role, and do it with eagerness. A cooperative effort like this would have a meaningful impact on an investor's experience and the way in which people view Wall Street. It makes perfect sense, and it's good business. Day-to-day policing is beyond the purview of the SEC and FINRA, and it would be a Herculean task for all fifty states to agree on cataloging crimes and standardizing punishments. Without denying the power of faith, it has been said that God helps those who help themselves. That truism applies to the securities industry just as it does to life.

Beyond rooting out its bad apples, Wall Street needs a total reset. Instead of safety first, it must shoot for the moon regarding enhanced customer relationships and public image. Personalized, periodic contact with clients is a must. It is amazing how many customers never hear from their advisors, let alone administrators and managers. This is Doing Business 101. Asking questions like "How are you?" "Where can we improve?" and "What can we change?" may be simple stuff, but it leaves a deep impression. Many businesses claim to be client-centric these days, but they don't do much to support that assertion.

Lastly comes the issue of money. Of course, money and wealth creation are central to innovation, growth, and our collective well-being, but contrary to a popular cliché, it (life) is not *all* about the money. For years, brokerage firms have engaged in recruiting wars, tossing about enormous signing bonuses as a way of attracting experienced advisors. In many cases, the bonuses are undeserved and out of line. Once advisors switch firms, they will say their old company was too large (or small), or the research department was weak, or there weren't any IPOs to offer clients, or any other big lie that ignores the obvious, i.e., it was all about the money.

The industry needs to take a close look at this practice of competitive recruiting. For one thing, it doesn't work. As it exists today, it is a zero-sum game, where one firm's win is another's loss. In the big picture, after ten or twenty years of this back and forth tug-of-war, the competitive landscape is largely unchanged, a virtual standoff. The only losers were investors. If you follow the money trail, you'll see it was the revenue generated by customers that made huge recruiting bonuses possible in the first place. Some common-sense reform—not collusion by brokerage firms, but sensible reform—is badly needed here. Recently, a few major firms have announced they will be putting the brakes on deals that involve large up-front payments. This is a step in the right direction. Sensible recruiting practices should involve long-term commitments and guarantees by all parties, and perhaps disclosure to clients as well.

Compensation as well needs to be reviewed. Client satisfaction and customer retention are key components of any business' ability to succeed, but they are completely invisible when it comes to advisor compensation, as is any other similar metric. Are you a team player? Have you enhanced your professional education? Are your customers making money? Do your clients think highly of you? Wall Street needs to rethink not just how much it compensates its advisors, but how it goes about doing so. Managing money is a complex, challenging job, and it is wrong to compensate financial advisors exclusively based on gross commissions or fees. They are not manual laborers doing piecework. Qualitative standards must be applied, just as they are for most professionals in other industries.

I reached out to gain the opinions of others. One of the more interesting came from international banker Oscar Jazdowski. He believes that enduring changes cannot be regulated or legislated—they can only result from a complete reset in cultural values. Some may think that the phrase "cultural values," when applied to Wall Street, is an oxymoron, but his point is well taken. His insights were thought-provoking and took me by surprise. We have repeatedly experienced the power of greed and its pernicious influence within society. In the *Treasure of the Sierra Madre*, Walter Huston speculated on what gold does to one's soul: "You lose your sense of values, and your character changes entirely."

Jazdowski pointed out that we are at the dawn of a revolution in artificial intelligence, one that could redefine work in general, the securities industry along with it. We have already seen in our lifetimes how advanced technologies have changed the characteristics of a typical job—one that is now safer, less demanding physically, and featuring a shorter workweek.

One hundred years ago, the most common occupations in the U.S. were farmer and domestic servant. What do you think they will be fifty years from now, two hundred years from now? Jazdowski speculates that AI holds such promise for society that the desire to accumulate ever-increasing amounts of money, something that has always been the fuel that powered Wall Street, may in time slowly subside. Perhaps his vision is utopian. But it does make sense that if technology is able to give society virtually everything it needs—food, shelter, healthcare, transportation, education, and cradle-to-grave social services—our obsession with money will likely fade away, and that, in turn, may instill a new value system in all of us, even the sometimes-sketchy characters that make their bones in financial services. The proposition is not that farfetched. The primary goal of the earliest human settlements was survival. A thousand years ago it was eternal salvation. Today, it is power through wealth. Tomorrow?

Keynote speaker, author, and executive coach Kim Curtin has a unique perspective. She calls for a spiritual awakening of sorts. This may seem airy-fairy to some, but in the end, we do have to ask what kind of society we wish to live in, and what standards of behavior that all of us—individuals, corporations, and government—must observe. Kim calls for an "increase in consciousness, causing those who have been out of integrity to acknowledge the responsibility they own for breaking the trust of consumers and to apologize for the breach of this trust. Second, it would cause Wall Street to express empathy to consumers for the costs they've suffered. Third, it would cause them to commit to now running their business in a way that honors and provides value to their customers, receiving profit from value and services provided, rather than by using creative manipulation."

She also raises an interesting challenge to the widely held belief that public companies should be run exclusively for the short-term benefit of their shareholders, not a combination of shareholders, customers, employees, and society. She has a point. I have often witnessed a company announce a stock buyback of say, $1 billion, only to end the year with more shares outstanding than had existed before the buyback took place.

What happened? The shares were reissued to executives who were cashing in their stock options, and the wealth that would have been distributed among all shareholders was redirected disproportionately to a handful of corporate officers and directors. I call this pattern of stock buyback/ option issuance a financial enema. Perhaps the imagery is a bit extreme, but it is accurate.

For now, Wall Street can certainly take steps to reshape its image and restore public trust, but only if it moves proactively. Taking the lead in reforming lending practices and high-frequency trading is essential. Prudence and ethical behavior are not optional; they are the core of any successful organization. Wall Street must demand excellence from all its employees, especially those in sensitive positions like analysts and financial advisors. It must walk the walk, and demonstrate that its integrity is present in every transaction and each customer relationship. Zero tolerance for bad behavior should mean exactly that. What matters more in business than one's reputation and customer relationships? Arguably, not much. Just because dinosaurs are passing from the scene in no way guarantees a utopian future. Now is the time to act, for Wall Street to clean house, and to reestablish the trust that has been lost.

AUTHOR BIOGRAPHY

● ● ●

JORY BERKWITS JOINED MERRILL LYNCH in 1972, and during a diverse and highly successful career has been recognized by *Barron's*, *Who's Who*, and various industry organizations for his many accomplishments in the investment industry.

Berkwits received his bachelor's degree from Columbia University and a master's degree from the University of Washington. Several years ago, he retired to Sarasota, Florida, where he is active in investing in private equity and mentoring small business owners through SCORE. Berkwits is also the author of *My Bittersweet Homecoming*.

Made in the USA
Columbia, SC
24 February 2018